The Gigantic Book of Golf Quotations

The Gigantic Book of Golf Quotations

Thousands of Notable Quotables
from Tommy Armour to Fuzzy Zoeller

EDITED WITH INTRODUCTIONS BY JIM APFELBAUM

FOREWORD BY ARNOLD PALMER

Skyhorse Publishing

www.skyhorsepublishing.com

10   9   8   7   6   5   4   3   2   1

Library of Congress Cataloging-in-Publication-Data
    The gigantic book of golf quotations : thousands of notable quotables
from Tommy Armour to Fuzzy Zoeller / edited with introductions
by Jim Apfelbaum ; foreword by Arnold Palmer.
        p.   cm.
    Includes bibliographical references and index.
    ISBN-13: 978-1-60239-014-0 (hardcover : alk. paper)
    ISBN-10: 1-60239-014-2 (hardcover : alk. paper)
    1. Golf—Quotations, maxims, etc.   I. Apfelbaum, Jim.

GV967.G55   2007
796.352—dc22

                                                    2007005352

Printed in the United States of America

Contents

Foreword

Golf is my life, and I have been around the game for as long as I can remember. I was three years old when I first started hitting balls, and I spent a lot of time around the sport as a young boy, mostly because my father was the head professional and greens keeper at the Latrobe Country Club in Pennsylvania. I'd ride in his lap while he was mowing the fairways with his tractor and eat lunch with him under the shade trees that grew on the course. Years later, when I was 12, I entered my first junior golf tournament and went on to play on the Latrobe High School team. Then, I was off to Wake Forest, at which point I had won a few amateur tournaments and started playing more on a national level. By the time I turned professional in 1955, I had won more than my fair share of titles, among them the Ohio Amateur, the Cleveland Amateur, the All-American Amateur, and best of all, the U.S. Amateur. And during my stints on both the regular and senior PGA Tours in the years to follow, I finished first in 73 events and added another 19 titles in non-sanctioned tournaments at home and abroad.

But golf for me was not only about playing in tournaments. I've always enjoyed a simple afternoon round with friends, and to this day, I love any excuse to play. In fact, it sometimes feels as if I have played every day of my adult life. And truth be told, that is not so far off.

All of this is to say that I have been around the game for a very long time. And being around golf so much, I have been lucky to have seen amazing places and witnessed extraordinary things, whether walking the fairways of Augusta National, say, or the streets of St. Andrews. I have also heard more than my share of thoughts and comments on the sport, both on the course and at the 19th hole afterwards, and the hilarity of those words as well as the depth of their meanings are what prompted me to write this Foreword. For golf is often as much about the interaction with your friends as it is the shots we are playing, and enjoying the way players are able to laugh at themselves as they chuckle at—and with—others. It is also about reading accounts of what happens to other people when they tee it up, whether for fun or in competition, and the things that come out of their mouths. Because we, as golfers, say the darndest things.

There is so much in this volume that will make you laugh, starting with comments from comedic geniuses like Bill Murray, Bob Hope, and David Feherty and moving to longtime journalistic observers of the game, such as Grantland Rice, Peter Doebereiner, and the fellow who wrote my biography a few years ago, Jim Dodson. The words of Buddy Hackett and Leslie Nielsen have understandably found their way into this book, and even men and women who are not noted for their wit and humor can bring down the house when the subject is golf. For example, Hank Aaron is not exactly a star at stand-up. But he can induce more than a few giggles when he says things like: "It took me 17 years to get 3,000 hits in baseball. I did that in one afternoon on the golf course."

But this publication of some 3,000 quotes is not only about laughs. It is also about insight into the game, from men like Ben Hogan and Bobby Jones who knew it intimately. It provides deeper takes on life itself, from the likes of Winston Churchill, President George H.W. Bush, and John D. Rockefeller. It even has a few lines from yours truly, as well as pearls of wisdom and wit from a few of my old competitors, like Jack Nicklaus and Gary Player as well as Billy Casper and Chi-Chi Rodriguez.

The Gigantic Book of Golf Quotations is the biggest and best compilation of thoughts on the game ever assembled. Culled from a variety of sources and edited by Jim Apfelbaum, they are sure to delight fans of the game for years to come.

I hope you enjoy it as much as I have.

—Arnold Palmer

The Gigantic Book of Golf Quotations

CHAPTER ONE

What is Golf?: Definitions

Isaac Newton had his apple. Grantland Rice saw the celluloid charge of the Apocalyptic Four Horsemen and produced the most famous lead in sports journalism. Gene Sarazen noticed airplanes lower their tails to rise and fashioned the sand wedge. So what could it have been? What inspired these crystalline insights into The Game? There must have been some backstory, for behind discovery's perfect diamond often rests a bituminous lump of hard experience. Did the heavens open as in golf they sometimes will? Or was there some lost ignominy, a series of accumulated hurts, another chilly dip on top of another exasperating yip?

Oddly enough, many of these profundities seem to owe their existence to logic. The findings appear to have sprung fully-formed. An easy birth. These, including just about anything from Byron Nelson, a modest and thoughtful man, suggest nothing if not the end result of years of dutiful lab work. Others have an existential, Zen-like, quality. The perception plucked from the expanse of the golf universe, a ripple across the water hazard that has always been there if only we were observant enough to notice.

Then there are those morsels suggestive of more turbulent origins. Dearly bought, roughly hewn, not so much a quote as an cathartic outburst, they evoke a wound, likely self-inflicted. On the one hand: mindful clarity, observations gleaned through diligent, ascetic, pursuit. On the other: those explosive, smoke billowing, glorious disasters. We're thankful for the result if the process may well have shortened the creator's lifespan.

Which to favor? As we read we're again reminded why the underdog is so memorable, so much more fun to be around. Discretion may be advisable. A safe distance can be best. Though difficult to maintain, mastering a look of feigned indifference is also recommended.

* * * * *

Golf is life. If you can't take golf, you can't take life.

—ANONYMOUS

Golf is a constant battle against par, and if you play it any other way, you're encouraging sloppy thinking and sloppy strokes. Ignore the social or business engagement on the golf course, therefore, and play medal whenever possible.

—GARY PLAYER
IN *SECRETS OF THE GOLFING GREATS*

Golf is a game whose aim it is to hit a very small ball into an even smaller hole, with weapons singularly ill-designed for the purpose.

—WINSTON CHURCHILL

Golf is the cruelest of sports. Like life, it's unfair. It's a harlot. A trollop. It leads you on. It never lives up to its promises . . . It's a boulevard of broken dreams. It plays with men. And runs off with the butcher.

—JIM MURRAY

Pro golf is dull. It's a chorus line of blond towheads you can't even tell apart.

—TOMMY BOLT

Golf is an open exhibition of overweening ambition, courage deflated by stupidity, skill soured by a whiff of arrogance.

—ALISTAIR COOKE

Golf is twenty percent mechanics and technique. The other eighty percent is philosophy, humor, tragedy, romance, melodrama, companionship, camaraderie, cussedness, and conversation.

—GRANTLAND RICE

Golf is a game that creates emotions that sometimes cannot be sustained with the club still in one hand.

—BOBBY JONES

Golf is a funny game. It's done much for health and at the same time has ruined people by robbing them of their peace of mind. Look at me, I'm the healthiest idiot in the world.

—BOB HOPE

Golf is the only game in which a precise knowledge of the rules can earn one a reputation for bad sportsmanship.

—PATRICK CAMPBELL

———•———

It [golf] is a test of temper, a trial of honor, a revealer of character. It means going into God's out of doors, getting close to nature, fresh air and exercise, a sweeping of mental cobwebs and a genuine relaxation of tired tissues.

—DAVID FORGAN,
AMATEUR GOLFER, BANKER, AND LIFETIME GOLF ENTHUSIAST
CHICAGO GOLF CLUB BY ROSS GOODNER

———•———

The ultimate analysis of the mystery of golf is hopeless—as hopeless as the ultimate analysis of that of physics or that of the feminine heart.

—ARNOLD HAULTAIN
THE GOLF BOOK

———•———

Golf tournaments are like teachers, and not because each deals with a course. Some tournaments make the pros work.

—DAVE ANDERSON
FROM *GOLF DIGEST*

Golf is like life in a lot of ways: The most important competition is the one against yourself. All the biggest wounds are self-inflicted. And you get a lot of breaks you don't deserve, both ways. So it's important not to get too upset when you're having a bad day.

—PRESIDENT BILL CLINTON
FROM *GOLF TODAY*

———◆———

Golf—the second best pastime that any sinner on earth can have.

—R.H. LYTTLETON

———◆———

Golf is a game of such monumental stupidity that anyone with a brain more active than a cantaloupe has difficulty gearing down to its demands.

—PETER ANDREWS

———◆———

Golf is not a funeral, though both can be very sad affairs.

—BERNARD DARWIN

———◆———

Golf is a lot like life. When you make a decision, stick with it.

—BYRON NELSON

I'm going to give you my secret to golf. You can't play a really great game unless you're so miserable that you don't worry over your shots . . . Look at the top-notchers. Come on, have you ever seen a happy pro?

—P.G. WODEHOUSE

It is a golf universe.

—TOM COYNE

Golf is to me what his Sabine farm was to the poet Horace—a solace and an inspiration.

—RAMSAY MACDONALD
BRITISH POLITICIAN

Golf is just the comedy side of what's going on in life. But, hey, this world is great. You can make fun of anything, from the tensest moments to the not so tense. Golf is a pressure game where funny and crazy things happen.

—BILLY ANDRADE

They say that life is a lot like golf—don't believe them. Golf is a lot more complicated.

—GARDNER DICKINSON

Mulligan: invented by an Irishman who wanted to hit one more 20-yard grounder.

—JIM BISHOP

The essence of golf is to say that it enhances the feeling that it is good to be alive. That's the first priority and absolute justification.

—PETER DOBEREINER
WORLDGOLF.COM

They call it golf because all of the other four-letter words were taken.

—RAYMOND FLOYD

Golf is so popular simply because it is the best game in the world at which to be bad . . . At golf, it is the bad player who gets the most strokes.

—A. A. MILNE
AUTHOR

Golf is a compromise between what your ego wants you to do, what experience tells you to do, and what your nerves let you do.

—BRUCE CRAMPTON

Golf is assuredly a mystifying game. Even the best golfers cannot step onto the first tee with any assurance as to what they are going to do.

—W. TIMOTHY GALLWEY

Golf is really three games. There's the long game, where women are at a disadvantage. There's the short game, where women are at no disadvantage at all . . . And there is the game that is eighteen holes in one.

—LOUISE SUGGS

Golf is a wonderful exercise. You can stand on your feet for hours, watching somebody else putt.

—WILL ROGERS

Golf is the only game where the worst player gets the best of it. He gets more out of it with regard to both exercise and enjoyment. The good player worries over the slightest mistake, whereas the poor player makes too many mistakes to worry over them.

—DAVID LLOYD GEORGE
BRITISH PRIME MINISTER

Golf is a game that needlessly prolongs the lives of some of our most useless citizens.

—BOB HOPE

Happiness is a long walk with a putter in your hand.

—WAYNE GRADY

A good one iron shot is about as easy to come by as an understanding wife.

—DAN JENKINS

Golf is a diabolical game. It's easy to make fun of something that's so bizarre, so painful, so humiliating . . . yet so joyous.

—KEN GREEN

In this case, golf is a means to an end. We can't change the course that someone's life has taken in the past, but through golf we can help mold that life and give it a more positive feeling.

—HALE IRWIN

Golf is more fun than walking naked in a strange place, but not much.

—BUDDY HACKETT

Golf is an ineffectual attempt to put an elusive ball into an obscure hole with implements ill-adapted to the purpose.

—PRESIDENT WOODROW WILSON

Pro golf is a parasitical business and they can do without us.

—WALTER HAGEN

It's a tan like mine. It tells you the player is spending a lot of time out on the fairway and the greens—and not in the trees.

> —LEE TREVINO
> ON THE SIGN OF A GOOD GOLFER

Golf is not sacred, and there is no use getting so gosh-darned solemn about it.

> —DON HEROLD
> AMERICAN HUMORIST, WRITER, ILLUSTRATOR AND AVID GOLFER

Golf is like an 18-year-old girl with the big boobs. You know it's wrong but you can't keep away from her.

> —VAL DOONICAN

Golf is golf. You hit the ball, you go find it. Then you hit again.

> —LON HINKLE

Golf is like a chain. You always have to work on the weakest links.

> —GEORGE ARCHER

It's a game of constant adjustment and the guy that adjusts the best is the best player.

—GENE LITTLER

Golf is a game in which attitude of mind counts for incomparably more than mightiness of muscle.

—ARNOLD HAULTAIN

Golf is just a game—and an idiotic game most of the time.

—MARK CALCAVECCHIA

Golf is assuredly a mystifying game. It would seem that if a person has hit a golf ball correctly a thousand times, he should be able to duplicate the performance at will. But this is certainly not the case.

—BOBBY JONES

Playing golf is like raising children: You keep thinking you'll do better next time.

— Roy McKie
Author

Local rules in golf: a set of regulations that are ignored by players on a specific course rather than by golfers as a whole.

— E.C. McKenzie
Humorist

Golf is a game of a lifetime.

— Tony Lema

Golf should be a fair test. If the average golfer shoots 90, he'll be comfortable. If he shoots 120, he'll want to give up the game.

— Robert Trent Jones, Sr.
Course Designer

Golf is like any other sports competition. There is not a whole lot of point to it unless someone suffers.

—Kevin Wohl

Yes, it is a cruel game, one in which the primitive instincts of man are given full play, and the difference between golf and fisticuffs is that in one the pain is of the mind and in the other it is of the body.

—Henry Leach

If anything could be better calculated to convince one of the essential lunacy of the human race, I haven't found it.

—Mike Seabrook
on golf

Golf is not a game of great shots. It's a game of the most misses. The people who win make the smallest mistakes.

—Gene Littler

The devoted golfer is an anguished soul who has learned a lot about putting just as an avalanche victim learned a lot about snow.

—DAN JENKINS

Golf is the Esperanto of sport. All over the world, golfers talk the same language—much of it nonsense and much unprintable—endure the same frustrations, discover the same infallible secrets of putting, share the same illusory joys.

—HENRY LONGHURST

It [golf] is a cure for care, an antidote to worry. It includes companionship for friends, social intercourse, opportunities for courtesy, kindliness and generosity to an opponent. It promotes not only physical health but moral force.

—DAVID FORGAN
AMATEUR GOLFER, BANKER, AND LIFETIME GOLF ENTHUSIAST,
CHICAGO GOLF CLUB BY ROSS GOODNER

Do your best, one shot at a time, and then move on. Remember that golf is just a game.

—NANCY LOPEZ

The course of true golf never did run smooth.

—HENNY YOUNGMAN
COMEDIAN

This is a game. That's all it is. It's not a war.

—JACK NICKLAUS

Golf is a game not just of manners but of morals.

—ART SPANDER

Golf is a game of situations.

—JOHN L. LOW

It seemed to me a form of tiddly-winks, stupid and silly, for never in my life had I known a sport that was not strenuous or violent, on his first impression of golf.

—CHARLES BLAIR MACDONALD

Great southpaw golfers are more scarce than a clear day in Los Angeles.
—JOE SCHWENDEMAN

Golf is a game, and talk and discussion is all to the interests of the game
. . . Anything that makes us think about it, talk about it, and dream about
it is all to the good and prevents the game becoming dead.
—ALISTER MACKENZIE

Golf is a game of upgrading and change.
—JIM MCLEAN
FROM *THE EIGHT-STEP SWING*

Golf keeps the heart young and the eyes clear.
—ANDREW KIRKALDY

Golf is like faith: it is the substance of things hoped for, the evidence of
things not seen.
—ARNOLD HAULTAIN

Golf is 90 percent inspiration and 10 percent perspiration.

—JOHNNY MILLER

Golf is a spiritual game. It's like Zen. You have to let your mind take over.

—AMY ALCOTT

Whatever anyone may care to say about golf, at least one thing is mercifully certain, namely it is a voluntary affair.

—HENRY LONGHURST

Then God says, 'Wait a minute, just so you don't forget.' A fleck of grass throws a putt off-line, the ball is struck in a tree or shoots this way or that. The elements, variables, the unexpected. That's golf.

—ANNETTE THOMPSON

Golf without mistakes is like watching haircuts. A dinner without wine.

—JIM MURRAY

The Londoner who declared golf a moral game is all wrong. Golf is anything but a moral pastime. It is essentially and in all its phases immoral. Golf is followed by a set of Cyrenaic sensuits as corrupt in their philosophy and profane in their doctrines as ever Aristippus was. . . .

—ST. LOUIS REPUBLIC EDITORIAL

Golf is a game of expletives not deleted.

—DR. IRVING A. GLADSTONE

Golf is a good walk spoiled.

—MARK TWAIN

Professional golf is the only sport where, if you win twenty percent of the time, you're the best.

—JACK NICKLAUS

Golf and women are a lot alike. You know you are not going to wind up with anything but grief, but you can't resist the impulse.

—JACKIE GLEASON
COMEDIAN

—◆—

Golf is like real estate, where there's a single key word: location, location, location. In golf it's putting, putting, putting.

—DAVID OGRIN

—◆—

Playing golf is like learning a foreign language.

—HENRY LONGHURST

—◆—

Golf is a fine relief from the tensions of office, but we are a little tired of holding the bag.

—ADLAI STEVENSON

[Golfers] are a special kind of moral realist who nip the normal romantic and idealistic yearnings in the bud by proving once or twice a week that life is unconquerable but endurable.

—ALISTAIR COOKE

Golf is essentially an exercise in masochism conducted out-of-doors.

—PAUL O'NEIL

Golf is very much like a love affair: if you don't take it seriously, it's no fun; if you do, it breaks your heart. Don't break your heart, but flirt with the possibility.

—LOUISE SUGGS

Golf combines two favorite American pastimes: taking long walks and hitting things with a stick.

—P.J. O'ROURKE

Golf is a hands game.

—HENRY COTTON

Golf is a lot like sex. Even when you cheat you still have to get it up and in. And that gets tougher and tougher to do every year.

  —BILLY ORVILE

Golf, and sometimes life, is full of new beginnings.

  —JAMES DODSON

Putting is like wisdom—partly a natural gift and partly the accumulation of experience.

  —ARNOLD PALMER

Golf is a game in which you claim the privileges of age and retain the playthings of childhood.

  —SAMUEL JOHNSON

Golf is the most useless outdoor game ever devised to waste time and try the sprit of man.

  —WESTBROOK PEGLER

Golf is the pursuit of the infinite.
—JIM MURRAY

A golf ball is like a clock. Always hit it at 6 o'clock and make it go toward 12 o'clock. But make sure you're in the same time zone.
—CHI-CHI RODRIGUEZ

Golf is a puzzle without an answer. I've played the game for 40 years and I still haven't the slightest idea how to play.
—GARY PLAYER

Golf is the only sport I know of where a player pays for every mistake . . . In golf, every swing counts against you.
—LLOYD MANGRUM

Golf is good for the soul.
—WILL ROGERS

Golf is an ideal diversion, but a ruinous disease.

—B.C. FORBES

———— ·✦· ————

Remember, the game is simple. The ball doesn't move. It simply sits and waits.

—STEVEN PRESSFIELD
FROM *THE LEGEND OF BAGGER VANCE*

———— ·✦· ————

The difference between golf and the government is that in golf you can't improve your lie.

—GEORGE DEUKMEJIAN
FORMER GOVERNOR OF CALIFORNIA

———— ·✦· ————

Golf is a game kings and presidents play when they get tired of running countries.

—CHARLES PRICE

———— ·✦· ————

Golf seems to me an arduous way to go for a walk. I prefer to take the dogs out.

—PRINCESS ANNE

Golf is a lot like sex. It's something you can enjoy all your life. And if you remain an amateur, you get to pick your own playing partners.

—JESS SWEETSER

Golf is the Great Mystery. Like some capricious goddess, it bestows its favors with what would appear an almost fat-headed lack of method and discrimination.

—P.G. WODEHOUSE
IN HIS BOOK *HEART OF A GOOF*

Golf is the worst drug in the world. You just keep coming back for more embarrassment.

—DEACON JONES
PRO FOOTBALL HALL OF FAMER

Golf is about how well you accept, respond to, and score with your misses much more so than it is a game of your perfect shots.

—DR. BOB ROTELLA

Good golf is simply a matter of hitting good shots consistently.

—GENE SARAZEN

❖

Golf is more exacting than racing, cards, speculation, or matrimony. In almost all other games you pit yourself against a mortal foe; in golf it is yourself against the world: no human being stays your progress as you drive your ball over the face of the globe.

—ARNOLD HAULTAIN
THE MYSTERY OF GOLF

❖

Golf is like a razor. You get just so sharp and then it begins to dull a little more the more you use it.

—DOUG SANDERS

❖

Golf . . . a young man's vice and an old man's penance.

—IRVIN S. COBB

Golf is a science, the study of a lifetime, in which you can exhaust yourself but never your subject.

—DAVID FORGAN

AMATEUR GOLFER, BANKER, AND GOLF ENTHUSIAST

[Golf] is like chasing a quinine pill around a cow pasture.

—WINSTON CHURCHILL

The difference between getting in a sand trap and getting in water is like the difference between an auto wreck and an airplane wreck. You can recover from one of them.

—BOBBY JONES

Hockey is a sport for white men. Basketball is a sport for black men. Golf is a sport for white men dressed like black pimps.

—TIGER WOODS

Golf is not, on the whole, a game for realists. By its exactitudes of measurement it invites the attention of perfectionists.

—HEYWOOD HALE BROUN
TUMULTUOUS MERRIMENT, 1979

———•———

The golf swing is like a suitcase into which we are trying to pack one too many things.

—JOHN UPDIKE

———•———

I regard golf as an expensive way of playing marbles.

—GILBERT K. CHESTERTON

———•———

Golf is like acting in that both require concentration and relaxation at the same time.

—JANE SEYMOUR

Golf is an awkward set of bodily contortions designed to produce a graceful result.

—TOMMY ARMOUR

Tennis is like a wonderful, longstanding relationship with a husband. Golf is a tempestuous, lousy lover; it's totally unpredictable, a constant surprise.

—DINAH SHORE

I can see the charm and temptation even now, for golf or any other pastime can be much more than a mere hitting of the ball; it can be, however poor a one, a life to be lived.

—BERNARD DARWIN

Golf is like solitaire. When you cheat, you cheat only yourself.

—TONY LEMA

Golf is the only-est sport. You're completely alone with every conceivable opportunity to defeat yourself.

—HALE IRWIN

Golfers make better lovers because they have such great touch. In golf you have to be good in all areas. You have to be powerful, be strong, have stamina, and be able to control yourself. All those things are important in making love.

—JAN STEPHENSON

Golf is not a game of good shots. It's a game of bad shots.

—BEN HOGAN

Golf is neither a microcosm of nor a metaphor of life. It is a sport, a bloodless sport, if you don't count the ulcers.

—DICK SCHAAP

If you watch a game, it's fun. If you play at it, it's recreation. If you work at it, it's golf.

—Bob Hope

Playing golf is a little like carving a turkey. It helps if you have your slice under control.

—Bob Orben
WRITER

In golf, driving is a game of free-swinging muscle control, while putting is something like performing eye surgery and using a bread knife for a scalpel.

—Tommy Bolt

Golf is 60 or 70 contestants over 200 acres doing unpredictable things at improbable times. It's an 18-ring circus without a ringmaster.

—Nick Seitz
WRITER

Undulation is the soul of golf.

—H.N. WETHERED

Golf is a non-violent game played violently from within.

—BOB TOSKI

There is one big difference. You're standing still in golf. Stand still in football and you're dead.

—HALE IRWIN
ON THE DIFFERENCE BETWEEN GOLF AND FOOTBALL

Golf is a game of the head as well as a game of the hands.

—JEROME TRAVERS
A LEADING AMATEUR GOLFER OF THE EARLY 20TH CENTURY

Golf is a day spent in a round of strenuous idleness.

—WILLIAM WORDSWORTH

The perfect game of golf has never been played. It's 18 holes in one.
—BEN HOGAN

Playing golf is like eating. It's something which has to come naturally.
—SAM SNEAD

It's a little like sex. One bad performance and you begin to wonder.
—JULIUS BOROS
ON LOSING HIS CONFIDENCE IN HIS GOLF GAME AT AGE 55

A golfer is someone with hoof and mouth disease. He hoofs it all day and mouths it all night.
—WILL ROGERS

This game is great and very strange.
—SEVE BALLESTEROS

In golf, humiliations are the essence of the game.

—ALISTAIR COOKE

Golfers are the only athletes who must dive through hundreds of spectators while in the middle of a game. It's like allowing fans to come out of the football stadium and ask for Joe Namath's autograph between plays.

—DAN SIKES

It's not your life, it's not your wife, it's only a game.

—LLOYD MANGRUM

Golf is like tennis. The game doesn't start until the serve gets in.

—PETER THOMSON

[G]olf offers an unusual combination of rigid specifications mixed with sometimes wild and unpredictable irregularities of nature . . . the constantly changing conditions and infinite variety of holes define the essence of the game.

—ROBERT TRENT JONES, SR.
IN HIS BOOK *GOLF BY DESIGN*

Golf is typical capitalist lunacy.

—GEORGE BERNARD SHAW

Golf is, in part, a game, but only in part. It is also part of a religion, a fervor, a vice, a mirage, a frenzy, a fear, an abscess, a joy, a thrill, a pest, a disease, an uplift, a brooding melancholy, a dream of yesterday, a disappointing today, and a hope for tomorrow.

—GRANTLAND RICE

Golf may be played on Sunday, not being a game within the view of the law, but being a form of moral effort.

—STEPHEN LEACOCK
FROM *WHY I REFUSE TO PLAY GOLF*

Golf is a peculiar game of a peculiar people.

—JOHN L. LOW

Don Quixote would understand golf. It is the impossible dream.

—JIM MURRAY

You go out and play your game. Sometimes it comes out as 68 and sometimes to 74. That's not fatalism, that's golf.

—PETER OOSTHERHUIS
AFTER BEING CALLED "FATALISTIC" RATHER THAN "ASSERTIVE"

Golf is a dumb game. Hitting the ball is the fun part of it, but the fewer times you hit the ball the more fun you have. Does that make any sense?

—LOU GRAHAM

In so many English sports, something flying or running has to be killed or injured; golf calls for no drop of blood from any living creature.

—HENRY LEACH
FORMER ADMIRAL OF THE FLEET AND FIRST
SEA LORD OF THE ROYAL NAVY

Golf is the indispensable adjunct of high civilization.
—ANDREW CARNEGIE
SCOTTISH BUSINESSMAN PHILANTHROPIST

Golf is a game for people who are not active enough for baseball.
—PRESIDENT WILLIAM HOWARD TAFT
THE FIRST OF MANY U.S. PRESIDENTS TO PLAY SERIOUS GOLF

Golf is a game in which you yell 'fore,' shoot six, and write down five.
—PAUL HARVEY

Too dull. It's a visual-neurological sport. It's so ridiculous.
—RALPH NADER

Golf, especially championship golf, isn't supposed to be fun, was never meant to be fair, and never will make any sense.

  —CHARLES PRICE

Golf remains, now as always, a sport geared toward fat men in plaid pants who think that *Fortune* magazine is racy.

  —JOE QUEENAN

CHAPTER TWO

Competition:
On Winning, Losing, and the
Pursuit of Excellence

Harvey Penick had seen enough of life that he was willing to accept that other forces could be at work. Winners, he said, were a "different breed of cat." The pun was unintentional. The belief was formed long before a prodigal cub with a feline nickname emerged to claim dominion over pro golf's manicured savannahs. The legendary teacher also spoke of it being one's time, the Man upstairs placing his arm around this one's shoulder, and not that one. Given golf's improbable finishes, enthralling as infuriating, divine intervention is as plausible an explanation as any.

Harvey may have known more than he let on. A painting hangs in the living room of a certain two-time Masters champion. Past the depiction of Ben Crenshaw famously crouched over the hole, emotions rising like a geyser, artist Opie Otterstad fittingly included the wizened teacher visage. He's peering out from one of Augusta National's majestic pines.

On his way to a less-celebrated if no less miraculous finale, Hale Irwin uncharacteristically four-putted from eight feet. Though it was early in the final round, he fell precipitously out of a tie for the lead. Spectators were then treated to the sight and sound of the three-time U.S. Open champion chewing himself out from under a small stand of trees. Much to his surprise, he later learned he'd won the tournament. The primal dressing down apparently had a cleansing, calming effect. After the implosion he resolved to merely play each shot in turn. That old cliché! Later, shrugging his shoulders, he was at a loss for words.

We recognize excellence when we see it. There are times we can even sense its approach. On rare occasions we find ourselves basking in its glow. Routinely inexplicable, there must be some explanation. It's enough to give a man pause. The more one sees in golf, the more likely one is to arrive at the conclusion that, as with most things, Harvey probably knew what he was talking about.

* * * * *

Winning isn't everything, but wanting it is.

  —ARNOLD PALMER

Winning isn't everything, but wanting it is.

No one remembers who came in second.

  —WALTER HAGEN

I really believe that when things are going your way, it is your destiny to win. So many great things happen.

  —SEVE BALLESTEROS
  GOLF DIGEST

Seve can have an off week and still win. But if Seve plays well and the rest of us play well, Seve wins.

  —BEN CRENSHAW
  ON GOLFER SEVE BALLESTEROS

He goes after a golf course like a lion at a zebra. He doesn't reason with it . . . He tries to hold its head under the water until it stops wriggling.

  —JIM MURRAY
  ON SEVE BALLESTEROS

When Jack Nicklaus told me I was playing Seve Ballesteros, I took so many pills that I'm glad they don't have drug tests for golfers.

—FUZZY ZOELLER
ON HIS RYDER CUP MATCH, WHICH HE HALVED

I think the biggest pressure comes from myself, I have very high expectations . . . I always feel like when I come to a tournament I want to be ready to play and that's one of the reasons I don't play as many events. I want my game to be top notch and I want every chance to win.

—ANNIKA SÖRENSTAM

I was criticized for years for being unsociable, but for me, how can you be mates with people you're trying to beat?

—NICK FALDO

That didn't really happen. It was a mirage. It was weird, like the whole thing wasn't happening.

—JOHNNY MILLER
AFTER WINNING THE 1994 AT&T PEBBLE BEACH NATIONAL PRO-AM

I know there's a lot of guys who would love to see me fail. Well, good. Let 'em. I'm glad.

—JOHN DALY

Always remember that however good you may be, the game is your master.

—J.H. TAYLOR

Someone has admirably described him in a championship as streaming ahead of the crowd like forked lightning and conveying a sense that thunderbolts are under his jurisdiction . . . There is indeed a murderous power about the man when he is really fighting for victory.

—HAROLD BEGBIE
ON J.H. TAYLOR

Hell, it ain't like losing a leg!

—BILLY JOE PATTON
ON LOSING THE MASTERS

Good golfing temperament falls between taking it with a grin or shrug and throwing a fit.

—SAM SNEAD

It's wonderful how you can start out with three strangers in the morning, play 18 holes and by the time the day is over you have three solid enemies.

—BOB HOPE

The average golfer doesn't play golf. He attacks it.

—JACK BURKE JR.

It's a heck of a lot harder to stay on top than it is to get there.

—TOM KITE

Every once in a while, you see Tiger Woods and David Duval playing the way they've played and you think it's easy to win. It's just not that easy.

—PAUL AZINGER

It seemed like every putt I hit, the hole got in the way.

—RONNIE BLACK
ON HITTING A 63 TO WIN THE TOURNAMENT.

———◆———

If a man can shoot 10 birdies, there's no reason why he can't shoot 18. Why can't you birdie every hole on the course?

—BEN HOGAN

———◆———

The answer to Hogan is, I fancy, that if Hogan means to win, you lose.

—HENRY LONGHURST

———◆———

Ben Hogan will keep winning championships as long as he wants to badly enough.

—BOBBY JONES

———◆———

Only way you beat Ben is if God wanted you to.

—TOMMY BOLT
ON BEN HOGAN

There's an old saying about match play, that three-up with two holes to play never wins.

—JIM APFELBAUM

It is there a psychology for winning? I don't understand the psychological function of the human mind sufficiently to answer that very well, except to say that winners are different. They're a different breed of cat.

—BYRON NELSON

It's great knowing how heavy the Wanamaker Trophy is.

—PAUL AZINGER
AFTER WINNING THE 1993 PGA CHAMPIONSHIP

Great champions have an enormous sense of pride. The people who excel are those who are driven to show the world and prove to themselves just how good they are.

—NANCY LOPEZ

Never give a golfer an ultimatum unless you're prepared to lose.

> —ABIGAIL VAN BUREN
> "DEAR ABBY"

———•———

You kind of play up to your competition. You're playing with the best players in the world, and your concentration and your focus goes to the next level.

> —MATT KUCHAR
> 1997 US AMATEUR CHAMPION

———•———

In those days, the money was the main thing, the only thing I played for. Titles were something to grow old with.

> —BYRON NELSON
> ON PLAYING TO WIN IN THE 1937 MASTERS

———•———

My caddie didn't want me to go for it. I looked at him and said: 'I don't ever want to win a golf tournament if that's the way to do it. I want to win like a champion.'

> —AMY ALCOTT
> ON HITTING A 3-IRON FROM HEAVY ROUGH TO THE FINAL
> GREEN WHEN SHE HAD A TWO-SHOT LEAD

If I ever get bored with golf, I'm going to start over and play left-handed.
—MICHELLE WIE

They must have been embarrassed that I won, because they canceled the tournament the next year.
—GARY MCCORD
AFTER THE HOGAN TOUR CANCELED THE GATEWAY OPEN IN 1992

I think professional golfers are the most competitive athletes of all. Every time out, we play against the whole league. The league never has a bad day either.
—JIM COLBERT

People ask me how good I would be with a strong back. But I've done pretty well with the one I have.
—FUZZY ZOELLER

I had a strange feeling. I do remember walking down the 15th fairway, which has always been something of a turning point in the event. I had a weird sensation that it was my tournament to win. It was strange, because under normal circumstances you feel like throwing up.

—DOTTIE MOCHRIE
ON WINNING THE 1992 NABISCO DINAH SHORE

Competitive golf has been the center of both our lives, and yet the differences between us—the factors that made us such intense and faithful competitors, I believe—are still as apparent to anyone who wishes to take time to look.

—ARNOLD PALMER
ON JACK NICKLAUS AND HIMSELF, FROM *A GOLFER'S LIFE*
WITH JAMES DODSON

To succeed at anything, you must have a huge ego. I'm not talking about confidence. Confidence is self-assurance for a reason. Ego is self-assurance for no good reason.

—FRANK BEARD

Yeah. I think when I play golf, yes, I think I have to make the world revolve around me. If you want to be the best at something, you have to make it revolve around what you are doing. Is that clear?

—JACK NICKLAUS
GOLF DIGEST

The truly great things happen when a genius is alone. This is true especially among golfers.

—J.R. COULSON

In golf, the best players prefer the strongest tests, where skill is most readily rewarded, inferior play is promptly penalized, and the gap between the best and the mediocre is widened.

—JOSEPH C. DEY
EXECUTIVE DIRECTOR OF THE UNITED STATES GOLF ASSOCIATION (1934–1968) AND FIRST COMMISSIONER OF THE PGA TOUR

When I'm in contention coming down to those last few holes . . . it is a miserable, sick, lonely feeling. You're so scared, sometimes you can't see. But when I can pull off a good shot on those holes, that's what I look forward to. And I figure I haven't won nearly enough.

> —SANDRA PALMER
> WINNER OF 21 LPGA EVENTS

In stroke play I don't particularly care what the guys I am playing with . . . do, because you're just trying to play the course. In match play I think you find yourself rooting against your opponent a lot more, because the difference between winning a hole could be the difference . . . [in] the match.

> —MARK CALCAVECCHIA
> *GOLF DIGEST*

I'm almost delighted I lost. I might have turned pro otherwise.

> —BILLY JOE PATTON
> ON LOSING THE MASTERS

I can't exactly describe it, but as I looked at the putt, the hole looked as big as a wash tub, I suddenly became convinced I couldn't miss. All I tried to do was keep the sensation by not questioning it.

—JACK FLECK
ON THE 1955 US OPEN, WHICH HE WON

Nine times out of ten, scores are very just bases on which to judge the respective merits of golfers.

—HERBERT WARREN WIND
IN THE BOOK *THE STORY OF AMERICAN GOLF*

I'm a perfectionist. I have to win. If I can't be best at anything I try I'd just quit.

—BETH DANIEL
DURING HER SECOND YEAR ON THE LPGA TOUR

. . . I have another reason for saying you should always play hard to win, apart from the fact that it improves your golf. I think you owe it to your opponent . . . I should feel insulted if I found out that my opponent had purposefully eased up because he felt sorry for me . . .

—GARY PLAYER
FROM *PLAY GOLF WITH GARY PLAYER*

Miss this little putt for fifteen hundred? I should say not.

—WALTER HAGEN
BEFORE SINKING A 10-FOOTER

Tommy Morris eclipsed his contemporaries and totally changed their conception of how well the game could be played—like Vardon, Jones and Hogan in later generations.

—MICHAEL HOBBS

[Great players] learn that they don't need to play their best golf to win. They only need to shoot the lowest score.

—RICK REILLY
IN HIS ESSAY "BANK SHOT"

It is hard work to play a game in the other fellow's country, and it seems that a probationary visit is needed before even the greatest can give of their best.

—BERNARD DARWIN
FROM *THE DARWIN SKETCHBOOK*

Seems I used to do everything like I was on a mission. If it was alcohol, I wanted to drink till I couldn't see straight. If it was golf, I wanted to beat everybody's brains out. If it was driving, I can get there faster'n you can . . . I was stubborn as hell. I had no direction.

—JOHN DALY

Until you win a tournament, you're just a day laborer, really working hard trying to get there.

—LOREN ROBERTS

That's how it should be in golf. OK, I'm trying to beat your brains in, but there still should be respect. Even if I'm not good enough on the day.

—ERNIE ELS
GOLF DIGEST

I knew if I could play 25, 30 tournaments, I'd show up with a chance to win; you have to have that confidence. I don't know if that's brash, but I always felt I had the capability to play well out here.

—WOODY AUSTIN
BEFORE WINNING THE 1995 BUICK OPEN

The kids on the Tour today are too good at losing. Show me a 'good loser' and I'll show you a 'seldom winner.'

 —SAM SNEAD

The glorious thing is that thousands of golfers, in park land, on windy downs, in gorse, in heather, by the many-sounding sea, enjoy their imbecilities, revel in their infirmities, and from failure itself draw that final victory—the triumph of hope.

 —R.C. ROBERTSON-GLASGOW

Hagen said that no one remembers who finished second. But they still ask me if I ever think about that putt I missed to win the 1970 Open at St. Andrews. I tell them that sometimes it doesn't cross my mind for a full five minutes.

 —DOUG SANDERS

To be a champion, you have to find a way to get the ball in the cup on the last day.

 —TOM WATSON

The mark of a great player is in his ability to come back. The great champions have all come back from defeat.

—SAM SNEAD

When a man misses his drive, and misses his second shot, and wins the hole with a birdie—it gets my goat.

—BOBBY JONES
AFTER LOSING TO WALTER HAGEN IN MATCH PLAY IN 1926

It's nice to have the opportunity to play for so much money, but it's nicer to win it.

—PATTY SHEEHAN

You're a good loser if you can grip the winner's hand without wishing it was his throat.

—HAL CHADWICK

Sometimes it's harder to play with a big lead. I've found that out myself. Instead of trying to win the golf tournament, you don't want to lose it. If guys are catching up . . . you kind of start to get nervous.

—VIJAY SINGH

I'm here and I can play, and I can play against anyone . . . I've proved that to myself over and over again. To me, I love having the opportunity to do it when I need to.

—ANNIKA SÖRENSTAM

I'm here because golf is my sport and I like to compete . . . Just by being here I'm already beginning to win.

—SEVE BALLESTEROS

I'm a very intense person. When I go after something, I want to go after it with everything I have. I want to push myself to the edge.

—GREG NORMAN

You have got to try to think, that guy is your enemy. That is the way competition is. You want to win. I didn't care who I played. But I respected everyone I played. And I'd like people to think I was fair.

    —SAM SNEAD
    GOLF DIGEST

Never let up. The more you can win by, the more doubts you put in the other players' minds the next time out.

    —SAM SNEAD

I dreamed I made 17 holes in one, and then on the 18th hole I lipped the cup and I was madder than hell.

    —BEN HOGAN

Having a good time is winning the tournament.

    —JAN STEPHENSON

The player who is going to win the most often is not the one superior in strength of distance, but the one who can make the fewest mistakes and keep out of as much trouble as possible, but when once in trouble can cope with any situation.

—ALEXA STIRLING
THE SO-CALLED "EMPRESS OF GOLF," SHE WON 3 US WOMEN'S
AMATEURS AND WAS THE CHILDHOOD GOLFING PARTNER
OF BOBBY JONES

This run doesn't have to end. If someone is going to beat me then I'm going to make sure they've worked for their victory. Let them come and get it from me.

—NICK FALDO

Winning tournaments is all great, these guys have all won tournaments. But what it boils down to is having the opportunity to walk the fairways with your heroes, with the true champions of the game.

—PETER JACOBSEN

It's always hard to sleep when you got a big early lead. You just lie there and smile at the ceiling all night.

—Dave Stockton

I know I can shoot low scores. The challenge is for me to shoot them more often.

—Bruce Lehnard

How can they beat me? I've been struck by lightning, had two back operations, and been divorced twice.

—Lee Trevino

There is a constant truth about tournament golf. Other men have to lose a championship before one man can win it.

—Dan Jenkins

He didn't beat me, sir. I beat myself, I beat myself.

—J.H. Taylor
WINNER OF 5 BRITISH OPENS, AFTER LOSING A MATCH

Absolutely everyone has done it, but there are few people who admit it.

    —DAVID FEHERTY

      ON CHOKING

Years from now I want people to be able to say: 'I saw Faldo play.'

    —NICK FALDO

It was a contest to see who could play the ugliest today, and I won . . . the contest, not the match.

    —STEWART CINK

      AFTER LOSING THE LEAD

I call my sand wedge my 'Half Nelson' because I can always strangle the opposition with it.

    —BYRON NELSON

While an effective golf swing is an essential ingredient to compete at the game's highest level, it is far from the only ingredient necessary to be a champion.

—TJ TOMASI
FROM *THE 30-SECOND GOLF SWING*

I know I made a lot of money, finished second on the Order of Merit, won three times, won the Ryder Cup, won the Dunhill Cup, but I was still very pissed off on Sunday, and I still am.

—SAM TORRANCE
ON NOT WINNING

I hope they regret it the rest of their lives.

—DAVID GRAHAM
INTERNATIONAL TEAM CAPTAIN AT THE INAUGURAL PRESIDENT'S CUP, CRITICIZING PLAYERS WHO OPTED NOT TO COMPETE

Al Geiberger should have to take a test to prove he's a member of the human race.

—LEE TREVINO
AFTER GEIBERGER SHOT A RECORD 59 AT THE DANNY THOMAS OPEN

We all think about winning, that's why we are out here . . . you just need some breaks to go your way, and when that happens, you better take advantage of it.

 —BILLY ANDRADE

Most golfers prepare for disaster. A good golfer prepares for success.

 —BOB TOSKI

More matches are lost through carelessness at the beginning than any other cause.

 —HARRY VARDON

I've never done that in the heat of battle. Usually, I do it in tournaments where I miss the cut.

 —GEORGE ARCHER
  ON HITTING AN EAGLE 2 ON HIS WAY TO WINNING A TOURNAMENT

I'll probably be hearing from the blooming Queen herself.

      —TONY JACKLIN
          WINNING HIS FIRST EVENT IN THE US

You haven't got a chance . . . I mean, I own the place!

      —DONALD TRUMP
          BEFORE A ROUND OF GOLF

This is what it's all about—competition, and I thrive on competition. I'm a very, very competitive person.

      —COLIN MONTGOMERIE

To my mind, Moe Norman is in the same league as Ben Hogan, Bobby Jones and Byron Nelson as a ball-striker and deserves the same kind of respect.

      —WALLY UHLEIN,
          CEO OF TITLEIST AFTER IT WAS ANNOUNCED HIS COMPANY WOULD
          PAY NORMAN $5,000 A MONTH FOR THE REST OF HIS LIFE

I'm not sure that the most talented player I ever saw wasn't myself.

—JOHNNY MILLER

I'm going to win so much money this year, my caddie will make the top twenty money winner's list.

—LEE TREVINO

If you guarantee them $20,000 for second place, they wouldn't take it. They must have the opportunity to win. If I were offered the same money, I'd grab it and stay home and watch the tournament on TV.

—FRANK BEARD
ON THE WINNING OBSESSION OF SEVERAL PLAYERS

Thank you. How did you do?

—BEN HOGAN
SAID TO CLAYTON HEAFNER, WHO FINISHED SECOND AT THE US 1951 OPEN, TWO STROKES BEHIND HOGAN

Why do I enjoy golf after 31 years, going out there and doing things that are necessary to be competitive—having practice, having to work, having to dedicate yourself? I guess it comes down to the competition. My personality . . . I'm not going to play if I'm not competitive.

—RAYMOND FLOYD
GOLF DIGEST INTERVIEW

Victory is everything. You can spend the money, but you can never spend the memories.

—KEN VENTURI

It's no fun getting up Sunday morning and being one of the first groups off and trying to figure out what flight you can make to get home. It's nice to be here late and have the opportunity to win.

—JIM FURYK

There is nothing—I speak from experience—in a round of either match or medal competition that bears down with quite the pressure of having continually to hole out putts of three and four feet . . . the kind left by overly enthusiastic approaches.

—BOBBY JONES

Golf is a game of days, and I can beat anyone on my day.

—FUZZY ZOELLER

Roberto, the clubs got heavy.

—LEE TREVINO
TO ROBERTO DE VICENZO AFTER LOSING A LEAD WITH
TWO HOLES TO PLAY

Twenty-five million people saw Roberto [De Vicenzo] birdie the 17th hole. I think it would hold up in court.

—JIMMY DEMARET
AFTER THE ARGENTINEAN WRONGLY SIGNED FOR A PAR ON THE HOLE
AND MISSED A PLAYOFF BY A STROKE

I lost that round in a bar.

—ROGER MALTBIE
ON SHOOTING A RECORD 92 AT A TOURNAMENT AFTER GOING OUT
DRINKING THE NIGHT BEFORE

All true games, I have said, are contests. But in golf the contest is not with your fellowman. The foe in golf is not your opponent, but great Nature herself, and the game is to see who will overreach her better, you or your opponent.

—ARNOLD HAULTAIN
THE GOLF BOOK

Par isn't good enough. Par is for wimps. These guys can really dispatch and destroy golf courses.

—TOM COYNE

I've always enjoyed the competition and playing against the best. That's why I came to the U.S. to play on this tour.

—SERGIO GARCIA

Golf is the most marvelous game. When I was at my tennis peak, there were half a dozen, say a dozen, guys who could give me a game. In golf, I can play against all but the most abject hacker and have a tough time.

—ELLSWORTH VINES

I think I fail a bit less than everyone else.

—JACK NICKLAUS

———•———

Walter Hagen had a sterling contempt for second place. He believed that the public only remembered a winner, that a man might as well be tenth as second when the shooting was over.

—HERBERT WARREN WIND

———•———

Every time I won, I wasn't sure what I could do. The ultimate shots, the ones you have to hit to win golf tournaments, were never certain with me.

—HALE IRWIN

———•———

Every golfer worthy of the name likes to think that he is just as good at the man-to-man competition as he is at shooting against par.

—BEN HOGAN

———•———

A good golfer has the determination to win and the patience to wait for the breaks.

—GARY PLAYER

The one thing that Hogan and Snead and I had in common was that we wanted to beat somebody.

—Byron Nelson

A lot of guys who have never choked have never been in the position to do so.

—Tom Watson

I'll shake his hand on the first tee and I'll shake his hand on the 18th green, but between those handshakes we are competitors and we'll be trying to beat each other as much as possible.

—Colin Montgomerie

I learned how to win by losing and not liking it.

—Tom Watson

If I'm destined to win, it's going to happen. I'm going to try my hardest.

—Michelle Wie

If your adversary is badly bunkered, there is no rule against your standing over him and counting his strokes aloud, with increasing gusto as their number mounts up; but it will be a wise precaution to arm yourself with the niblick before doing so, so as to meet him on equal terms.

—HORACE HUTCHINSON

When their names are mentioned, which is all too infrequently, there is almost invariably a shade of sadness that accompanies the names of men who are remembered not as winners but as losers.

—HERBERT WARREN WIND
ON MACDONALD SMITH, LEO DIEGEL AND HARRY COPPER, WHO ARE EXCELLENT GOLFERS WHO NEVER WON A NATIONAL CHAMPIONSHIP

It's not whether you win or lose—but whether I win or lose.

—SANDY LYLE

I'm a perfectionist. I want to be as good as I can.

—KARRIE WEBB

I'm tired of giving it my best and not having it be good enough.

—JACK NICKLAUS
AFTER LOSING THE BRITISH OPEN BY ONE SHOT IN 1977

Consistent winners refuse to wait for breaks to happen.

—JACK WHITAKER

Whenever there are winners, there must be losers. In golf the winner is the man who brings the lowest score in stroke play, or who scores lower on more holes than his opponent in match play.

—HERBERT WARREN WIND
IN THE BOOK *THE STORY OF AMERICAN GOLF*

I see no reason why a golf course cannot be played in 18 birdies. Just because no one has ever done that doesn't mean it can't be done.

—BEN HOGAN

My frustration centers on not being able to play as well as I once did. I still could play regularly, but don't want to. I was out there from 1955 through 1969. That's fifteen years of motels and competitive pressure.

—MICKEY WRIGHT
IN A *GOLF DIGEST* INTERVIEW

My game was my business and as a business it demanded constant playing in the championship bracket, for a current title was my selling commodity.

—WALTER HAGEN
FROM HIS AUTOBIOGRAPHY *THE WALTER HAGEN STORY*

But then there's a little part of me that says, 'You know what? I still think I can get better, I still think I can do this and that.' That's what keeps me going.

—ANNIKA SÖRENSTAM

I get bored easily. I like challenges. I've played against men my whole life. I want to play against the best players in the world, men and women.

—MICHELLE WIE

There is no other loser in sport who has shown himself to be as gracious and warm as Nicklaus has shown himself to be.

—HERBERT WARREN WIND

If money titles meant anything, I'd play more tournaments. The only thing that means a lot to me is winning. If I have more wins than anybody else and win more majors than anybody else in the same year, then it's been a good year.

—TIGER WOODS

I'm happy out of my mind. I like beating a lot of people.

—MICHELLE WIE

I'm trying as hard as I can, and sometimes things don't go your way, and that's the way things go.

—TIGER WOODS

Every golfer has a little monster in him. It's just that type of sport.

—FUZZY ZOELLER

If you want to beat someone out on the golf course, just get him mad.

—DAVE WILLIAMS
GOLF COACH

———•———

You don't want to see him hitting 5-woods while you're swinging a driver. You don't want to see him draining 40-foot putts twice on the front nine. You don't want to see him splashing bunker shots within three feet for up-and-down. Really, you don't want to see him, period.

—MICHAEL WILBON
ON TIGER WOODS, "TIGER FINDS WAY TO EXCLUSIVE CLUB,"
WASHINGTON POST

———•———

I've heard players speak proudly of fifth-place finishes. If you can be happy with fifth, it could be that you don't have what it takes to win.

—MICKEY WRIGHT
ON THE LPGA TOUR IN 1976

I was tryin's to get so far ahead I could choke and still win, but I had to keep on playin'.

—LEE TREVINO
ON BEING CHASED BY JACK NICKLAUS IN THE 1968 US OPEN

I guess deep inside, I'm still twenty years old and feel I can make every putt I look at. The goal, even though it isn't a realistic one, is to putt my best every day.

—TIGER WOODS
FROM HIS BOOK *HOW I PLAY GOLF*

About five weeks a year I play my best golf. The rest of the time I play like Johnny Hack out there.

—FUZZY ZOELLER

I always wanted to be the best I could be at whatever I did. I didn't want to be the number one golfer in the world. I just wanted to be as good as I could be. I work hard, I push myself hard, and I probably even expect too much of myself.

—GREG NORMAN

I guess I must have choked.

—BERT YANCEY
AFTER HIS FINAL ROUND COST HIM THE 1968 US OPEN
CHAMPIONSHIP

Every time I'd get close to a major prize, my hands would begin to shake, and for a moment or two, when it counted most, the demons of doubt would whisper in my ear and I honestly wondered if I could win again.

—ARNOLD PALMER
ON THE DECLINE OF HIS GAME

I'm the best and I'll thank you to remember that.

—HARRY VARDON

A competitor will find a way to win. Competitors take bad breaks and use them to drive themselves just that much harder. Quitters take bad breaks and use them as reasons to give up. It's all a matter of pride.

—NANCY LOPEZ

I beat Tiger Woods by five strokes—but he was only six at the time.
—GREGG ZAUN
KANSAS CITY ROYALS CATCHER, ON COMPETING AGAINST
WOODS AS A JUNIOR

If you look at most of the guys, it looks like their peak years are in their 30s. Hopefully, that'll be the case for me. Obviously, there's a lot deeper competition, a lot more work I need to get done. I need to work very hard to accomplish those goals, but ultimately it's winning major championships that I want to do.
—TIGER WOODS

Here is a philosophy of boldness to take advantage of every tiny opening toward victory.
—ARNOLD PALMER

No, I don't go places for sentiment—I have that at home. I came here believing I had a chance . . . to win.
—BEN HOGAN
ASKED AT AGE 53 IF HE CAME TO THE MASTERS FOR
SENTIMENTAL REASONS

On iron shots, he's so far ahead of anyone else that I don't even know who rates second.

> —FRANK BEARD
> ON BEN HOGAN BEING THE BEST IRON SHOOTER EVEN AT AGE 53

Running through all his golf is that vein of pugnacity. Archie Compston is always prepared to meet anybody, anywhere, any time for any sum, and will walk on the first tee with an unbounded belief in his own ability to win.

> —E.M. COCKELL
> ON ARCHIE COMPSTON

I'd like to thank Tom and Ed for missing all those putts.

> —FUZZY ZOELLER
> AFTER WINNING THE 1979 MASTERS DUE IN PART TO SOME
> MISSED PUTTS BY TOM WATSON AND ED SNEED

Too much tax.

> —ISAO AOKI
> ON NOT TAKING ADVANTAGE OF A CONDO HE WON IN
> THE UNITED STATES FOR SHOOTING A HOLE-IN-ONE

I'm the best. I just haven't played yet.

—MUHAMMAD ALI
ON GOLF

A win is a win. It's just some events have more significance than others. That's all it is. But the title is the title.

—GREG NORMAN

Tommy Armour is a great golfer—a superlative golfer. But he is something more than that—he is a personage. He has what it takes to stand out from the herd.

—CLARENCE BUDDINGTON KELLAND

Who's going to be second?

—WALTER HAGEN
SAID COMMONLY BEFORE A TOURNAMENT BEGAN

If I had to go play holes or golf courses or golf tournaments that have defeated me in my career, I wouldn't have time for anything else.

> —RAYMOND FLOYD

He's going to have to play a lot better next year or he's going to have to watch a lot of me.

> —BRENT MUSBURGER
> RESPONDING TO JOHN DALY'S CRITICISM

I retired from competition at twenty-eight, the same age as Bobby Jones. The difference was that Jones retired because he beat everybody. I retired because I couldn't beat anybody.

> —CHARLES PRICE

I missed the nine-hole cut.

> —DAVE MARR
> ON SHOOTING A 70 IN AN EXHIBITION MATCH WHERE NICKLAUS
> SHOT 66, SNEAD SHOT 64, AND BOROS SHOT 62

January shoots low when the money's high.
—LEE TREVINO, ON JANUARY'S CLUTCH PLAY

Hush-a-bye, baby, pretty one, sleep;

Daddy's gone golfing to win the club sweep.

If he plays nicely (I hope that he will)

Mother will show him her dressmaker's bill.

Hush-a-bye, baby, safe in your cot;

Daddy's come home, and his temper is hot.

Cuddle down closer, baby of mine;

Daddy went round in a hundred and nine!

—ANONYMOUS

I play with friends, but we don't play friendly games.
—BEN HOGAN

The problem is, I'm already over $2 million in spending.

—CHI-CHI RODRIGUEZ
ON HAVING REACHED A MILLION DOLLARS IN CAREER EARNINGS

Be brave if you lose and meek if you win.

—HARVEY PENICK

You hear that winning breeds winning. But no winners are bred from losing. They learn that they don't like it.

—TOM WATSON

Golf is war. And like all wars, if you're not looking to win you probably shouldn't show up.

—CAPTAIN BRUCE WARREN OLLSTEIN

I like trying to win. That's what golf is all about.

—JACK NICKLAUS

The only emotion Ben shows in defeat is surprise. You see, he expects to win.

> —JIMMY DEMARET
> ON FRIEND BEN HOGAN

I look into their eyes, shake their hand, pat their back, and wish them luck, but I am thinking, 'I am going to bury you.'

> —SEVE BALLESTEROS

I can tell right away if a guy is a winner of a loser just by the way he conducts himself on the course.

> —DONALD TRUMP

. . . and again Paradise played its part, this time a less heavenly one, because he robbed me of a hole by playing what I still think is one of the best shots I ever saw, with a wooden club off a wet road, right over the woods and onto the green . . .

> —BERNARD DARWIN
> ON DEFEATING HORACE HUTCHINSON IN MATCH PLAY IN 1900

Over the first three rounds you're playing the course. In the final round, if you're in contention, you're playing the man.

—JACK NICKLAUS

I've taken some pleasure out of being the little guy who has beaten the big fellows. At match play, don't think that isn't an advantage, because a big guy would rather lose to a big guy.

—PAUL RUNYAN

I have an agenda, to beat 53 other guys.

—COLIN MONTGOMERIE

In the case of all game players, yearbooks and books of scores are the only things to count in the long run, when the time of living memory is past: the names of 'uncrowned kings' are apt to fade and be forgotten.

—BERNARD DARWIN
ON GOLFERS WHO FAIL TO WIN

If you ever see a man who has tied with another for a medal, in the luncheon interval with a biscuit and a lemon soda, you may go out and bet your modest half-crown against that man with a light heart.

—HORACE HUTCHINSON
1890

He plays with the frigidity of dry ice. He is the most merciless of all the modern golfers.

—GENE SARAZEN
ON BEN HOGAN

I've always made a total effort, even when the odds seemed entirely against me. I never quit trying; I never felt that I didn't have a chance to win.

—ARNOLD PALMER

There are questions all the time, every week, whether people know me or not. It's not just annoying, it hurts. I'm not trying to make errors, to miss a shot, but it happens. Every ounce of me is out there trying to be the best.

—PAT BRADLEY
EARLY IN HER LPGA HALL OF FAME CAREER

The sweetest two words are 'next time.' The sourest word is 'if.'

—CHI-CHI RODRIGUEZ

———◆———

When talents are equal, it's that extra effort that makes the difference in the close ones. In almost every endeavor, success failure depends on execution, precision, inches, seconds, unbelievable skill, unbelievable performances, unbelievable happenings.

—JACK WHITAKER

———◆———

Forget it. I can beat any two players in this tournament by myself. If I need any help, I'll let you know.

—BABE ZAHARIAS
REASSURING HER NERVOUS PARTNER PEGGY KIRK BELL AT THE START OF A FOUR-BALL EVENT

———◆———

Honestly, I don't feel like I'm here to prove anything. I'm here to play golf. I know where I'm at on the money list. You know where I'm at. I'm here to reach my own goals, play my own game. I don't look at it that way. I see it as an opportunity for me.

—ANNIKA SÖRENSTAM

On paper, they should be caddying for us. But that isn't what this is about. It's about bringing your game to the event . . . and they bring it.

—Payne Stewart
DESCRIBING THE EUROPEAN RYDER CUP TEAM

Do I wish I was longer? Sure. I'll get longer, but everybody else will, too. It was a power game last year, and I finished fourth on the money list, so it can be done.

—Jim Furyk

I don't care what anybody says. The first tournament is not the hardest one to win. It's always the second one.

—John Daly

I asked myself the question I always ask when the heat is really on: For all the cash, what shot would you play?

—Jim Colbert
GOLF DIGEST

There are always some fellows in there against you, shooting just as good golf or better.

—BEN HOGAN
ON WHAT DROVE HIM TO BE THE BEST

Forget your opponents; always play against par.

—SAM SNEAD

I love the challenge and I love coming down the stretch and making the shots you need to . . . It's just the extra excitement, knowing there are just a few holes left and having to hit the perfect shot. That's when all my adrenaline starts kicking in, on the back nine because that's when it matters.

—ANNIKA SÖRENSTAM

I worked for my money, why shouldn't they? Why should I support them now—if I get sick, are they going to feel an obligation to support me?

—LOUISE SUGGS
ON HER OPPOSITION TO SHARING PURSES WITH
GOLFERS IN A TOURNAMENT

Arnold Palmer is the most aggressive player in the history of golf. Some guys, if they're behind six or seven strokes, they start playing for fourth place. Arnold could be behind six or seven strokes and the last day he'd go out and try to shoot zero.

—CHARLIE SIFFORD

Actually, Ben didn't leave himself much time for laughter. I can't recall him ever finding humor in anything that happened on the golf course. Golf was his business—a tough business, full of disappointments.

—FRED CORCORAN
ON BEN HOGAN

The main problem with keeping your eye on the ball is you have to take your eye off your opponent.

—BRUCE LANSKY

I never knew what top golf was like until I turned professional. Then it was too late.
—STEVE MELNYK

———•———

He comes onto a tee looking like a prize fighter climbing into the ring ready for a world championship bout.
—CHARLES PRICE
ON ARNOLD PALMER

CHAPTER THREE

The Mental Game:
On Motivation, Risk, Control, Luck, and Getting "In the Zone"

Shrouded in mist, impervious as Everest stands golf's eternal (and infernal!) frontier. For most of us the expanse between the ears presents a fitful ascent, our breathing affected with each plodding step. A field of untapped riches, the mental game resists Man's indefatigable attempts to reach and secure the summit, defying (alas) even his steadfast faith in technology.

Various practitioners of the healing and black arts now direct a cottage industry ministering to the seeker. They load him down with stores of metaphorical maps, picks, shovels, and divining rods. Ah, but the journey must necessarily be a solitary trek. The prospector, no matter how well equipped, travels alone to stake his claim.

Why the weekend 59er should expect to strike gold when the game's immortals forlornly continue to dig in the hot sun long after their claim has run dry calls into question not only our sanity, but theirs. And, then, when it's least expected, after, say, the sixth try at qualifying school (in the case of Masters' winner Mike Weir), or when we're finally—this time for good—going to pack it in, something catches our eye in the streambed. We visualize a positive result, listen to the tape and recite the mantra as directed. Lo and behold the shot materializes in the mind's eye. The ball does what it's told, the impossible putt falls. Amidst the sifted sand a glistening nugget appears in our pan—Eureka!

We're again smitten with the fever. And so the trek continues though fool's gold lines the trail.

"It is a compulsive game," observed Henry Longhurst, who understood.

* * * * *

Ninety percent of golf is played from the shoulders up.

> —DEACON PALMER
> GOLF PRO AND FATHER TO ARNOLD PALMER

Jimmy Demaret and I had the best sports psychologist in the world. His name was Jack Daniels and he was waiting for us after every round.

> —JACKIE BURKE
> CRITICIZING MODERN PLAYERS FOR USING MENTAL COACHES

Unlike any other game player, the golfer can go virtually alone into the breach and have himself a tilt. It is just he and the golf course, and the latter essentially passive. The golfer is Don Quixote attacking a windmill, a windmill that is literally, and . . . figuratively, himself.

> —AL BARKOW, 1974
> *GOLF'S GOLDEN GRIND: A HISTORY OR THE TOUR*

We really have to play with 15 clubs. The 14 in our bag and the 15th in our head.

> —GREG TWIGGS

I've got to go out there and try to figure out how I'm going to play, how I'm going to manage my game, and how I'm going to beat everybody else in the field, and that's how I think out there.

—VIJAY SINGH

The mark of a champion is the ability to make the most of good luck and the best of bad.

—ANONYMOUS

Everyone has his own choking level, a level at which he fails to play his normal golf. As you get more experienced, your choking level rises.

—JOHNNY MILLER

I think that to score in golf is a matter of confidence. If you think you cannot do it, then there is no chance that you will.

—HENRY COTTON

When facing a hazard, focus your attention sharply on your target, not the hazard.

 —Dr. Bob Rotella
  Sports Psychologist

All golfers . . . get to the stage where they feel that they have reached the limit of their capabilities and that they cannot improve any further . . . There is no way of telling yourself that this kind of streak will come to an end, it's just a matter of perseverance.

 —George Will
  From *Good Advice for Men and Women Golfers*

The only shots you can be sure of are those you've had already.

 —Byron Nelson

This game is so elusive. You try to maintain the peaks and level up the valleys.

 —Tom Watson

You have to be calm and collected, he says. Golf, if you will excuse his using a long word, is a psychological game. Have a picture in your mind, he says, of the right way of hitting through the ball and you can do it.

> —JOHN P. MARQUAND
> ON LOSING THE 1986 MASTERS TO JACK NICKLAUS
> FROM *THE WAY THE BALL BOUNCES*

In golf you almost always beat yourself or are destroyed by the game.

> —AL BARKOW

Fact one: anyone with normal coordination can become the best putter in the world. Fact two: great putting can make up for many other faults during a round. But no one putts well day-in and day-out if they don't first believe they are a great putter.

> —PIA NILSSON
> COACH OF THE SWEDISH NATIONAL GOLF TEAM

When we first arrived, some of the players were talking about how nervous they were. I squelched that right away. I want no negativity. I wanted everything and everybody up. I told them if they were nervous I would get them some vaseline for their teeth to quiet the chattering noise.

> —JOANNE CARNER

In golf, as in no other sport, your principal opponent is yourself.

　　—HERBERT WARREN WIND

———◆———

The mind messes up more shots than the body.

　　—TOMMY BOLT

———◆———

Of the mental hazards, being scared is the worst. When you get scared, you get tense.

　　—SAM SNEAD

———◆———

There's a heightened sense of pressure on every shot, and there's no sense denying it. Recognize it, and deal with it.

　　—MIKE WEIR

———◆———

I've quit worrying about poor shots. I just tell myself, 'Relax, Bozo. If you can't have fun, you shouldn't be out here.'

　　—PATTY SHEEHAN

The best way to win any important event is to play just as one would play a private round at home, and not endeavor to accomplish the performance of a lifetime. There is such a thing as trying too hard; it begets anxiety, which is usually fatal—especially in putting.

—HARRY VARDON

As a golfer, you feel like you're perpetually on the rack [in foursomes]. Mentally, it's very difficult.

—BEN CRENSHAW

I believe that the very best thing I do—better than my setup, better than my backswing turn, better than my downswing turn—is to visualize a perfect shot in my mind every time I step up to the ball.

—JOHN DALY
FROM *GRIP IT AND RIP IT*

When I play my best golf, I feel as if I'm in a fog, standing back watching the earth in orbit with a golf club in my hands.

—MICKEY WRIGHT

You have to understand, I don't play golf for fun. It's my business. When the mailman starts delivering mail on his off day, that's when I'll start playing golf for the hell of it.

—LEE TREVINO

I think a lot of people have high expectations of me, but I have high expectations of myself.

—MICHELLE WIE

Golf puts a man's character on the anvil and his richest qualities—patience, poise, restraint—to the flame.

—BILLY CASPER

The word is control. That's my ultimate—to have control.

—NICK FALDO

Success depends almost entirely on how effectively you learn to manage the game's two ultimate adversaries: the course and yourself.

—JACK NICKLAUS

Golf is at least fifty percent mental game, and if you recognize that it is the mind that prompts us physically, then we can almost say that golf is entirely a mental game.

—PETER THOMSON

I've been down six before, but I've never been six down and won. You've got to stay positive, and that's all I wanted to do.

—TIGER WOODS

With a fine sea view, and a clear course in front of him, the golfer should find no difficulty in dismissing all worries from his mind, and regarding golf, even it may be indifferent golf, as the true and adequate end of man's existence.

—ARTHUR JAMES
FIRST EARL OF BALFOUR, GOLF

When you are young and facing a fifty-to-one shot through an opening in trees with a two-iron you say, 'What the heck?' and try it. You are so gifted physically and so ungifted mentally.

—RAY FLOYD

Through the ball we are all the same. We just have different ways of getting it there.

—CHARLES COODY

———◆———

That's the key when you do pick a club—to be decisive. If you make an indifferent swing, you're not sure when you're hitting the shot, you're not going to like what happens. You just have to pick your club and trust it and go ahead and hit it.

—MIKE WEIR

———◆———

It's easy to keep things going when you're rolling in a bunch of birdie putts.

—JIM FURYK

———◆———

I go into the locker room and find a corner by myself and just sit there. I try to achieve a peaceful state of nothingness that will carry over onto the golf course. If I get the feeling of quiet and obliviousness within myself, I feel I can't lose.

—JANE BLALOCK
LPGA AND SENIOR LPGA TOUR MEMBER

These guys have no fear? Not to them, it's not; they've been doing it all their lives.

—BUTCH HARMON

To play well you must feel tranquil and at peace. I have never been troubled by nerves in golf because I felt I had nothing to lose and everything to gain.

—HARRY VARDON

It's funny . . . you need a fantastic memory in this game to remember the great shots and a very short memory to forget the bad ones.

—GARY McCORD

The ego is everything. And if you can't get that pumped up regularly, you can't last.

—DAVE MARR

If you're not just a little bit nervous before a match, you probably don't have the expectations of yourself that you should have.

—HALE IRWIN

I had always suspected that trying to play golf in the company of big-time pros and a gallery would be something like walking naked into choir practice.

—DAN JENKINS
WRITER

The trouble with me is I think too much. I always said you have to be dumb to play good golf.

—JOANNE CARNER

Seeing the line is a curious thing and I am free to confess I do not well understand it. I suppose it's one of those psychological phases of golf.

—BOBBY JONES

We're also still walking around with the same mental demons. A 4-foot putt to win will never get any less petrifying.

—DAVID FEHERTY

If you're stupid enough to whiff, you should be smart enough to forget it.

—ARNOLD PALMER

Psychologically, the driver is very important. If you hit your tee ball well, it fills you with confidence. On the other hand, if you smash a couple of drives into the trees, your confidence can be shaken.

—HARVEY PENICK
HARVEY PENICK'S LITTLE RED BOOK BY HARVEY PENICK
WITH BUD SHRAKE

Once the golfing champion allows himself to suspect that playing a superb round is not the be-all and end-all of life he is lost.

—ANONYMOUS

If the mind is full of fear or failure—a dread of the next approach, a persistent thought of three putts although the green is still far away—then . . . there is but one thing that can at all help and that is to see the humor of the situation.

> —JOYCE WETHERED

Making a million or having the return of his laundry delayed by fiscal factors, nothing bothers Hagen. He could relax on a hot stove.

> —TOMMY ARMOUR
> ON WALTER HAGEN

Listen to your heart and your gut. That small voice inside you. How often have you left the house knowing you've forgotten something, and it turns out you have? Intuition is very powerful, and certainly it's true in golf.

> —NICK FALDO

My ability to concentrate and work toward that goal has been my greatest asset.

> —JACK NICKLAUS

It's nice to get under par and play with house money for a change. You can love a place, but you still have to perform.

—Curtis Strange

It is a game in which the whole temperamental strength of one side is hurled against the strength of the other, and the two human natures are pressing bitterly and relentlessly last.

—Henry Leach

If you expect a bad lie for even one second, the gods will know it and give you a bad lie.

—Michelle Wie

After a golfer has been out on the circuit for a while he learns how to handle his dating so that it doesn't interfere with his golf. The first rule usually is no woman-chasing after Wednesday.

—Tony Lema

Nicklaus not only enjoys a tremendous advantage percentage-wise but also holds a substantial psychological edge over his opponents with his long ball.

—ARNOLD PALMER

I have been trying to listen to my heart more on the golf course when I make decisions about a shot. However, my heart just isn't beating loud enough.

—HALE IRWIN
ON THE LINE OF PUTTS

I'm not really interested in sports psychology. It makes me feel like a crazy person.

—MICHELLE WIE

A few disasters resulting from a desire to display brilliant technique are enough to harden even the most sensitive nature . . . Once the round is under way, the business at hand becomes that of getting results. Nothing else matters.

—BOBBY JONES

Champions, at every level, play by targeting. Every shot is a target-player interaction where the player connects to the target through the senses, making the connection a multisensorial experience.

—TJ Tomasi
FROM *THE 30-SECOND GOLF SWING*

However unlucky you may be, it really is not fair to expect your adversary's grief for your undeserved misfortunes to be as poignant as your own.

—Horace Hutchinson

I say this without any reservations whatsoever: It is impossible to outplay an opponent you can't outthink.

—Lawson Little

I do not remember any other golfer who did not consider himself, on the whole, a remarkably unlucky one.

—Sir Walter Simpson

My luck is so bad that if I bought a cemetery, people would stop dying.

—ED FURGOL
ON HIS GOLF LUCK

———•—•———

On the golf course, a man may be the dogged victim of inexorable fate, be struck down by an appalling stroke or tragedy, become the hero of an unbelievable melodrama, or the clown in a sidesplitting comedy—any of these within a few hours.

—BOBBY JONES

———•—•———

The greedy golfer will go too near and be sucked into his own destruction.

—JOHN L. LOW
SCOTTISH AMATEUR GOLFER, GOLF WRITER AND ARCHITECT

———•—•———

Every day in every way I am getting better and better and, believe it or not, you did. What Benny wants you to say is simply that every day in every way your golf is getting better. Say it two thousand times and then go out and see what happens.

—JOHN P. MARQUAND
FROM *THE WAY THE BALL BOUNCES*

I've always felt that I had to prove myself. I've never felt people thought that much of me, I guess.

—BETH DANIEL
LPGA TOUR PLAYER

Too much ambition is a bad thing to have in a bunker.

—BOBBY JONES

If you travel first class, you think first class and are more likely to play first class.

—RAY FLOYD

Anyone who hasn't been nervous, or hasn't choked somewhere down the line, is an idiot.

—CARY MIDDLECOFF

You have to take this game through so many labyrinths of the mind, past all the traps, like: 'Will my masculinity be threatened if I hit the ball well and still shoot 72?'

—MAC O'GRADY

The loss of enthusiasm—I think that happens to everybody when they don't play well. I'm not one of those guys who can be confident and happy when they're not playing well. It got to be a vicious circle. I wasn't playing well, so I wasn't confident.

> —CURTIS STRANGE
> EXPLAINING HIS SLUMP AFTER WINNING BACK-TO-BACK US OPENS IN 1988 AND 1989

Confidence is what you need in golf.

> —JOHN P. MARQUAND
> FROM *THE WAY THE BALL BOUNCES*

He's made one of the greatest attempts to play of any athlete I've seen.

> —PAYNE STEWART
> ON PAUL AZINGER'S VALIANT FIGHT AGAINST CANCER IN 1994

In competition you must be yourself . . . If you're the joking sort, go ahead and joke. If you're the serious sort, there's no need to pretend not to be.

> —HARVEY PENICK
> FROM *HARVEY PENICK'S LITTLE RED BOOK*

I believe most of us would be restored to golfing health all the more quickly if we could make for ourselves a self-denying ordinance, and refrain from thinking for a minimum of one whole round.

    —BERNARD DARWIN

The excellence of anyone's game depends on self-control.

    —ALEX MORRISON

It is hard to know you don't have the game to win, and that making the cut is the best you can hope for . . . you never have rhythm. Then you lose confidence. You are what you believe you are.

    —SEVE BALLESTEROS
    GOLF DIGEST

You're embarrassed. You're in a fog. You're standing in front of the world and it's like you're playing the hole naked.

    —TOM WIESKOPF
      DESCRIBING HIS THOUGHTS ON HIS WAY TO THE 12TH HOLE AT THE
      1980 MASTERS

For true success, it matters what our goals are. And it matters how we go about attaining them. The means are as important as the ends. How we get there is as important as where we go.

—YOUNG TOM MORRIS

———◆———

The golfer, though, stands alone. He starts and finishes the deed; every shot he plays is a one-on-one confrontation with his own nervous system, power of concentration, ego.

—AL BARKOW

———◆———

Concentration comes out of a combination of confidence and hunger.

—ARNOLD PALMER

———◆———

Let's face it, 95 percent of this game is mental. A guy plays lousy golf, he doesn't need a pro—he needs a shrink.

—TOM MURPHY

Better scoring is out there for you if you want it. But you have to go get it. You have to earn it. And in the words of the greatest mind in golf, Yoda, 'Try not. Do, or do not. There is no try.'

—DAVE PELZ
FROM DAVE PELZ'S SHORT GAME BIBLE

The number one guys have to be almost totally self-centered. They have to possess an incredible burning for success. They have to ignore their friends and enemies and sometimes their families and concentrate entirely on winning.

—FRANK BEARD
SENIOR TOUR PLAYER

Hit the shot you know you can hit, not the one you think you should.

—DR. BOB ROTELLA
SPORTS PSYCHOLOGIST

Too many people carry the last shot with them. It is a heavy and useless burden.

—JOHNNY MILLER

It's OK to have butterflies. Just get them flying in formation.

  —FRANCISCO LOPEZ

Of all the hazards, fear is the worst.

  —SAM SNEAD

It's nice to worry about playing golf and not all the other stuff.

  —JOHN DALY
   ON HIS TROUBLES OFF THE COURSE

The excellence of anyone's game depends on self control.

  —ALEX MORRISON
   A NEW WAY TO BETTER GOLF

I'm just going to play as hard as I can [today]. Try as hard as I can. You know whatever happens happens, and hopefully it will be a good round.

  —DAVID LEADBETTER

When I play, my mind-set is that I can beat everyone . . . [But] I don't really think I'm the best yet.

—MICHELLE WIE

Show me someone who gets angry once in a while, and I'll show you a guy with a killer instinct. Show me a guy walking down the fairway smiling, and I'll show you a loser.

—LEE TREVINO

I told him, 'I promise you one thing: You'll never meet another person as tough as you.' He hasn't. And he won't.

—EARL WOODS
ON HIS SON, TIGER

Memories like that help. We all have something like that we can pull upon. Maybe not in a match-play situation, but in some kind of tournament where you did something that maybe you weren't sure you would be able to pull it off. That can become infectious.

—JUSTIN LEONARD

Every great player has learned the two Cs: how to concentrate and how to maintain composure.

—BYRON NELSON

Most of us have a real warped idea of the amount of control we have over anything. It's not that we can't control certain aspects of this game, it's that we think we can control everything. That's where our error is.

—ANNETTE THOMPSON

Before mental skills can really make a difference, a golfer has to develop swing skills and course management.

—CAROL MANN

Aggressive play is a vital asset of the world's greatest golfers. However, it's even more important to the average player. Attack this game in a bold, confident, and determined way, and you'll make a giant leap toward realizing your full potential as a player.

—GREG NORMAN

If I didn't putt well, it was 80s for me every time . . . I was hooking the ball from fear, not from my swing. I was wearing myself out mentally on the course, physically on the range.

—IAN BAKER-FINCH

But the butterflies in the stomach have hatched, and as we take our stance the line of the putt wriggles and slips around like a snake on glass.

—JOHN UPDIKE
ON THREE- AND FOUR-FOOTERS

I don't have any particular hang-ups about superstitions. I did try them all, but they didn't work.

—KATHY WHITWORTH

Seve Ballesteros is a rare kind of guy. He's an excitable golfer who can still concentrate.

—LARRY NELSON

I'm waiting for the day when everything falls into place, when every swing is with confidence, and every shot is exactly what I want. I've been close enough to smell it a couple times, but I'd like to touch it. Then I think I would be satisfied.

—TOM WATSON

The fundamental problem with golf is that every so often . . . the odds are that one day you will hit the ball straight, hard, and out of sight. This is the essential frustration of this excruciating sport.

—COLIN BOWLES
AUTHOR

The biggest challenge you face on the tee—even before you decide what kind of shot you want to hit—is changing your mind-set from 'driving range' to 'on the course.'

—JOHNNY MILLER

Nobody can know what's in my heart. Nobody can know what I'm thinking. I know what I've got to do.

—JOHN DALY

All athletes, when they get in pressure situations, revert to what they know. I don't think you are going to revert to mechanics. I think you revert to feel.

—JACK NICKLAUS
GOLF DIGEST, 1991

The dollars aren't important . . . once you have them.

—JOHNNY MILLER

I sometimes lose control of my emotions so completely that I don't know where I am or that it's me hitting the ball.

—MICKEY WRIGHT

I have only one goal in golf—to leave it with my sanity.

—JOE INMAN
MEMBER OF THE PGA TOUR

After taking the stance, it is too late to worry. The only thing to do then is to hit the ball.

—BOBBY JONES

That's a dream scenario. No surprises. No distractions, no shenanigans, nothing to have to keep an eye on or out for. No problems with pace of play or gamesmanship. Just golf.

—JIM APFELBAUM

When I first came on tour, it terrified me to hit the first drive. I was lucky if I kept it in play. That feeling has disappeared for the most part, but I still feel it once in a while.

—LON HINKLE

Be decisive. A wrong decision is generally less disastrous than indecision.

—BERNHARD LANGER

Golf should make you think, and use your eyes, your intelligence, and your imagination. Variety and precision are more important than power and length.

—JACK NICKLAUS

I don't think I'm afraid of anybody out there. I just think, you know, it's really up to me how I play.

—VIJAY SINGH

I know my limitations in golf. Payne [Stewart] used to be able to hit a 1-iron so high that it would land so soft, like a wedge. Me, I don't even carry a 1-iron. In my work life, hopefully I can hit a high 1-iron.

—DONALD TRUMP
GOLF DIGEST

If you want it, get it and spend it. It's only money, not something to worship. If you run out, go out and get some more.

—MARK CALCAVECCHIA

You create your own luck by the way you play. There is no such luck as bad luck. Fate has nothing to do with success or failure, because that is a negative philosophy that indicts one's confidence, and I'll have no part of it.

—GREG NORMAN

You must attain a neurological and biological serenity in chaos. You cannot let yourself be sabotaged by adrenaline.

—MAC O'GRADY
ON PLAYING GOOD GOLF

The trouble with golf is you're only as good as your last putt.

—DOUG SANDERS
PGA PRO

A goal is not the same as a desire, and this is an important distinction to make. You can have a desire you don't intend to act on. But you can't have a goal you don't intend to act on.

—YOUNG TOM MORRIS

I felt something heavy. It was not that I was not feeling well. Maybe you could call it pressure.

—AYAKO OKOMOTO
AFTER FAILING TO WIN THE MAZDA-PGA CHAMPIONSHIP

If she's dumb enough to play, I'm dumb enough to let her.

—Mrs. Tillie Stacey
mother of Hollis Stacey, when Hollis played with
tendonitis in her right wrist

———•———

A tournament goes on for days. It is played at a dangerously high mental pressure. Golf makes its demands on the mind. A golfer is terribly exposed in almost every way. The responsibility is his and there is no way to camouflage this, no hope of jettisoning it.

—Peter Alliss
Aliss Through the Looking Glass

———•———

The most rewarding things you do in life are often the ones that look like they cannot be done.

—Arnold Palmer

———•———

I became more and more aware of the feeling of the game, of how it was to walk from shot to shot, how it was to feel the energy gathering as I addressed the ball, how the golf links smelled.

—Michael Murphy
from *Golf in the Kingdom*

The other truth about golf spectatorship is that for today's pros it all comes down to the putting, and that the difference between a putt that drops and one that rims the cup, though teleologically enormous, is intellectually negligible.

—JOHN UPDIKE
THE GOLF BOOK

—◆—

We have to be pretty self-centered and confident in ourselves to be successful on the Tour. We have strong personalities—maybe even more so than other professions—because we have to depend solely on our abilities.

—BETSY KING

—◆—

The simpler I keep things, the better I play.

—NANCY LOPEZ

—◆—

It's very important to take the lead early on. You want to set the pace. It's great to have the momentum on your side. It's tough to fight from behind.

—ANNIKA SÖRENSTAM

Confidence in golf means being able to concentrate on the problem at hand with no outside interference.

—TOM WATSON

Golf has probably kept more people sane than psychiatrists have

—HARVEY PENICK

The shank—of all the golfing diseases, shanking is by far the most outrageous in its devastating results.

—ROGER WETHERED
FROM *THE GAME OF GOLF*, 1931

To control his own ball, all alone without help or hindrance, the golfer must first and last control himself. At each stroke, the ball becomes a vital extension, an image of one's innermost self.

—JOHN STUART MARTIN
FROM *THE CURIOUS HISTORY OF THE GOLF BALL*

I'll tell you one thing about chasing a little white ball. Make what you want out of it, but it's all on the greens—and half of that's in your head.

 —TOM WEISKOPF

I wouldn't be here if there wasn't a golf tournament here. They're all the same—greens, tees. I'm here because there's money to be won.

 —LEE TREVINO
  RESPONDING TO A GALLERY MEMBER WHO ASKED WHETHER
  HE LIKED PINEHURST NO. 2

I accept the fact that I'm going to miss it sometimes. I just hope I miss it where I can find it.

 —FUZZY ZOELLER
  FROM *THE SWING: MASTERING THE PRINCIPLES OF THE GAME*

He's a genius, but it's definitely a flawed genius. You know that quote about how God doesn't give you everything? With Monty, it's the inability to control himself at given moments.

 —DENIS PUGH
  ON COLIN MONTGOMERIE

The next time you see a good player stalking backward and forwards on the green, do not be led away by the idea that he is especially painstaking, but rather pity him for a nervous individual who is putting off the evil moment as long as he possibly can.

—TED RAY

You've got to gamble every once in a while in a round of golf. I'm not afraid to screw up.

—FUZZY ZOELLER

Maintain a childhood enthusiasm for the game of golf.

—CHI-CHI RODRIGUEZ

In those days [the 1930s] the money was the main thing, the only thing I played for. Championships were something to grow old with.

—BYRON NELSON

You don't realize the pressure you're under trying to make the cut. By Sunday you feel as if you were in a prize fight.

—DAVE STOCKTON

If you have to remind yourself to concentrate during competition, you've got no chance to concentrate.

—BOBBY NICHOLS

My ultimate ambition is to be able to afford to retire from the game because it drives me berserk.

—DAVID FEHERTY

If I can visualize something, then it is easier for me to work there . . . I need to see things. Goals are things I can understand, I can touch.

—ANNIKA SÖRENSTAM

Try to feel that you are looser and more decisive on the eighteenth hole than you were on the first. Feel more likely to coin the last tournament of the season than the first.

—DR. BOB ROTELLA

———

My caddie dared me to try it, but I didn't think it was worth losing a ball.

—IAN WOOSNAM
AFTER PLAYING PARTNER JOHN DALY HIT A 421-YARD SHOT

———

When I joined the Tour I studied the best players to see what they did that I didn't do. I came to the conclusion that the successful players had the Three Cs: Confidence, Composure, Concentration.

—BOB TOSKI

———

Don't let the bad shots get to you. Don't let yourself become angry. The true scramblers are thick-skinned. And they always beat the whiners.

—PAUL RUNYAN

Sometimes things work out on the golf course and sometimes they don't. Life will go on.

—GREG NORMAN

The first one was okay. The second one was pretty tough.

—GENE SAUERS
AFTER JOHN COOK CHIPPED IN TWO STRAIGHT
PLAYOFF HOLES TO BEAT SAUERS

Every day I try to tell myself that this is going to be fun today. I try to put myself in a great frame of mind before I go out—then I screw it up with the first shot.

—JOHNNY MILLER

Golf is the only game that pits the player against an opponent, the weather, the minutest details of a large chunk of local topography, and his own nervous system, all at the same time.

—MIKE SEABROOK

Sometimes thinking too much can destroy your momentum.

—TOM WATSON

A hundred years of experience has demonstrated that the game is temporary insanity practiced in a pasture.

—DAVE KINDRED
COLUMNIST

The first thing you gotta learn about this game, Doc, is it isn't about hitting a little white ball into some yonder hole. It's about inner demons and self-doubt and human frailty and overcoming all that crap.

—RON SHELTON
FROM HIS SCREENPLAY FOR THE FILM *TIN CUP*

Walk the course and annotate your scorecard with distances before an important match. It will save you the element of doubt as you prepare to hit your shots.

—DR. BOB ROTELLA

There is no shape nor size of body, no awkwardness nor ungainliness, which puts good golf beyond reach. There are good golfers with spectacles, with one eye, with one leg, even with one arm. In golf, while there is life there is hope.

—SIR WALTER SIMPSON
THE ART OF GOLF

You can talk to a fade but a hook won't listen.

—LEE TREVINO

Remember you have to be comfortable. Golf is not a life or death situation. It's just a game and should be treated as such. Stay loose.

—CHI-CHI RODRIGUEZ

Thinking instead of acting is the number-one golf disease.

—SAM SNEAD

It may be a little bit more nerve-wracking to be standing on the tee and announced as defending champion and you've got to go out there and play well, but a lot of guys ride on that, they love that thrill, and I do.

—VIJAY SINGH

It takes years to build up your confidence, but it hardly takes a moment to lose it. Confidence is when you stand over a shot and know you're going to make it because you've done it time and time again.

—JACK NICKLAUS

I love to watch *Oprah*, *Geraldo*, all the shows about dysfunctionals. That's my psychoanalysis. I realized I wasn't as bad as I thought.

—MAC O'GRADY
PGA TOUR PROFESSIONAL

There are people better coordinated than I am and with more ability, but if I had to choose, I'd take somebody with confidence over somebody with natural talent.

—SANDRA PALMER
1975, IN "SANDRA PALMER CAN HANDLE THE PRESSURE,"
BY SARAH BALLARD, *SPORTS ILLUSTRATED*

The three things I fear most in golf are lightning, Ben Hogan, and a downhill putt.

> —SAM SNEAD

You all think I'm out here for my score. I'm not.

> —FUZZY ZOELLER

I've tried to pay attention and not look around so much. But there's a lot to look at.

> —FRED COUPLES
> ON CONCENTRATION IN GOLF

The person I fear most in the last two rounds is myself.

> —TOM WATSON

I just try to put it on the fairway, then the green and not three putt.

> —PETER THOMSON
> ON HIS GAME

When you get right down to it, golf is about one thing—putting the ball in the hole. And when you break it down even further, all you can do is hit the ball, go find it, and hit it again.

—Annika Sörenstam
From *Every Shot Must Have a Purpose*

———◆———

When you play golf, just play golf. Here's you, here's the ball, there's the target. Go to it. Hit the ball to the target as best you can. Find the ball and do it again. Experience, adjust, experience, adjust.

—Chuck Hogan

———◆———

First tee ball at those things is more daunting to me than any business deal.

—Donald Trump
on playing at Pro-Am Tournaments

———◆———

The more you miss, the worse it gets. The worse it gets, the more likely you are to miss again.

—Dave Pelz
1997, from the article, "You Need a Ritual," *Golf* magazine, with James A. Frank

If there's something I know now that I wish I knew earlier in my career, it would be that I wish I hadn't been in such a hurry to play, had learned to wait, to be more patient. But that wasn't my nature.

—HARRY "LIGHTHORSE" COOPER

On the putting green the mind can be grave source of trouble. Begin to dislike the look of a putt, and the chances of holing it at once become less.

—JOYCE WETHERED

The number-one thing about trouble is . . . don't get into more.

—DAVE STOCKTON

I don't derive satisfaction from trying to satisfy other people's expectations. I am not out to prove anything to you or to anybody else. I am out to prove it to me.

—DAVID DUVAL

What makes a great captain? Twelve great players. My job is to get them matched up and motivate them so they make me look good. If they play good, we all look great. If they don't, I look dumb.

—CURTIS STRANGE
AFTER BEING ELECTED THE US RYDER CUP CAPTAIN

It's not artificial and no tricks about it. Either you hit the fairway or you're going to be in trouble.

—MIKE WEIR

The most important facets of golf are careful planning, calm and clear thinking and the ordinary logic of common sense.

—PETER THOMSON
PRO GOLFER AND MEMBER OF THE WORLD GOLF HALL OF FAME

A golfer chokes when he lets anger, doubt, fear, or some other extraneous factors distract him before a shot.

—DR. BOB ROTELLA
FROM *GOLF IS NOT A GAME OF PERFECT*

Its power as a symbol is so complex and labyrinthine, so capable of lending itself to the psyche of each and every player, that once an attempt like this has begun to comprehend its inner meaning, all bearings may be lost.

  —MICHAEL MURPHY
   ON GOLF
   FROM *GOLF IN THE KINGDOM*

I think that I always adhere to my old theory that a controlled shot to a closely guarded green is the surest test of any man's golf.

  —A.W. TILLINGHAST

The zone is a funny area . . . What you see, well, it's more like what you don't see. You don't see anything but a four-inch-wide strip right in front of your face. Everything else disappears. The tents are gone, everything is gone. And it takes a while to get out of it.

  —PATTY SHEEHAN
   ON THE FOCUSED STATE KNOWN AS "THE ZONE"

It is commitment that separates the three levels of golfers—those who can't play, those who can play sometimes (usually when there is no pressure), and those who can play no matter what's at stake.

—TJ TOMASI
FROM *THE 30-SECOND GOLF SWING*

He doesn't need a challenge, I think that is the worst misconception going. That the number-one golfer needs a number-two golfer to push him. Tiger is pushed by history and by records and by his own goals. He doesn't need anybody pushing him.

—EARL WOODS

You seem to forget that luck is a part of the game and a good golfer must be good at all parts of the game.

—WALTER TRAVIS
WHEN IT WAS SUGGESTED THAT HE LOST THE US AMATEUR
BECAUSE OF AN OPPONENT'S LUCK

I tend to be a nervous, anxious player in the first place, so I've found that if I just think about taking the club back away from the ball very slowly it helps focus my attention and improves the pace of my swing.

  —RUSS COCHRAN

People think Trevino's loosey goosey. In fact he's tight as a drum. They think he's relaxed. Really, he's so intense he has to talk and joke constantly to relieve the tension.

  —DALE ANTRUM
   ON LEE TREVINO

For this game you need, above all things, to be in a tranquil frame of mind.

  —HARRY VARDON

Competitive golf is played mainly on a five-and-a-half-inch course, the space between your ears.

  —BOBBY JONES

If you can't laugh at yourself, then how can you laugh at anybody else? I think people see the human side of you when you do that. I don't think it's healthy to take yourself too seriously.

—PAYNE STEWART

In the game of life it's a good idea to have a few early losses, which relives you of the pressure of trying to maintain an undefeated season.

—LEE TREVINO

If I never win a major or never hit another golf ball again, I can look back and say I'm successful. I only need to look at my house to know that. I didn't inherit it . . . I earned it.

—COLIN MONTGOMERIE

Do you know how many times I've had some guy on a Toro lawnmower on my butt as the sun is going down and I'm trying to make a six-footer to make the cut?

—DENNIS TRIXLER
JOURNEYMAN GOLFER

Relax? How can anybody relax and play golf? You have to grip the club, don't you?

> —Ben Hogan

You can flop it up there and look like a hero, but it is all luck.

> —Tiger Woods
> ON HIS CHIP SHOT AFTER COMING FROM BEHIND
> TO WIN THE 1994 US Amateur

Give luck a chance to happen.

> —Tom Kite

Good players have the power to think while they are competing. Most golfers are not thinking even when they believe they are. They are only worrying.

> —Harvey Penick

I'm a strong believer in fate. And I believe it's not over. Anything is possible.

> —Justin Leonard

Try to think where you want to put the ball, not where you don't want it to go.

—BILLY CASPER

The muttered hint, 'Remember, you have a stroke here,' freezes my joints like a blast from Siberia.

—JOHN UPDIKE

Thinking you are going to win the Crosby Pro-Am with a high handicap makes as much sense as leaving the porch light on for Jimmy Hoffa.

—BILL HARRIS

Moderation is essential in all things, madam, but never in my life have I failed to beat a teetotaler.

—HARRY VARDON
ON BEING ASKED TO JOIN THE TEMPERANCE MOVEMENT

Having a great golf swing helps under pressure, but golf is a game of scoring.

—JERRY PATE

Laddie, a blind hole is blind only once to a man with a memory.
—TOMMY ARMOUR

When you play the game for fun, it's fun. When you play it for a living, it's a game of sorrows.
—GARY PLAYER

You have the hands, now play with the heart.
—ROBERTO DE VICENZO
TO SEVE BALLESTEROS, BEFORE HE WON THE 1979 U.S. OPEN

When the big four-oh jumps up and grabs you, you realize there's only a limited amount of time left. It brings a sense of urgency.
—LANNY WADKINS
ON WINNING TWO TOURNAMENTS AT AGE 40

Golf pros, almost to a man, are conservative. Perhaps this is forced on them by the game they play. Golf is a game of considered judgment, careful ball placement and strategy, the avoidance of hazards. Most who play are not prone to take chances.

—AL BARKOW
ON THE NATURE OF THE TOUR

Splosh! One of the finest sights in the world: the other man's ball dropping in the water—preferably so that he can see it but cannot quite reach it and has therefore to leave it there, thus rendering himself so mad that he loses the next hole as well.

—HENRY LONGHURST

If you must, let your practice swing be the one where you think of mechanics. Once your mechanics feel right, take a trial swing to concentrate on the target and the feel.

—DR. BOB ROTELLA
SPORTS PSYCHOLOGIST

Either a wise man will not go into bunkers, or, being in, he will endure such things as befall him with patience.

—ANDREW LANG

If I can just keep playing steady and build on the momentum, anything can happen. I'm hitting enough quality shots. I feel confident.

—MIKE WEIR

In golf you've got two continuously merciless competitors, yourself and the course.

—TOMMY ARMOUR

You just know. You've got the feel. Everything is right: Your clothes look good, your hair's perfect and you managed to shave your legs that day without cutting yourself.

—PATTY SHEEHAN
ON THE FEELING JUST BEFORE A HOT STREAK

First you've got to be good, but then you've got to be lucky.

—HARRY COOPER

————◆————

Next to the idiotic, the dull unimaginative mind is the best for golf.

—SIR WALTER SIMPSON

————◆————

If you are going to continue to rely on somebody every time, you never end up doing it yourself.

—JACK NICKLAUS
GOLF DIGEST 1991, ON TEACHERS

————◆————

It got to where I just hated to go out to the golf course . . . There was panic and fear because I didn't know where the ball was going or whether I'd even hit it! To actually fear playing golf after having done so well is a terrible experience.

—KATHY WHITWORTH
DESCRIBING WHAT IT WAS LIKE SLUMPING

Peter Alliss used to say I hit miracle shots. I never thought that. Miracles don't happen very often; I was hitting those shots all the time.

—SEVE BALLESTEROS
GOLF DIGEST

❖

I know how to choke. Given even a splinter-thin opportunity to let my side down and destroy my own score, I will seize it. Not only does ice water not run through my veins, but what runs there has a boiling point lower than body temperature.

—JOHN UPDIKE
GOLF DIGEST, 1995

❖

Concentration is not an element that should be applied all the way around a golf course. It is not the least bit important until you are ready to shoot. There's plenty of time to concentrate when you step up to the ball.

—JULIUS BOROS
FROM *HOW TO PLAY PAR GOLF*

So if you visit Chicago, enjoy the many great courses, the Midwestern friendliness, and the city's other amenities. But if a stranger with a goofy swing wants to play for more than loose change, take a pass. It's a long walk back to your hotel in bare feet.

—MIKE ROYKO

I'm not the kind of person who will back down because people don't want me here . . . I'm not really sure that I get a lot of extra attention and stuff like that, but if I do, that's great.

—MICHELLE WIE

It's all about the bottle, the British term meaning the ability to be in a situation and feel comfortable, be in control and have the mental toughness to get the job done.

—NICK FALDO

I compare the pressure of a golf shot with making an extra point in basketball. The player starts from a full stop, and that rim doesn't move.

—HARVEY PENICK

A leading difficulty with the average player is that he totally misunderstands what is meant by concentration. He may think he is concentrating hard when he is merely worrying.

—R.T. JONES

The least thing upset him on the links. He missed short putts because of the uproar of the butterflies in the adjoining meadows.

—P.G. WODEHOUSE

Things have come out well and we can enjoy this, but golf is an unpredictable game and we shouldn't become relaxed.

—SEVE BALLESTEROS

One thing about golf is you don't know why you play bad and why you play good.

—GEORGE ARCHER

When you are on the golf course, you're the boss.

—EARL WOODS

I used golf as a Zen exercise. I learned that a person who is able to concentrate and focus can do almost anything.

—T-BONE BURNETT

But there is a difference between playing well and hitting the ball well. Hitting the ball well is about thirty percent of it. The rest is being comfortable with the different situations on the course.

—MICKEY WRIGHT
WINNER OF THE RECORD 13 LPGA TOUR TOURNAMENTS IN 1963

I try to be semi-humble. If I started going around saying how good I was, everything would go wrong.

—JOHNNY MILLER

It just happened that the hole got in the way. I was trying to make a 4 and I made a 3.

—FUZZY ZOELLER
EXPLAINING A LUCKY EAGLE 3

Don't be in such a hurry. That little white ball isn't going to run away from you.

—PATTY BERG

He started thinking, 'My Dad's going to pass me on the money list.'

—BOB DUVAL
SENIOR TOUR PRO, ON THE MOTIVATION BEHIND
HIS SON DAVID'S THREE-TOURNAMENT WINNING STREAK

Success is a choice; therefore, so is failure.

—BOB BRUE

There are 30 million golfers out there and they all suck. So I'm just going to tell them how bad I am and how good these guys are and have fun with it.

—GARY MCCORD

At first a golfer excuses a dismal performance by claiming bad lies. With experience, he covers up with better ones.

—P. BROWN

Water creates a neurosis in golfers. The very thought of this harmless fluid robs them of their normal powers of rational thought, turns their legs to jelly, and produces a palsy of the upper limbs.

—PETER DOBEREINER
WRITER

Other major American sports may be more consistently exciting, but no game has greater potential than golf for producing the cosmic gasp.

—TOM BOSWELL

Every golfer scores better when he learns his capabilities.

—TOMMY ARMOUR

In golf, as in life, the attempt to do something in one stroke that needs two is apt to result in taking three.

—WALTER CAMP
LEGENDARY COLLEGE FOOTBALL COACH

He could shoot 66 wearing tweed pants and no underwear.
> —ANONYMOUS
> ON HOW TOUGH LLOYD MANGRUM WAS

Most of us have a real warped idea of the amount of control we have over anything. It's not that we can't control certain aspects of this game, it's that we think we can control everything. That's where our error is.
> —ANNETTE THOMPSON

Concentration comes out of a combination of confidence and hunger.
> —ARNOLD PALMER

Pressure is playing for $50 a hole with only $5 in your pocket.
> —LEE TREVINO

I go to the first tee scared to death every day. The peaks do not seem to last as long as the valleys in this game.
> —J.C. SNEAD

We create success or failure on the course primarily by our thoughts.

—GARY PLAYER

Ask yourself how many shots you would have saved if you never lost your temper, never got down on yourself, always developed a strategy before you hit, and always played within your own capabilities.

—JACK NICKLAUS

Golf has its drawbacks. It is possible, by too much of it, to destroy the mind.

—SIR WALTER SIMPSON
THE ART OF GOLF

Golfers are the greatest worriers in the world of sport.

—BILLY CASPER

The more good rounds you play on a golf course, the more good memories you have to draw upon when you need to.

—MIKE WEIR

Readers are reminded that the word 'yip' was invented by T.D. Armour the great teacher of golf . . . Armour defines 'yips' as a 'brain spasm which impairs the short game.' 'Impairs' is a euphemism.

—STEPHEN POTTER
IN HIS BOOK *GOLFSMANSHIP*, 1968

If we had to play Augusta National in one hour, the best athlete would win the Masters. But as it is, they give us time to hang ourselves. Every swing is a 'thought shot.' So instead of the best athlete, you end up with the best thinker as the winner.

—JOE INMAN
MEMBER OF THE PGA TOUR

While, on the whole, playing through the green is the part most trying to the temper, putting is that most trying to the nerves.

—ARTHUR JAMES
FIRST EARL OF BALFOUR

I shot a wild elephant in Africa thirty yards from me, and it didn't hit the ground until it was right at my feet. I wasn't a bit scared. But a four-foot putt scares me to death.

—SAM SNEAD

The most advanced medical brains in the universe have yet to discover a way for a man to relax himself, and looking at a golf ball is not the cure.

—MILTON GROSS

I find a better way to let it go. I do something physical to feel better, like slam the club in the rough, slam my bag, or slap a tree.

—TOM LEHMAN
ON DEALING WITH FRUSTRATION ON THE COURSE

Golf cannot be played in anger, or in any mood of emotional excess. Half the golf balls struck by amateurs are hit, if not in rage, surely in bewilderment, or gloom, or cynicism, or even hysterically—all of those emotional excesses which must be contained by a professional.

—GEORGE PLIMPTON

If Bolt had a head on his shoulders, he would have been the best golfer who ever lived.

> —BEN HOGAN
> ON THE TEMPER OF TOMMY BOLT

I'm about five inches from being an outstanding golfer. That's the distance my left ear is from my right.

> —BEN CRENSHAW

The clubs were not the problem. My brain was.

> —PAYNE STEWART
> ON HIS TERRIBLE 1994 SEASON

Golf is a thinking man's game. You can have all the shots in the bag, but if you don't know what to do with them, you've got troubles.

> —CHI-CHI RODRIGUEZ

Basically, it's the inability to make your hands obey the commands your mind gives them.

—JOHNNY MILLER
ON THE 'YIPS'

Excessive golfing dwarfs the intellect. And this is to be wondered at, when we consider that the more fatuously vacant the mind is, the better for play. It has been observed that absolute idiots play the steadiest.

—SIR WALTER SIMPSON
FROM *THE ART OF GOLF*

I will admit that if you are in the category of self-proclaimed world's worst putters, you may have a little more mental work to do than the novice who doesn't judge himself or herself as either good or bad . . . There's no lid on the hole for anyone.

—JOHN DALY
FROM *GRIP IT AND RIP IT* BY JOHN DALY AND JOHN ANDRISANI

Set a thief to catch a thief. Set the mind to watch the mind it becomes in moments of excitement full of fancies, fears or useless wandering ideas and it may be no easy task to tie it down to the matter at hand.

  —JOYCE WETHERED

Serenity is knowing that your worst shot is still pretty good.

  —JOHNNY MILLER

There's times when you can get off to a start like that, look up on the board and see guys getting off to a good start. You want to go out and try to force things and try to make some birdies. I stayed patient and just let it happen.

  —JIM FURYK

If you're playing well, they could probably put the pin on the cart path and you'd get it close.

  —MIKE SULLIVAN

I've got a lot to think about—and all weekend to think about it.

—DAVID DUVAL

AFTER MISSING HIS FIRST CUT IN TWO YEARS

The average golfer, I can say flatly, lacks the ability to concentrate, which probably is the most important component of any good game. I believe the ability to concentrate is the difference in skill between the club player and the golf professional, even more than the shot-making process.

—DOW FINSTERWALD

I was young and righteous, but you cannot become a champion without the ability to cope with your emotions. That is the most important factor in becoming a winner. This is what it's all about—being able to control every emotion: elation, dejection, fear, greed, the whole lot.

—MICKEY WRIGHT

CHAMPION OF THE 1952 US GIRL'S JUNIOR

That way you can understand why you're driving yourself crazy.

—ALLISON FINNEY
LPGA PRO, EXPLAINING WHY SHE MAJORED IN PSYCHOLOGY

—◆—

I had a reputation for being tough. You had to be when you were Italian.

—GENE SARAZEN

The History of the Game: From Shillelagh-Wielding Scottish Shepherds to the Present

There is, it's true, some circumstantial evidence regarding the Orient, hardly more convincing, though, than the fanciful sagas of the lonely shepherd whiling away the hours amongst his flock. (No self-respecting Blackface ewe would give two a side.) People have clearly been spending idle moments whacking small round objects to various ends with sticks since ancient times. Without more compelling evidence, those absorbed with the game's genesis must look to that small but influential Atlantic island with disreputable plumbing. The southern region has given us many gifts, among them the herbaceous border and the presumption of innocence. Its rugged northern tier has also delivered to the world two rich, enduring, and distinctly Highland bequests. It is a remarkable achievement, for not only has Scotland nurtured golf but also its lifeblood: single malt whisky.

The two may not be unrelated. Those who sip a dram after 18 holes on a true links recognize one as the ideal salve for the other. A chart graph would reflect a companion spiral of activity in the rise of distilling during the 1400s, a time of both active trade with the Netherlands where Kolven, an early golf antecedent was popular, and a time of intense Scottish interest in golf; perhaps its first plausible boom.

Beginning in 1457, we have the series of parliamentary proclamations from James II, III and IV, banning *Golfe*, among other sports, as a dodge from the more important task of improving one's archery skills. Royal condemnation would hardly have been merited were the game not such a diverting distraction.

Both Scotch and golf are individualistic, acquired tastes, not for the meek and extremely diverse. Each comprise keen subtleties; at times teasing, at others, as one single malt purports to taste, "smooth as tiger claws." In the face of centuries of rampant progress, each has remained supremely satisfying, conducive to restorative bouts of introspection, despair, and camaraderie.

* * * * *

We borrowed golf from Scotland as we borrowed whiskey. Not because it is Scottish, but because it is good.

> —HORACE HUTCHINSON

* * *

Think of teeing off in the land where bairns cut their teeth on niblicks and brassies, and the nineteenth hole still thrives—bonny Scotland, the gowfer's paradise.

> —FROM AN ADVERTISEMENT IN *GOLF ILLUSTRATED*
> FOR THE WHITE STAR LINE, 1929

* * *

Ever since golf began—Scottish historians have settled on the year 1100 as a reasonable date of birth—the game has been an enigma.

> —HERBERT WARREN WIND

* * *

In golf the cardinal rules are arbitrary and not founded on eternal justice. Equity has nothing to do with the game itself. If founded on eternal justice the game would be deadly dull to watch and play.

> —CHARLES BLAIR MACDONALD

In the homeland of golf, Scots played for centuries on terrain that was entirely natural. These natural links of Scotland form the foundation of the practice of golf architecture even today.

—GEOFFREY S. CORNISH
GOLF ARCHITECT AND WRITER

Golf is a plague invented by the Calvinistic Scots as a punishment for man's sins. As General Eisenhower discovered, it is easier to end the Cold War or stamp out poverty than to master this devilish pastime.

—JAMES RESTON

Scotland is a peculiar land that is the birthplace of golf and sport salmon fishing, a fact that may explain why it is also the birthplace of whisky.

—HENRY BEARD
HUMORIST

Of this diversion the Scots are so fond, that, when the weather will permit, you may see a multitude of all ranks, from the senator of justice to the lowest tradesman, mingled together, in their shirts, and following the balls with utmost eagerness.

> —THOMAS SMOLLETT
> 1771

Golf is an exercise which is much used by the Gentlemen of Scotland. A large common in which there are several little holes is chosen for the purpose. It is played with little leather balls stuffed with feathers; and sticks made somewhat in the form of a handy-wicket.

> —BENJAMIN RUSH
> AMERICAN FOUNDING FATHER

That he is today a respected and self-respecting, prosperous member of society is largely due to the generations of professionals which arose in the early nineties with J.H. as their natural born leader.

> —BERNARD DARWIN
> ON J.H. TAYLOR'S IMPACT ON PROFESSIONAL GOLFERS

Golf was invented by some Scotsman who hit a ball, with a stick, into a hole . . . The game today is exactly the same, except that it now takes some ninety-odd pages of small type to ensure that the ball is hit, with the stick, into the hole . . . without cheating.

—A.S. GRAHAM

In the old days the pins were simply sticks of wood to which skeins of scarlet worsted were attached.

—DOROTHY CAMPBELL HURD
ON NORTH BERWICK AT THE START OF THE TWENTIETH CENTURY

Here one makes clubs fine and noble.
Play colf with pleasure, not brawls.
Play for a pint or a gallon.
Let the winter be cold and hard,
We play the ball just the same.

—HOUSE SIGN IN HARLEM,
1650

The golf links lie so near the mill

That almost every day

The laboring children can look out

And watch the men at play.

   —Sarah N. Cleghorn

    1915, on child labor and golf

Golf is gaining so enormously in popularity, and so many now take an interest in the matches of good, and especially of professional players.

   —Horace Hutchinson

    1890

It is decreeted and ordained . . . that the Fute-ball and Golfe be utterly cryed downe, and not to be used. And as tuitching the Fute-ball and the Golfe, to be punished by the Barronniss un-law.

   —James II of Scotland

    1457

The rules are based on three fundamental principles: That the golfer must play the ball as it lies, play the course as he finds it, and finally, where neither of the first two principles can apply, settle all questions by fair play.

—JOSEPH C. DEY
EXECUTIVE DIRECTOR OF THE UNITED STATES GOLF ASSOCIATION (1934–1968) AND FIRST COMMISSIONER OF THE PGA TOUR

The Rules of the game of golf change over time in some aspects that affects scores, but the basic character of the game has not changed.

—JOHN COMPANIOTTE
FROM *GOLF RULES AND ETIQUETTE SIMPLIFIED*

Fute-ball and Golfe be abused in time cumming, and that the buttes be made up, and schuting used.

—JAMES III OF SCOTLAND
1471

It is statute and ordained that in na place of the Realme there be used Fute-ball, Golfe, or uther sik unproffitable sportes.

—JAMES IV OF SCOTLAND
TO PARLIAMENT IN EDINBURGH, MAY 16, 1491

John Gardiner, James Bowman, Laurence Chalmers, and Laurence Cuthbert confess that they were playing golf . . . in time of preaching after noon on the Sabbath. The Session rebuked them, and admonished them to resort to the hearing of the Word diligently on the Sabbath in time coming, which they promised to do.

—Kirk Session of Perth
1599

James Waldie to have plaid att the golfe with the herds of Mulben; being found guilty they were rebuked for making so little conscience of the Lord's day, and ordained to make their publick repentance three Lord's days.

—Kirk Sessions of Boharm
1658

Golf was a game supported by rich men who did the hiring and firing. The pros were servants.

—Al Barkow
ON THE LOW STATUS OF PROS IN GOLF'S BEGINNINGS

From its earliest beginnings, golf has been a gentleman's game—to be played as much for the sake of the game as for the contest.

—Tony Lema

❖

Never since the days of Caesar has the British nation been subjected to such humiliation.

—Lord Northbourne
at the presentation ceremonies after
Walter Travis became the first American
to win the British Amateur in 1904

❖

Ye will remember to bring with you ane dossen of commoun golf ballis to me and David Moncrieff.

—Letter from the Orkneys
1585

I was playing golf the other day
That the Germans landed;
All our troops had run away,
All our ships were stranded;
And the thought of England's shame
Altogether spoilt my game.

> —ANONYMOUS

———•———

It is splendid that you should be following in the footsteps of Lafayette and Churchill. However, a senior member asks me to remind you that we are twenty years more ancient that the First Continental Congress, and maybe you should get your priorities straight.

> —KEITH MACKENZIE
> FROM THE ROYAL & ANCIENT GOLF CLUB OF ST. ANDREWS TO
> ALISTAIR COOKE, WHO CHOSE TO ADDRESS THE US HOUSE
> OF REPRESENTATIVES ON THE BICENTENNIAL OF THE FIRST
> CONTINENTAL CONGRESS OVER HIS SPEECH AT THE
> ST. ANDREWS ANNUAL DINNER

The ball people with their balls shall post themselves along the canal from the bridge in front of Master Arent Goes.

—MAGISTRATES OF BERGEN OP ZOOM
1461

Na inhabitants, be thameselffis, thair children, servands, or fameleis, be sene at ony pastymes or gammis within or without the toun upoun the Sabbath day, sic as golf, aircherie, rowbowliss, penny stane, katch pullis, or sic other pastymes.

—EDICT OF EDINBURGH COUNCIL
1592

Unlike many other sports, golf does not enjoy the privilege of knowing its exact birthright.

—IAN MORRISON
AUTHOR

Those little bastards have no idea how hard we worked and how little money we made. We made the Tour what it is today and they don't even know it.

—JERRY BARBER
ON YOUNGER PGA TOUR PLAYERS

—•—

The feeling toward the golf professionals in this country was such that the winner of the 1898 U.S. Open, Fred Herd, was required to put up security for the safe keeping of the trophy. It was feared he would pawn the trophy for drinking money.

—AL BARKOW
ON THE LACK OF RESPECT FOR GOLF PROFESSIONALS
IN GOLF'S EARLY DAYS

—•—

When I was in that streak, I didn't do anything but play golf. That's why I think it was more fun in our time. It was hard, but people like to be challenged. They like it hard.

—BYRON NELSON
GOLF DIGEST

More camaraderie as a whole in the big group. There weren't that many players. A lot of them played tour in the winter and had a club job. It was basically a two-pro system. It wasn't as big a business as it is today.

—RAYMOND FLOYD
1994
ON HIS EARLY DAYS ON THE TOUR, *GOLF DIGEST*

Nobody strikes the ball on the streets with clubs with lead or iron heads.

—ORDINANCE OF ZIERIKZEE
1429

The soldier, having sought the bubble reputation in the cannon's mouth, may earn laurels on a field which shall be bloodless and receive at least a purer pleasure from deftly landing his ball in the hole that ever came to him from letting daylight into his fellow mortals.

—DR. PROUDFOOT
1890

I remember making rulings on other players in a tournament I was competing in. In this day and age, you'd probably get sued for something like that.

—BETSY RAWLS
REMEMBERING THE DAYS WHEN SHE WAS AN LPGA EXECUTIVE

Walter Hay, goldsmith, accusit for playing at the boulis and golff upoun Sondaye in the tyme of the sermon.

—*RECORD OF ELGIN*, 1596
ACCUSING A GOLDSMITH OF PLAYING GOLF ON SUNDAY

To my mind, these two [Young Tom Morris and Bobby Jones] are the greatest golfers in history, both as to execution, clean sportsmanship, courtesy, equable temperament, and most attractive personality.

—CHARLES BLAIR MACDONALD
1928

After the Restoration, James Duke of York was sent to Edinburgh, and his favourite pastimes appear to have been torturing of the adherents to the Covenant, and the playing of golf on the Links of Leith.

—JOHN ROBERTSON

I think more of the golf rules stink. They were written by the guys who can't even break a hundred.

—CHI-CHI RODRIGUEZ

Racism in golf reared its head in America as early as 1896. In the second U.S. Open, held that year at Shinnecock Hills, a group of professionals threatened to boycott play if John Shippen, of black and Indian parentage, was allowed to compete . . . Theodore Havemeyer [USGA President] refused to bar him.

—BUD DUFNER

In the old days, who wanted to see a pro play? All he did was play when a member wanted a mercenary as his advisor.

—HERB GRAFFIS
FAMOUS AMERICAN GOLF WRITER AND ADMINISTRATOR

The 1922 U.S. Open was the first USGA event with an admission fee for spectators. In less than four years, thanks to the popularity of Bobby Jones and other players, those fees became the organization's chief source of income.

—*GOLF* MAGAZINE
DECEMBER 1994

———•———

Old Tom is the most remote point to which we can carry back our genealogical inquiries into the golfing style, so that he may virtually accept him as the common golfing ancestor who has stamped the features of his style most distinctly on his descendants.

—HORACE HUTCHINSON
1900 ON OLD TOM MORRIS

———•———

I had a good chance to get in the Masters if I finished good. And I was going good. Suddenly I was intercepted by five white men who started following me around. They threw their beer cans at me and called me 'nigger' and other names.

—CHARLIE SIFFORD
AFRICAN-AMERICAN GOLFER DESCRIBING HIS EXPERIENCE
AT THE 1959 GREENSBORO OPEN

David Gray pewdarer and Thomas Saith tailour being callit comperit, and, being accusit for prophaning of the Saboth day in playing at the gouf eftir nune, confest the samin; and because thai war nocht apprehendit with the lyik fault of befoir, thair war admonished nocht to do the samin heireftir.

—St. Andrews' Kirk Sessions
1598

The King [Charles I] was nowhere treated with more honor than at Newcastle, both he and his train having liberty to go abroad and play at Goff in the Shield Field, without the walls.

—John Sykes
1833

At this meeting, it was possible for the serious-minded to make a comparison between the English and Scottish swing, and the opinion was the Scottish swings were quicker and shorter.

—The First Ladies' Golf Union
FROM A MEETING OF THE UNION IN 1895

Whoever plays ball with a club shall be fined 20 shillings or their upper garment.

—THE MAGISTRATE OF BRUSSELS
1360

According to the Captain of the Honourable Company of Edinburgh Golfers, Hoylake, or Westward Ho meant that you lost the hole, except on medal days when it counted as a rub of the green.

—HERBERT WARREN WIND

Tennis is not in use amongst us, but in lieu of that, you have that excellent recreation of goff-ball than which truly I do not know a better.

—THE MARQUIS OF ARGYLL
1661

Hail, Gutta-Percha! precious gum!

O'er Scotland's links lang may ye bum;

Some proud pursed billies haw and hum,

And say ye'er douf at fleein';

But let them try ye fairly out,

Wi' ony balls for days about,

Your merits they will loudly tout,

And own they hae been leein'.

—WILLIAM GRAHAM
  1848

Indoor golf is to be one of the features of the athletic work of many young society girls this winter. They are the younger girls . . . but they have already been exposed to the contagion of golf, and they will prepare . . . to be genuine fanatics by the time their school duties are over.

—*THE NEW YORK TIMES*
  NOVEMBER 14, 1897

In order to preserve the balance between power and the length of holes and in order to retain the special features of the game, the power of the ball should be limited.

> —THE ROYAL AND ANCIENT RULES OF GOLF COMMITTEE
>   RECOMMENDATION, 1919

When a ball lies on clothes, or within one club length of a washing tub, the clothes may be drawn from under the ball and the tub removed.

> —THE RULES OF GOLF
>   ISSUED BY THE ROYAL & ANCIENT GOLF CLUB FOR HAZARDS
>   CAUSED BY TOWNSWOMEN WHO CLEANED THEIR APPAREL
>   IN THE SWILCAN BURN, 1851

A game . . . first recorded in Scotland in the 15th century, and played under codified rules since the middle of the 18th century; now consisting of hitting a golf ball, using an array of golf clubs, by successive strokes to each of nine or eighteen holes on a golf course.

> —THE RULES OF GOLF
>   PUBLISHED BY THE ROYAL AND ANCIENT GOLF CLUB IN
>   ST. ANDREWS, SCOTLAND, AND THE UNITED STATES GOLF
>   ASSOCIATION IN FAR HILLS, NEW JERSEY

Na, na, we're na goin t'eat in the kitchen.

—WILLIE ANDERSON
BEFORE THE 1901 US OPEN, WHEN THE PROS COULDN'T EAT
IN THE CLUBHOUSE

The example of public-spirited park commissioners of New York . . . in providing public links in Van Cortlandt Park, is bearing good fruit.

—C. TURNER, 1896
FROM AN ARTICLE IN *THE OUTING* ON THE OPENING OF THE FIRST
MUNICIPAL PUBLIC GOLF COURSE IN THE UNITED STATES

King Charles I is said to have been fond of the exercise of the golf. While he was engaged in a party of golf on the Links of Leith, a letter was delivered into his hands, which gave him the first account of the rebellion in Ireland.

—WILLIAM TYTLER
1792

Gentlemen, this beats rifle shooting. It is a game I think might go in our country.

—WILLIAM K. VANDERBILT
IN BIARRITZ AT THE END OF THE 19TH CENTURY, AFTER OBSERVING
WILLIE DUNN HIT SEVERAL PRACTICE SHOTS

Linksland is the old Scottish word for the earth at the edge of the sea . . . You see, the game comes out of the ocean, just like man himself! Investigate our linksland. Michael, get to know it. I think you'll find it worthwhile.

—MICHAEL BAMBERGER
FROM *STARK*

There's a widely held respect for the game, for fellow competitors, and for its history that's very appealing.

—BOB COSTAS

What golf has of honor, what it has of justice, of fair play, of good fellowship, and sportsmanship—in a word, what is best in golf—is almost surely traceable to the inspiration of the Royal & Ancient.

—ISAAC GRAINGER

CHAPTER FIVE

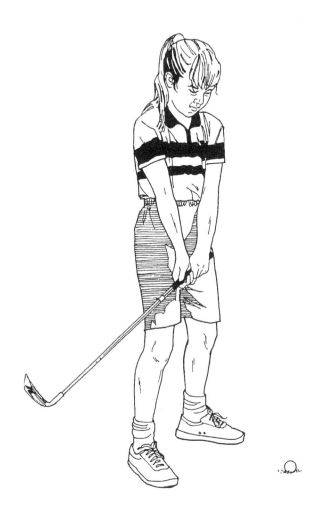

Humble Beginnings: Famous Players On Their Golfing Origins

Their self-deprecating jibes always got a laugh, the stories now retold so often as to be romanticized. Funny and touching the first time around, reflection suggests a darker root. Juan, better known as Chi-Chi, suffered from childhood malnutrition. Escaping the Puerto Rican cane fields, he became a caddie at nine. Like his "merry" and very determined friend of Mexican descent, Lee Trevino, he escaped poverty's grip via a tour with Uncle Sam.

Across the Spanish-speaking world, the youngest of four brothers honed his game hitting pebbles on the beach in northern Spain. Sneaking onto a course and playing in the dark remains his fondest childhood memory. Severiano's skill with a three-iron, with which he later performed miracles from greenside bunkers and other improbable lies, was honed from necessity and invention. The Ballesteros boys milked cows, gathered eggs from their own chickens, and grew their own vegetables. It was an experience not markedly different from that of another prodigal golfer from an earlier generation growing up in hardscrabble western Pennsylvania. The Palmers also grew chickens to eat.

This stereotypical pastime of the rich would provide for these men from the other side of the tracks. That a young and untested South African, Gary Player, far from home, slept rough in a bunker emits a Dickensian whiff that stretches modern credulity. What we can be certain of is that these men, and others, have found in golf a rich palate for personal expression. Each has forged his own way to bask in the democratic glories of a democratic game. The deserving merit and reap their prize, a fitting tribute to both golfer and game.

* * * * *

I do not recall the first time I hit a golf ball, or hit at one; and as I recall it the game did not make much of an impression on me.

  —BOBBY JONES

When Tiger was six months old, he would sit in our garage, watching me hit balls into a net. He had been assimilating his golf swing. When he got out of the high chair, he had a golf swing.

  —EARL WOODS

The best year of my life was when I was eleven. I got straight As, had two recesses a day, and the cutest girlfriend, and won thirty-two tournaments that year. Everything's been downhill since.

  —TIGER WOODS

I started to play golf when I was three . . . Six years later, Dad loaded the family belongings into a Model-A Ford pickup and moved all of us west [from South Dakota] to California where the plan was . . . to play year-round on real grass courses.

  —MARLENE BAUER HAGGE
   THE YOUNGEST PLAYER TO WIN AN LPGA EVENT, AGE 18, IN 1952

When I was three . . . my father put my hands in his and placed them around the shaft of a cut-down women's golf club. He showed me the classic overlap, or the Vardon grip . . . and told me to hit the golf ball . . . 'Hit it hard boy. Go find it and hit it again.'

—ARNOLD PALMER
1999, *A GOLFER'S LIFE*

I needed to be pushed. As a youngster I didn't recognize my true ability or talents . . . Sure, I said I was going to the golf course, but when I got my driver's license, man, as soon as I got out of sight, I took the next left.

—PAT BRADLEY
LPGA HALL OF FAMER

It took her at least two years to learn to respect the short game and realize that even the top players have to be able to get down in two from off the green. Then her chipping and putting started to improve, and, of course, her scoring did.

—BETSY RAWLS
ON MICKEY WRIGHT

I was so poor, I grew up under a sign that said, 'Made in Taiwan.'

—CHI-CHI RODRIGUEZ

My family was so poor they couldn't afford any kids. The lady next door had me.

—LEE TREVINO

From the time you're a junior, adults keep telling you about patience and hard work and using your head, but until you've been knocked down a few times and have to get back on your feet all by yourself, you probably haven't learned the lessons.

—MIKE WEIR

I had played poorly for two years and started thinking, 'Gee, maybe I'll do something else.' Then I saw my friends going to work every day and realized that my life wasn't so bad. I've been more patient with my golf ever since.

—STEVE PATE

I had a natural golf swing, they said. With proper instruction, I could hit a golf ball as far, if not farther, than any of the women golfers. Dad was elated. As I came off the course after that round, my destiny was settled. I would become a golfer.

—GLENNA COLLETT VARE
CHAMPION OF A RECORD 6 US WOMEN'S AMATEURS

Golf, like measles, should be caught young, for, if postponed to riper years, the results may be serious.

—P.G. WODEHOUSE
FROM *A MIXED THREESOME*, 1922

Gary, lad, what you want to do is go home to Johannesburg, forget about golf, and get yourself an honest job.

—ADVICE GIVEN TO HALL OF FAMER GARY PLAYER AFTER MISSING THE CUT AT A 1955 TOURNAMENT

In the summer of 1968, a young golfer from Texas experienced something that would forever change his life. Not only did I fall in love with formal tournament competition, but I was enraptured with so many other facets of the game: the different courses, the people, the history and traditions.

—BEN CRENSHAW

My father had the Arabic attitude that, to enter heaven, he had to have a son to close his eyes. When I arrived, he was displeased. And it was made known to me from the word naught that, as a woman, I was inferior in every way.

—ENID WILSON
THREE-TIME WINNER OF THE BRITISH LADIES (1931–1933) AND
TWO-TIME WINNER OF THE ENGLISH LADIES' (1928, 1930)

I used to sling the old golf club quite a distance. Tony (my brother) and I used to be dreadful. We would spend twenty minutes or longer trying to retrieve a club one of us had thrown into a tree.

—LAURA DAVIES
LPGA TOUR PLAYER

People begin playing for many reasons—exercise, because a friend plays, an injury has made some more physical game impossible, business contacts or often because the game is played in such beautiful surroundings.

—MICHAEL HOBBS
GOLF FOR THE CONNOISSEUR

When I joined the tour in 1964, I told my wife I wanted to play five years. Instead, I've played five careers.

—GEORGE ARCHER

I'd probably been up to 250, but I just happened to be at 215 at the time. I'd probably be the fat lady in a circus right now if it hadn't been for golf. It kept me on the course and out of the refrigerator.

—KATHY WHITWORTH
ON HER PORTLY YOUTH

I started in engineering and switched to business for my major. If I had stayed for my junior year, I'd have had to switch to basket weaving. It was getting tough.

—NANCY LOPEZ
ON WHY SHE LEFT TULSA UNIVERSITY TO JOIN THE LPGA TOUR

Being left-handed isn't really so different anymore. It's not like when I was a kid.

—MIKE WEIR

If I'm going to play golf, I might as well play for the money.

—ARNOLD PALMER
UPON TURNING PRO

People think growing up in the hills was a handicap I had to overcome. In a lot of ways it gave me [an] . . . advantage that has lasted me to this day. Just like with that stick, I'd have to overcompensate for just about everything; sticks for clubs, acorns for balls . . .

—SAM SNEAD

I got my golfing education from the drubbings. And very lately I have come to a sort of Presbyterian attitude toward tournament golf; I can't get away from the idea of predestination.

—BOBBY JONES
1927, IN HIS AUTOBIOGRAPHY DOWN THE FAIRWAY

Little Bobby Jones of Atlanta is really a fine player, and shows every indication of becoming a tremendous great one, once he is master of himself, which must come with maturity.

—A.W. TILLINGHAST
WHEN JONES WAS 14 YEARS OLD

I was the world's worst salesman.

—JOE DURANT
ON WHY HE GAVE PRO GOLF ANOTHER CHANCE

Of all the golfers in the world I cannot believe that anyone will make a greater impact upon the championships than this very tough, determined young man. The world is at his feet and he is only 21 years of age.

—PAT WARD THOMAS
ON JACK NICKLAUS

Why do I love kids so much? Because I never was a kid myself. I was too poor to be a child, so I never really had a childhood. The biggest present I ever got was a marble.

—CHI-CHI RODRIGUEZ

Whenever we left our apartment to go play in Canada or Australia, we couldn't afford to keep the apartment. So every year we had to get our stuff and pile it in a storage locker for $50 a month. Then we'd find another apartment.

—MIKE WEIR

I thought everybody was named Labron and Byron, talked with a Texas accent, and said, 'Nice shot, padnah.'

—AMY ALCOTT
ON HOW SHE OPTED TO CHOOSE GOLF OVER TENNIS AT AGE 9

I learned by copying. My father used to take Roger and me to watch golf when we were youngsters, and I tried to copy the good players' rhythm. Then, when I began playing fairly well, I played a lot with Roger and his friends from Oxford.

—JOYCE WETHERED
LEADING WOMEN'S GOLFER IN THE 1920s AND 1930s

Betsy studied and played golf. I played golf, partied, and studied a little.

—BETH DANIEL
ON BEING A COLLEGE TEAMMATE OF BETSY KING

The first time I grabbed a golf club, I knew that I'd do it for the rest of my life.

—MICHELLE WIE

I started out as a private, but after beating the colonels a few times, I rose to sergeant.

—LEE TREVINO
ON PLAYING GOLF IN THE MARINES

One of the things that my parents have taught me is never listen to other people's expectations. You should live your own life and live up to your own expectations, and those are the only things I really care about.

—TIGER WOODS

The hardest thing was being young and coming onto the tour right out of high school and a very close home environment. I think the thing I missed most was my mother's homemade soup.

—AMY ALCOTT
ON HER EARLY DAYS IN THE LPGA TOUR

What's entered my mind more than anything else is guys like Curtis Strange and Hubert Green missed their first time. It's kind of like, if you're ready for it, you'll get through with no problem, and if you're not, you won't.

—DAVID DUVAL
ON MISSING THE CUT AT THE 1993 PGA TOUR QUALIFYING SCHOOL

When I was growing up, they had just found radio.

—ARNOLD PALMER
WHEN ASKED IF HE WATCHED SPORTS ON TELEVISION AS A CHILD

Here boy, give me the bag. I'll go down the fairway and you stay here and find the ball. You'd better find it, too, or don't come back.

—ERICKSON PERKINS
A ROCHESTER BANKER, TO THE GREAT WALTER HAGEN
DURING HIS CADDIE DAYS

I probably wouldn't have gone if not for the golf scholarship. Got to admit, I just walked through school as a conduit to the Tour.

—CHARLES COODY
AMERICAN GOLFER, ON THE MERITS OF ATTENDING TCU

There aren't too many frat parties out on tour.
—TIGER WOODS
ON WHY HE WAS RELUCTANT TO LEAVE COLLEGE AND JOIN THE PROS

If you really want to get better at golf, go back and take it up at a much earlier age.
—THOMAS MULLIGAN

I owe much to having seen her play when I was just coming to understand golf a little. She put the kindling in the fire that was beginning to burn.
—GLENNA COLLETT VARE
ON ALEXA STIRLING

I fancy that having at first played the game almost entirely by the light of nature he [Gene Sarazen] took to thinking about it. That is a thing that has almost got to happen to any good young golfer at some time.

—BERNARD DARWIN

———•———

Forget the PGA Tour. There's no money in it.

—TITANIC THOMPSON
ADVICE TO LEE TREVINO IN 1966

CHAPTER SIX

The Difficulty, Nature, Values, and Character-Building Spirit of the Game

It's one of only two golf entries in the original Oxford Dictionary of Quotations. Bernard Darwin, who penned the introduction in 1941, and handled the Dickens, chose wisely, in this case borrowing an anecdote from the great golf evangelist, Charles Blair McDonald. But what a daunting task! Limited to just two picks to cover the sum total of golf wisdom. Impossible!

Excised long ago from subsequent editions, the selection must've appealed to Darwin on several levels. It conveys both wit and sagacity. It takes place in St. Andrews, then as now a seat of scholarship and golf. Perhaps too much may be made of this, but one can sense that the tale might also have been suggestive of a time, place and even an attitude that Darwin wished immortalized. Its tribute to applying the old bean alone assures its pertinence. There is the social role reversal, and, finally, most of all, there is comeuppance delivered with the characteristic candor for which caddies throughout the world, and especially at the Old Course, are renowned. Yes, all these might conceivably have "pushed" Bernardo's buttons.

Our dramatis personae: the anonymous professor, presumably accustomed to calling the shots, and his gruff caddie-teacher. The lesson is not going well, the professor "not a promising pupil." Willie Lang, "fairly out of patience," speaks:

Ye see, Professor, as long as ye are learning thae lads at the College Latin and Greek it is easy work, but when ye come to play golf ye maun hae a heid! (You must have a head!)

Aye! To which we might add and ye maun hae still.

* * * * *

Is my friend in the bunker or is the bastard on the green?

—ANONYMOUS

—•—

Sneaky cheaters are people who suffer from that old devil 'low self-esteem'; and are lured to cheat at golf in the same way they might drift into alcoholism. They are looking for ways to justify the internal image.

—PETER ANDREWS
GOLF WRITER AND COMMENTATOR, "CHEATERS BOLD
AND SNEAKY," *GOLF DIGEST*

—•—

Out here, guys bitch about everything. They even bitch about the ice cream.

—ED DOUGHERTY
ON THE PGA TOUR

—•—

Golf should be essentially a game of good fellowship; it should, and generally does, constitute a bond of union between any strangers who casually meet.

—H.S.C. EVERARD
1890

What's the point of washing off your ball when teeing off on a water-hazard hole?

—BRUCE LANSKY
AUTHOR

Everyone cheats when they first start playing golf. A lot of people don't ever stop.

—FRANK BEARD
SENIOR TOUR PLAYER

It's a slow process. You can't go from struggling, having trouble holing putts, to making everything just like that. If I keep making good putts here and there, feeling confident, consistent over the ball, it's going to be important.

—SERGIO GARCIA

It takes six years to make a golfer: three to learn the game, then another three to unlearn all you have learned in the first three years. You might be a golfer when you arrive at that stage, but more likely you are just starting.

—WALTER HAGEN

Golf is the cruelest game, because eventually it will drag you out in front of the whole school, take your lunch money and slap you around.
>   —RICK REILLY

— • —

Don't forget to maintain your strengths.
>   —JIM COLBERT
>   *GOLF DIGEST*

— • —

If, then, happy men ought to play golf, what of miserable men? Let them also become golfers. 'What!' the reader exclaims, 'shall a man in misery take to golf?' Yes, most assuredly!
>   —DR. PROUDFOOT
>   1890

— • —

I am the most fortunate, failed golfer in the world.
>   —TOM COYNE

A professional will tell you the amount of flex you need in the shaft of your club. The more the flex, the more strength you will need to break the thing over your knee.

—STEPHEN BAKER

'Who is the best lefthand player you ever saw?' said Mr. Bliss, himself a lefthander and playing the game of his life. 'Never saw one that was worth a damn,' Harry Vardon replied.

—MICHAEL HOBBS

Stroke play is my second favorite form of golf, and by quite a long way. It is not the play itself that puts me off, it is the task of marking a card.

—PETER DOBEREINER

Have you ever actually listened to golfers talking to each other? Looked good starting out . . . Better direction than last time . . . Who's away? . . . It sounds like visitors' day at a home for the criminally insane.

—PETER ANDREWS

It taught me perseverance, it taught me not to cheat—no easy thing for a boy when he's two down and his ball is deep in the woods.

—JAMES RESTON
ON THE LESSONS OF GOLF

The number of shots taken by an opponent who is out of sight is equal to the square root of the sum of the number of curses heard plus the number of swishes.

—MICHAEL GREEN
PRO ON THE EUROPEAN TOUR

Hey, is this room out of bounds?

—ALEX KARRAS
AFTER HITTING A GOLF BALL THROUGH THE
CLUBHOUSE WINDOW AT RED RUN GC

Seve did not win the right way, you see. That's to say, he did not win the way Nicklaus won, with self-control, conservative strategy, methodical Germanic doggedness and endless patience. The virtues of the king can, unconsciously, become the only acceptable virtues.

—THOMAS BOSWELL
ON WHY BALLESTEROS WASN'T IMMEDIATELY ACCEPTED IN THE U.S.

I don't enjoy playing video golf because there is nothing to throw.

—PAUL AZINGER

My game is so bad I've got to hire three caddies—one to walk the left rough, one for the right rough, and one down the middle. And the one in the middle doesn't have much to do.

—DAVE HILL

Do I have to know rules and all that crap? Then forget it.

—JOHN DALY

The biggest liar in the world is the golfer who claims that he plays the game merely for exercise.

—TOMMY BOLT

Two things I take very seriously in life. My golf game and my relationship with God. Neither one is simple.

—CHERYL LADD

It's been a funny week. It took me three days to play 18 holes.

  —HALE IRWIN

———————

If Charles II felt any way troubled, he was at least allowed to have re-course to the distractions of golf.

  —SAMUEL R. GARDINER
   1894

———————

Pick up the ball, have the clubs destroyed, and leave the course.

  —VISCOUNT CASTLEROSSE
   BRITISH JOURNALIST, AFTER TOPPING THREE STRAIGHT BALLS

———————

One reward golf has given me, and I shall always be thankful for it, is introducing me to some of the world's most picturesque, tireless, and bald-faced liars.

  —REX LARDNER

If profanity had an influence on the flight of the ball, the game of golf would be played far better than it is.

  —HORACE HUTCHINSON

———•———

If you are going to throw a club, it is important to throw it ahead of you, down the fairway, so you don't have to waste energy going back to pick it up.

  —TOMMY BOLT

———•———

The most exquisitely satisfying act in the world of golf is that of throwing a club. The full backswing, the delayed wrist action, the flowing follow-through, followed by that unique whirring sound, reminiscent only of a passing flock of starlings, are without parallel in sport.

  —HENRY LONGHURST

———•———

Pain and suffering are inevitable in our lives, but misery is an option.

  —CHIP BECK
  ON THE VICISSITUDES OF GOLF

Would that I could hand on unimpaired the great game as it was my good fortune to know it.

—CHARLES BLAIR MACDONALD

A great deal of unnecessarily bad golf is played in this world.

—HARRY VARDON

It's how you deal with failure that determines how you achieve success.

—DAVID FEHERTY

It's like playing in a straitjacket. They just lay you upon the rack and twist on both ends.

—BEN CRENSHAW
ON THE DIFFICULTY OF THE GAME

I don't fear death, but I sure don't like those three-footers for par.

—CHI-CHI RODRIGUEZ

Golf may be played on Sunday, not being a game within view of the law, but being a form of moral effort.
—STEPHEN LEACOCK

Tommy [Bolt] threw clubs with class.
—DON JANUARY

I'm hitting the woods just great, but I am having a terrible time hitting out of them.
—HARRY TOSCANO

No sport is so underrated in terms of dedication needed and skill required. It's you against everyone, and yet you alone against the course.
—BARBARA BALDWIN
WRITER, OBSERVING HER TEENAGE SON PLAYING GOLF

Many play golf, and one odd effect of that pursuit is that they return to work manifestly stupider than they were. It is, I think, the company of other golfers.

     —G.W. Lyttleton

Ladies and gentlemen, I three-putted seven times this week!

     —Meg Mallon
         before throwing her putter into the lake at
         the Walt Disney World's Eagle Pines Golf Course

With any other sport or pastime golf compares favorably.

     —Sir Walter Simpson

You can't always be playing well when it counts. You'll never win golf tournaments until you learn how to score well when you're playing badly.

     —Jim Barnes
         advice to Bobby Jones

I made nothing happen very slowly.

—GARY MCCORD
ON HIS THIRTEEN-YEAR CAREER

Real golfers go to work to relax.

—GEORGE DILLON
GOLF COURSE ARCHITECT

As good a golfer as Tiger is, he's a better person.

—EARL WOODS

The bored haughty face that she turned to the world concealed something
. . . and one day I found out what it was . . . At her first big golf tournament there was a row that nearly reached the newspapers—a suggestion
that she had moved her ball from a bad lie in the semifinal round.

—F. SCOTT FITZGERALD, 1923
THE GREAT GATSBY

There is one man who ought never to appear on a golfing green. And this is the good man. The immaculate creature whose life is spent seeing his neighbor's faults and comparing them with his own wonderful perfection, is quite out of place among golfers.

—DR. PROUDFOOT
1890

Tell me honestly: do you know anyone who truly likes to play golf? Oh, I suppose there are some people who derive pleasure from golf just as there are certain kinds of individuals who enjoy being snapped in the rib cage with knotted towels.

—PETER ANDREWS

There were no 'two Gerald Fords,' there was no other agenda, no secret life. An avid golfer to the end, he would never move his ball to improve his lie when no one was looking. To me that was the central theme of his character.

—DAVID HUME KENNERLY

The modern player is getting more non-confrontational all the time. A lot of guys don't want to look at the leader boards, or even pay much attention to what the players they're paired with are doing.

—JOHNNY MILLER
GOLF DIGEST, 1991

When you lose your swing, you might just as well quit walking around in the sun and get in the shade.

—JIMMY DEMARET

People who are great in other sports, whom I have worked with, always say that golf is the toughest game they've ever played because it's not just athleticism that enables them to become great. Golf is far more than that.

—DAVID LEADBETTER

You don't have the game you played last year or last week. You only have today's game. It may be far from your best, but that's all you've got. Harden your heart and make the best of it.

—WALTER HAGEN

If I had cleared the trees and drove the green, it would've been a great shot.

—SAM SNEAD

I think after four hours you should pick your ball up and walk in, and if you haven't finished, that's tough.

—COLIN MONTGOMERIE

The more you play golf, the less you know about it.

—PATTY BERG

The game embarrasses you until you feel inadequate.

—BEN CRENSHAW

The first step in building a solid, dependable attitude is to be realistic, not only about your inherent capabilities, but also about how well you are playing to those capabilities on any given day.

—BYRON NELSON

As every golfer knows, no one ever lost his mind over one shot. It is rather the gradual process of shot after shot watching your score go to tatters . . . knowing that you have found a different way to bogey each one.

—THOMAS BOSWELL

Never refer to your partner as The Load, Hooky or Old Shanks here, that I got saddled with, or Three-putt. When he says: 'I'm doing the best I can,' never say: 'That's exactly what I was afraid of.'

—JIM MURRAY

The game was easy for me as a kid. I had to play a while to find out how hard it is.

—RAYMOND FLOYD

Golf is the hardest game in the world. There is no way you can ever get it. Just when you think you do, the game jumps up and puts you in your place.

—BEN CRENSHAW

Every round I play, I shorten my life by two years.

—TOMMY NAKAJIMA

I wish I had played it yesterday. When you don't know where you're going, you're sort of at the mercy of the course a little bit. And my caddie is, I think he's dead by now. I had a couple guys following him the last few holes.

—BILL MURRAY

Golf isn't like other sports where you can take a player out if he's having a bad day. You have to play the whole game.

—PHIL BLACKMAR

It is more satisfying to be a bad player at golf. The worse you play, the better you remember the occasional good shot.

    —NUBAR GULBENKIAN
    1972

———•———

If you are caught on a golf course during a storm and are afraid of lightning, hold up a 1-iron. Not even God can hit a 1-iron.

    —LEE TREVINO

———•———

It's good sportsmanship to not pick up lost golf balls while they are still rolling.

    —MARK TWAIN

———•———

Many men are more faithful to their golf partners than to their wives and have stuck with them longer.

    —JOHN UPDIKE

Getting nothing is not the end of the world. I've gotten my share. So I'm tickled pink just to be here.

—FRED COUPLES

Wind and rain are great challenges. They separate the real golfers. Let the seas pound against the shore, let the rain pour.

—TOM WATSON

There are certain things you don't believe in. The Easter Bunny. Campaign promises. The Abominable Snowman. A husband with lipstick on his collar. And a guy who tells you he shot a 59 on his own ball. Out of town, of course.

—JIM MURRAY

The score a player reports on any hole should always be regarded as his opening offer.

—ANONYMOUS

I don't even know if there was a Mulligan. But he gave his name to a wonderful gesture—letting you play a bad first drive over, and no penalty.

> —REX LARDNER
> FROM *OUT OF THE BUNKER AND INTO THE TREES*

All my life I wanted to play golf like Jack Nicklaus, and now I do.

> —PAUL HARVEY
> AFTER NICKLAUS SHOT 83 IN THE 1981 OPEN

Golf is probably the only known game a man can play as long as a quarter of a century and then discover it was too deep for him in the first place.

> —SEYMOUR DUNN

I have often been gratefully aware of the heroic efforts of my opponent not to laugh at me.

> —BERNARD DARWIN

It's definitely been a learning experience, not just in golf but in general. The biggest adjustment has been not knowing where I'm going, how I'm going to get there . . . and when I get to a new town it seems as though I get lost every time.

—VICKI GOETZE
WINNER OF THE 1989 AND 1992 US WOMEN'S AMATEUR,
ON ADJUSTING TO THE TOUR

The toughest thing I've ever had to do in golf is hit the ball off that first tee with thousands of people watching and having no idea where the ball was going.

—BYRON NELSON

All good players have good hands. And I'm afraid you have to be born with them.

—DAVE STOCKTON

I feel like I've been beaten up by the neighborhood bully.

—MAC O'GRADY
AFTER A BAD ROUND

For me, the worst part of playing golf, by far, has always been hitting the ball.

    —DAVE BARRY

I get pissed off. I simply do not understand someone who hits a ball that lands behind a tree and can look at and say, 'Well, that's golf.'

    —SIMON HOBDAY
    SENIOR TOUR PRO, ON BAD SHOTS

I never win a match . . . I spend my life out of bounds. I never even count my strokes.

    —P.G. WODEHOUSE
    FROM *THE LONG HOLE*

You learn about self-control and dealing with bad bounces.

    —CHET EDWARDS
    U.S. CONGRESSMAN
    ON LEARNING LIFE LESSONS THROUGH GOLF

I probably have forgotten more about golf than I have ever learned.

—JACK NICKLAUS

Golf is based on honesty. Where else would you admit to a seven on a par three?

—JIMMY DEMARET

Golf inflicts more pain than any other sport. If you're the sort of person whose self-worth is tied up in how you play, golf will cut you to the core of who you are.

—JAMES E. LOEHR
SPORTS PSYCHOLOGIST

While it is true that some amateur golfers are unwittingly or unwillingly duped, badgered, or coerced into playing a round of golf, an incredible 97 per cent of the dummies actually report to the first tee on a voluntary basis.

—GEOFF HOWSON
FROM *GOLF*

Those who the gods seek to destroy first, learn how to play golf.
—LESLIE NIELSEN

We play many tournaments that effectively eliminate thought. You have traps on both sides of the flat fairway and traps on all four sides of the green. You step up and aim at the center of an obvious target every time. You have no options, no room for strategy.
—DAVID GRAHAM
PGA TOUR AND SENIOR PGA TOUR MEMBER

It's like a cold slap in the face. You're mad and you're not trying to protect anything out there anymore.
—MARK McCUMBER
ON THE EFFECTS OF A QUADRUPLE BOGEY

Setting goals for your game is an art. The trick is in setting them at the right level, neither too low nor too high.
—GREG NORMAN

Here are two basic rules which should never be broken. Be subtle. And don't, for God's sake, try to do business with anyone who's having a bad game.

—WILLIAM DAVIS

The rest of the field.

—ROGER MALTBIE
WHEN ASKED WHAT HE WOULD HAVE TO SHOOT IN ORDER TO WIN

My goal for 1987 is to go the whole year without being fined.

—MAC O'GRADY

I learned early that whatever I got out of life, I'd have to go out and get for myself. And the physical aptitude I possessed gave me the means at the beginning. However, I had to create a paying market for that ability to play golf.

—WALTER HAGEN
FROM HIS AUTOBIOGRAPHY *THE WALTER HAGEN STORY*

If you call on God to improve the results of a shot while it is still in motion, you are using 'an outside agency' and subject to appropriate penalties under the rules of golf.

—HENRY LONGHURST

Maybe it is good enough that we are against doping, that simply being against cheating is all we reasonably can offer. Even if sports such as pro golf still tell us they are drug-free and they don't need testing at all.

—RICK TELANDER

Few learn golf in a lifetime.

—GRANTLAND RICE

Next to sunburn, a visit to the dentist, or a wasp sting on the privates, nothing gives a man more masochistic satisfaction than a round of golf.

—ARCHIE COMPSTON
PGA PRO

Golf is a game in which the ball lies poorly and the players well.

    —ART ROSENBAUM

Now I can see I can't make anything.

    —JACK NICKLAUS

      ON HIS NEW CONTACT LENSES

The world's number-one tennis player spends 90 percent of his time winning, while the world's number-one golfer spends 90 percent of his time losing. Golfers are great losers.

    —DAVID FEHERTY

I think anyone who has a lot of given talent probably has a lot of pressure on them. I get mad when people say I'm a waste of talent. They don't realize how hard I work.

    —BETH DANIEL

      LPGA TOUR PLAYER, ON THE PRESSURE OF THE TOUR

No one has ever conquered this game. One week out there and you are God; next time you are the devil.

—JULIE INKSTER
MEMBER OF THE LPGA TOUR

Success in golf depends less on strength of body than upon strength of mind and character.

—ARNOLD PALMER

I can airmail the golf ball a long distance, but sometimes I don't put the right address on it.

—JIM DENT

No other game is more capable of evoking a person's total commitment.

—MICHAEL MURPHY
FROM *GOLF IN THE KINGDOM*

I may know I am better than an 18, but the computer absorbs my scores . . . and continues to tell me that is what I am. Therein lies the tragedy of golf. We know what we should be, but there is always some number telling us what it is.

—PETER ANDREWS

I gave [golf] up soon after I married. I claimed it was a supreme sacrifice, but the development of a cancerous slice probably had more to do with it.

—MICHAEL HOBBS
FROM *GOLF FOR THE CONNOISSEUR*

That round of golf was like a first date. She didn't care for me and I didn't like her. I tried to kiss her, but she slapped me. I was afraid to come back for a second date.

—MAC O'GRADY
ON WITHDRAWING FROM A TOURNAMENT AFTER SHOOTING 79

Old-time golfers insist that there is nothing more satisfying in the game of golf than the crisp snap of a hickory-shafted club breaking sharply across the player's knee.

—HENRY BEARD
HUMORIST

Talking to a golf ball won't do you any good. Unless you do it while your opponent is teeing off.

—BRUCE LANSKY
AUTHOR

There's something haunting about getting up at dawn and walking a golf course, checking pin placements. It's easy to lose track of reality.

—ERNEST CREAMY CAROLAN
LONGTIME CADDIE FOR MANY GREATS,
INCLUDING ARNOLD PALMER AND BEN HOGAN

Golfers should not fail to realize that it is a game of great traditions, of high ideals of sportsmanship, one in which a strict adherence to the rules is essential.

—FRANCIS OUIMET

I have a tip that can take 5 strokes off anyone's golf game. It's called an eraser.

—ARNOLD PALMER

———◆———

You are meant to play the ball as it lies, a fact that may help to touch on your own objective approach to life.

—GRANTLAND RICE

———◆———

Some people say I play erratic golf. What they mean is I frequently play lousy.

—TOM SHAW

———◆———

A kid grows up a lot faster on the golf course. Golf teaches you how to behave.

—JACK NICKLAUS

After an abominable round of golf, a man is known to have slit his wrists with a razor blade and, having bandaged them, to have stumbled into the locker room and inquired of his partner, 'What time tomorrow?'
> —ALISTAIR COOKE

In football . . . some coaches have stated, when you throw a pass, three things can happen, two of them are bad. In golf, there is no limit.
> —MARINO PARASCENZO
> WRITER

The hardest part was getting in and out of the car and buckling and unbuckling the seatbelt 90 times.
> —DON "SNOWSHOE" THOMPSON
> AFTER HITTING A BALL AT 44 COURSES IN 12 CONSECUTIVE HOURS

I've got a new idea. Try the fairways.
> —PRESIDENT BILL CLINTON
> SAID TO ONE OF HIS FOURSOME WHO HIT A BAD SHOT

The humor of golf is a divine comedy . . . Like all sources of laughter it lies in contrast and paradox; in the thought of otherwise grave men gravely devoting hours and money to a technique which so often they, apparently alone, do not know they can ever master.

—R.C. ROBERTSON-GLASGOW
BRITISH WRITER AND CRICKETER

I hit some crummy shots. And when I hit some good shots, I hit crummy putts.

—RICK FEHR
ON HIS FINAL-ROUND 73 IN THE 1985 US OPEN

Golf is the infallible test. The man who can go into a patch of rough alone, with the knowledge that only God is watching him, and play his ball where it lies, is the man who will serve you faithfully and well.

—P.G. WODEHOUSE

I've injured both my hands playing golf and they're okay now, but my brain has always been suspect.

—BOB MURPHY

Men who would face torture without a word become blasphemous at the short 14th. It is clear that the game of golf may well be included in that category of intolerable provocations which may legally excuse or mitigate behaviour not otherwise excusable.

—A.P. HERBERT
ENGLISH WRITER AND ACTIVIST

Why don't you come down here and play with me! Come on, come on. You and your kid too. I'll give you two a side and play your low ball.

—TOMMY BOLT
YELLING AT GOD, AFTER MISSING A SHORT PUTT

Heck no. It's from the six rounds of golf I played in the last five days.

—BOBBY RAHAL
RACE CAR DRIVER, WHEN ASKED IF HIS SORE BACK
WAS CAUSED BY AN ACCIDENT IN HIS CAR

It's easy to see golf not as a game at all but as some whey-faced, nineteenth-century Presbyterian minister's fever dream of exorcism achieved through ritual and self-mortification.

—BRUCE MCCALL

He enjoys that perfect peace, that peace beyond all understanding, which comes at its maximum only to the man who has given up golf.

    —P.G. WODEHOUSE

Because golf exposes the flaws of the human swing—a basically simple maneuver—it causes more self-torture than any game short of Russian roulette.

    —GRANTLAND RICE

No matter what calamities befall him in everyday life, the true hacker still needs the pressure and inconvenience of . . . hours of trudging in wind or rain or sleet or sun . . . hacking at a white pellet that seems to have a mind of its own and a lousy sense of direction.

    —TOM O'CONNOR

The game itself is so absorbing and the challenge faced by the competitors so daunting, I think one could be led to conclude an ascetic lifestyle is best.

    —JIM APFELBAUM

Golf gets people outdoors, the sort of people who should be kept indoors.
—LINDA SMITH

How would you like to meet the top 143 people at what you do each week in order to survive?
—BRUCE CRAMPTON
PGA PRO

Anyway, a man who cannot take a thrashing in good part is usually intolerable when he is doing the thrashing.
—GARY PLAYER
FROM *PLAY GOLF WITH GARY PLAYER*

I've seen lifelong friends drift apart over golf simply because one could play better but the other counted better.
—STEPHEN LEACOCK

Golf's a hard game to figure. One day you slice it, shank it, hit into all the traps and miss every green. And then the next day, you go out and for no reason at all you really stink.

—BOB HOPE

A wife can sometimes be a deterrent to a good game of golf.

—EARL WOODS

Try to remember that a person may be a most indifferent golfer, and yet be a good Christian gentleman, and in some respects worthy of your esteem.

—HORACE HUTCHINSON
FROM *HINTS ON GOLF*

I'm a firm believer in the theory that people only do their best at things they truly enjoy. It is difficult to excel at something you don't enjoy.

—JACK NICKLAUS

Anyone taking up golf has to realize at the outset that it is an appallingly difficult game to play well.

    —PETER RYDE
    WRITER

There is no better game in the world when you are in good company, and no worse game when you are in bad company.

    —TOMMY BOLT

To such a perfect putter as Mr. Travis, who would putt if need were with an umbrella or walking-stick, doubtless there are no difficulties.

    —ARTHUR POLTOW
    ILLUSTRATED OUTDOOR NEWS (1906)

Golf does strange things to other people, too. It makes liars out of honest men, cheats out of altruists, cowards out of brave men, and fools out of everybody.

    —MILTON GROSS

A golf ball can stop in the fairway, rough, woods, bunker or lake. With five equally likely options, very few balls choose the fairway.

—JIM BISHOP

We can get so much out of golf. I know I have, and I'd like to see the same for you. Golf is the game of a lifetime, one in which you can get better and better. It's not what you do that counts, but what you attempt to do.

—GEORGE KNUDSON
CANADIAN PGA PRO

I should have guessed that any Russian who had yielded to such a capitalist diversionary activity such as golf would have been, on his first homecoming, bundled off to Siberia, where he'd have been condemned to play golf with a red ball and a snow sled.

—ALISTAIR COOKE
FROM *WORKERS, ARISE! SHOUT FORE*

The thing that sets golf apart from the other sports is that it takes self-confidence, an ability to rely totally on yourself.

—JACK NICKLAUS

I've had a good day when I don't fall out of the cart.

—BUDDY HACKETT
COMEDIAN

I think he probably enriched more lives than anyone else I have ever known. He enriched mine beyond measure.

—HERBERT WARREN WIND
ON BOBBY JONES

The game requires a certain cold toughness of mind, and absorption of will. There was not an athlete I talked to from other sports who did not hold the professional golfer in complete awe, with thanksgiving that golf was not their profession.

—GEORGE PLIMPTON

In any other sport, it's considered semi-honorable, even chuckle-creating, to cheat.

—JIM MURRAY

Sometimes the game of golf is just too difficult to endure with a golf club in your hands.

     —BOBBY JONES

Men capable of governing empires fail to control a small white ball, which presents no difficulties whatever to others with one ounce more brain than a cuckoo clock.

     —P.G. WODEHOUSE
       FROM *HEART OF A GOOF*

I guess there is nothing that will get your mind off everything like golf will. I have never been depressed enough to take up the game, but they say you can get so sore at yourself that you forget to hate your enemies.

     —WILL ROGERS

We learn so many things from golf. How to suffer, for instance.

     —BRUCE LANSKY

I think, number one, I'd like people to think that I tried hard. I was a mean cuss probably at times. But you can't go on the course and say, Hello, Minnie. Hello, Joe. How are the kids? No, you can't do that.

—SAM SNEAD
GOLF DIGEST

I tried to make a one, but I made two of them instead.

—AL KELLEY
SENIOR TOUR GOLFER, ON GETTING AN 11 ON A PAR 5 HOLE

I expect to hit five bad shots.

—WALTER HAGEN
ON HOW HE EXPECTS TO PLAY EVERYDAY

Match play really exposes your character, who you are and how much of a will to win you have in your heart . . . It also exposes what kind of weaknesses your game has.

—JOHNNY MILLER

In a team sport, you can go out and make your own breaks. You can make a tackle. You can jump up and block Julius Erving's shot. In golf, you're all alone. Sometimes it's hard. I can't run out and jump on Jack Nicklaus's back.

—ANDY NORTH

Sometimes you lose your desire through the years. Any golfer goes through that. When you play golf for a living, like anything in your life, you are never going to be constant, at the top.

—TOM WATSON
AT THE 1994 BRITISH OPEN AT TURNBERRY

Golf and sex are the only things you can enjoy without being good at them.

—JIMMY DEMARET

What an achievement it would be to set forth, properly and for all time, the glories of a golf tournament, the subtleties of mood, the severities of the strain, the infinite complexity and the pure simplicity that taken together make up the most stimulating sporting event of all.

—MARK MCCORMACK

Eighteen holes of match play will teach you more about your foe than nineteen years of dealing with him across the desk.

—GRANTLAND RICE

It is the most individual of all sports, and no amount of camaraderie prior to the match can change the fact that you're in it alone.

—BARBARA BALDWIN
WRITER, OBSERVING HER TEENAGE SON PLAYING GOLF

Oh hang it! With so many things to be thought of all at once, steady play is impossible.

—SIR WALTER SIMPSON

The way I putted, I must have been reading the greens in Spanish and putting them in English.

—HOMERO BLANCAS

I don't know the traffic regulations of every city I get to either, but I manage to drive through without being arrested.

>—LLOYD MANGRUM
>ON BEING PUNISHED AS A RESULT OF NOT KNOWING THE RULES

When I left the course after a round this year, a lady told me my biorhythms were off. I told her my golf game was off.

>—JACK NICKLAUS
>FROM THE VIDEO *BAD GOLF MY WAY*

No matter what happens—never give up a hole . . . In tossing in your cards after a bad beginning you also undermine your whole game, because to quit between tee and green is more habit-forming than drinking a highball before breakfast.

>—SAM SNEAD

I won't say my golf is bad, but if I started growing tomatoes, they'd come up sliced!

>—MILLER BARBER

Put me on a putting green in Miami for a week and I'll kill more tourists than the Fontainebleau.

—GEORGE LOW

The golfer has more enemies than any other athlete. He has fourteen clubs in his bag, all of them different; 18 holes to play, all of them different, every week; and all around him is sand, trees, grass, water, wind and 143 other players.

—DAN JENKINS
ON THE PGA TOUR

Nobody ever looked up and saw a good shot.

—DON HEROLD
AMERICAN HUMORIST, WRITER, ILLUSTRATOR AND AVID GOLFER

I don't suppose that any of the pro or amateur golfers who were combat soldiers, Marines, or sailors will soon be able to think of a three-putt green as one of the really bad troubles in life.

—LLOYD MANGRUM
VETERAN OF THE D-DAY INVASION AND THE BATTLE OF THE BULGE

Golf courses are the best place to observe ministers, but none of them are above cheating a bit.

—JOHN D. ROCKEFELLER

If a man can take five or six bogeys in a row, or a succession of flubbed shots without blowing his stack, he is capable of handling any situation.

—JIMMY DEMARET

People who say golf is fun are probably the same people who rationalize the game by saying they play it for their health. What could be fun about a game in the entire history of which nobody has ever shot the score he thought he should have?

—CHARLES PRICE

If I had my way, no man guilty of golf would be eligible to any office of trust under the United States

—H.L. MENCKEN

Golf giveth and golf taketh away, but it taketh away a hell of a lot more than it giveth.

—SIMON HOBDAY

There shouldn't be any cups, just flagsticks. And then the man who hit the most fairways and greens and got the closest to the pins would be the tournament winner.

—BEN HOGAN

If golfers can run around and crow when they make a birdie, I think it would be just as proper to lie down on the green and cry when you make a bogey.

—J.C. SNEAD

If there is any larceny in a man, golf will bring it out.

—PAUL GALLICO

Golf is a game where guts, stick-to-itiveness and blind devotion will always net you absolutely nothing but an ulcer.

> —TOMMY BOLT

I think I'll change my grip.

> —BILL THOMAS
> AFTER BREAKING THE WINDSCREENS OF TWO PASSING CARS

Golf has more rules than any other game, because golf has more cheaters than any other game.

> —BRUCE LANSKY

It is impossible to imagine Goethe or Beethoven being good at billiards or golf.

> —H.L. MENCKEN

The income tax has made more liars out of the American people than golf has.

> —WILL ROGERS

It [championships] is something like a cage. First you are expected to get into it and then you are expected to stay there. But of course, nobody can stay there.

—BOBBY JONES
EXPLAINING WHY HE RETIRED FROM COMPETITIVE GOLF IN 1930
AT AGE 28

When you give all your time and all your resources to golf and you still can't hit the ball straight, it literally breaks your heart.

—TOM COYNE

Where's Tonya Harding when you need her?

—SCOTT HOCH
ON BEING BEATEN BY DAVID DUVAL

We all suffer, of course we do. You try and talk it up to give yourself confidence but, my goodness, it's hard work.

—COLIN MONTGOMERIE

No game designed to be played with the aid of personal servants by right-handed men who can't even bring along their dogs can be entirely good for the soul.

—BRUCE MCCALL
"THE CASE AGAINST GOLF", FROM *ESQUIRE*

———•———

There's going to come at least one point when you want to throw yourself in the nearest trash can and disappear. You know you can't hide. It's like walking down the fairway naked. The gallery knows what you've done, every other player knows, and worst of all, you know.

—HALE IRWIN

———•———

The average player would rather play than watch. Those who don't play can't possibly appreciate the subtleties of the game. Trying to get their attention with golf is like selling Shakespeare in the neighborhood saloon.

—BOB TOSKI

———•———

If you want to increase your success rate, double your failure rate.

—TOM WATSON

Golf is the hardest game in the world to play and the easiest to cheat at.
—DAVE HILL

My golf is improving. Yesterday I hit the ball in one!
—JANE SWAN

Dishonesty is a rarity in golf. I think that I know the reason why. While there may be training aids to assist you when you practice, and anyone can benefit from good instruction and playing tips, once you're on the course you make each shot by yourself.
—JOHN COMPANIOTTE
FROM *GOLF RULES AND ETIQUETTE SIMPLIFIED*

Golf teaches success and failure. Neither lasts long.
—GLENN KUMMER

Good golfers are good golfers largely because they have learned and accepted that, no matter how fine the gun's firing action, unless it is aimed correctly it won't deliver the missile to the target.

—JOHN JACOBS

Golf lacks something for me. It would be better if once in a while someone came up from behind and tackled you just as you were hitting the ball.

—RED GRANGE
    FOOTBALL LEGEND

If you pick up a golfer and hold it close to your ear, like a conch shell, and listen—you will hear an alibi.

—P.G. WODEHOUSE

There is an old saying: If a man comes home with sand in his cuffs and cockleburs in his pants, don't ask him what he shot.

—SAM SNEAD

When making a match, do not try to get a greater allowance of strokes than that to which you are entitled on your handicap, alleging your opponent that the said handicap is an unfair one.

—HARRY VARDON
FROM *SOME GENERAL HINTS*

———•———

Looks like Generation X is turning into Generation Selfish.

—LANNY WADKINS
ON THE PLAYER PAY CONTROVERSY AT THE 1999 RYDER CUP

———•———

What in the world am I doing in a golf course where guys shoot 61?

—BEN HOGAN
ON TRAILING TWO OBSCURE GOLFERS WHO SHOT 61S IN THE FIRST
ROUND OF A TOURNAMENT

———•———

I sent Gary [Player] a telegram recently. I asked him if he turned over a new leaf.

—TOM WATSON
ON ACCUSING GARY PLAYER OF ILLEGALLY UNCOVERING
A BALL FROM UNDER A LEAF DURING A SKINS GAME

Golf wasn't meant to be fair.

> —PETE DYE
> GOLF COURSE ARCHITECT

Of all the games man has devised, supposedly for his enjoyment, golf is in a class by itself in the anguish it inflicts.

> —HERBERT WARREN WIND

I wasn't playing well, and I fought my swing forever, and I was sick of it, and I was getting worse and said, 'To hell with it.'

> —CURTIS STRANGE
> ON HIS REASONS FOR QUITTING THE TOUR

The myth is better than the reality. I'm in golf purgatory. I can't play enough rounds to get my handicap up where it belongs.

> —CHRIS CHOCOLA
> U.S. CONGRESSMAN

I had to learn how to play out of bunkers because I used to be in so many of them.

—KEN VENTURI

I never cussed much. That's a bunch of bullshit.

—TOMMY BOLT
ON CURSING

Gripes! They're going to have to hire a third person just to smile for us.

—CURTIS STRANGE
ON BEING PAIRED WITH LANNY WADKINS

I've been around the game a long time. Par doesn't give a damn about pride. I've seen par wring pride's neck.

—DAN JENKINS
IN RESPONSE TO THE PRESIDENT SAYING HE HAS TOO MUCH PRIDE TO
TAKE A MULLIGAN, *GOLF WITH THE BOSS*

I wish to goodness I knew the man who invented this infernal game. I'd strangle him. But I suppose he's been dead for ages. Still, I could go and jump on his grave.

> —P.G. WODEHOUSE
> FROM *HEART OF A GOOF*

I haven't been playing very well, but nobody cares but my wife. It's good to be under par for the start.

> —CURTIS STRANGE

Sudden success in golf is like the sudden acquisition of wealth. It is apt to unsettle and deteriorate the character.

> —P.G. WODEHOUSE

For every up in this game, there's twenty downs.

> —BRIAN DAVIS

I tell myself that Jack Nicklaus probably has a lousy curveball.

—BOB WALK
FORMER MAJOR LEAGUE PITCHER, ON HOW HE
HANDLES GOLFING FRUSTRATION

How could anyone working eight-to-five generate sympathy for anybody who could win $50,000 in a week?

—HUBERT GREEN

No, I can't. I guess I could win if everybody else broke their leg or something.

—NOLAN HENKE
ASKED IF HE COULD WIN THE 1991 US OPEN
WHILE ONLY ONE SHOT OFF THE LEAD

There is only one thing worse than playing the way I am. That's not playing at all.

—ARNOLD PALMER
DURING A SLUMP IN HIS MID-40s

It's so ridiculous to see a golfer with a one-foot putt and everybody is saying 'Shhh' and not moving a muscle. Then we allow nineteen year-old kids to face a game-deciding free throw with seventeen thousand people yelling.

—AL MCGUIRE
HALL OF FAME BASKETBALL COACH

The two qualities that helped most: honesty about my game, and a sense of humor.

—JOYCE WETHERED
WINNER OF FIVE CONSECUTIVE ENGLISH WOMEN'S
AMATEUR CHAMPIONSHIPS

First comes my wife and children. Next comes my profession—the law. Finally, and never as a life itself, comes golf.

—BOBBY JONES

I don't want 400 members telling me what to do and only talking to me when something goes wrong.

—CHI-CHI RODRIGUEZ
ON WHY HE WOULD NEVER BE A GOLF PRO AT A COUNTRY CLUB

It never occurs to Arnold that the ball won't go in the hole, but I'm always surprised when it does.

—GENE LITTLER
COMPARING HIS PUTTING PHILOSOPHY WITH ARNOLD PALMER'S

A curious thing I have noticed about golf is that a festering grievance sometimes does wonders for a man's drive.

—P.G. WODEHOUSE

Anyone taking up golf has to realize at the outset that it is an appallingly difficult game to play well.

—PETER RYDE

The stories of bad scores rarely start with, 'I ripped one down the middle.'

—COLIN MONTGOMERIE

I always tried to remind myself of the great number of times I would follow a sequence of bad shots with a good one—or even a great one. As long as this was a possibility, I reasoned, then why not expect good ones to follow the bad ones . . .

—SAM SNEAD

On tour we get paid for performance. If we don't play well, our income falls dramatically. If we get hurt and have to sit out a season, there's no income at all.

—TOM KITE

Qualifying competitions are dull things unless they are cruel.

—BERNARD DARWIN

A good player prays for wind every day, but not too earnestly.

—JOHN L. LOW
CONCERNING GOLF

When God wants to play through, you let him.

—LEE TREVINO

The setting up of a golf shot can be as ponderous as the loading of a Roman siege catapult, with interminable adjustments to range and aim before finally the carcass of a dead horse is hoisted into the middle launcher.

—PETER DOBEREINER

I used to play golf with a guy who cheated so badly that he once had a hole in one and wrote down zero on his scorecard.

—BOB BRUCE
SENIOR PGA TOUR MEMBER

In other games you get another chance. In baseball you get three cracks at it; in tennis you lose only one point. But in golf the loss of one shot has been responsible for the loss of heart.

—TOMMY ARMOUR

Playing the game I have learned the meaning of humility. It has given me an understanding of the futility of human effort.

  —ABBA EBAN

He plays just like a union man. He negotiates the final score.

  —BOB HOPE
   ON PLAYING GOLF WITH GEORGE MEANY

I think it's sort of the reason I want to play golf at all. The reason that anybody keeps going out and plays this impossible ridiculous game. As hard as golf is, as expensive it is, it is difficult.

  —TOM COYNE

We learned to play foursomes from the Americans. For years, every time we had a shot to play, we would always confer with our partner . . . really, sharing the responsibility. The Americans never did that. Each played her own game and took responsibility for the shot.

  —JOHN BAILEY
   HUSBAND OF DIANE BAILEY, CAPTAIN OF THE 1986 CURTIS CUP TEAM

Running through the Rules are underlying principles that, like the steel rods which lie below the surface of reinforced concrete, serve to bind together the brittle material and to give it strength.
— RICHARD S. TUFTS

I played so bad, I got a get-well card from the IRS.
— JOHNNY MILLER
ON HIS TERRIBLE 1977 SEASON

The only way of really finding out a man's true character is to play golf with him. In no other walk of life does the cloven hoof so quickly display itself.
— P.G. WODEHOUSE

I try to work with God as a partner.
— GARY PLAYER

When the great snooker player Joe Davis saw his first game of golf the putting puzzled him. 'Why,' he asked his golfing friend, 'don't they knock the ball into the hole the first time?'
— ANONYMOUS

Par is a designation of excellence.

> —ROBERT SOMMERS
> WRITER

———•———

You know they have a saying around the racetrack that if you have eight cheap horses and run them against each other eight times, you'd have eight different winners. Sound like the PGA Tour to you?

> —JIM MURRAY

———•———

But in the end it's still a game of golf, and if at the end of the day you can't shake hands with your opponents and still be friends, then you've missed the point.

> —PAYNE STEWART

———•———

The object of golf is not just to win. It is to play like a gentleman, and win.

> —PHIL MICKELSON

———•———

It's nice to be well liked, but it's even better to be well liked and respected.

> —MEG MALLON
> 1991 US WOMEN'S OPEN CHAMPION,
> 1990 LPGA'S "MOST POPULAR PLAYER"

After the shot is played, the moment is lost forever. So every shot is important, every shot is once-in-a-lifetime.

—MICHAEL BAMBERGER
FROM STARK

The only problem in major golf is, as ever 'how to score,' for nearly all the players setting out on the circuits can hit the ball. That is no problem. It is the scoring which counts.

—HENRY COTTON

Golf gives you an insight into human nature, your own as well as your opponent's. Eighteen holes of match or medal play will teach you more about your foe than will eighteen years of dealing with him across a desk.

—GRANTLAND RICE

The score is important, of course. And the discovery that you are superior to another golfer is satisfying. But when your score is bad and the other fellow beats you, golf still has been a blessing to you. The score isn't the 'be all and end all.'

—TOMMY ARMOUR

I'm more proud of my reputation than the fact that I won a lot of tournaments.

—Byron Nelson
Golf Digest

If we are to preserve the integrity of golf as left to us by our forefathers, it is up to all of us to carry on the true spirit of the game.

—Ben Crenshaw

Bobby Jones was the most genuinely modest person I have ever met. When one had talked with him a short time he gave you the feeling that the only difference between your game and his was that he had been much more lucky.

—Raymond Oppenheimer
Captain of the 1951 European Walker Cup team

I don't want somebody to ask, 'How many tournaments did Annika Sörenstam win?' I would rather they say she was a great athlete, she loved sportsmanship and she loved what she did. If they know my name, then they will know I played good golf.

—Annika Sörenstam

I think the golfer who fails to clean up his mess in a sand trap should be banned from the game . . . The absence of a rake is no excuse for not smoothing the sand. You can take care of the marks easily with the back of a club.

—Jack Nicklaus

The reality of life as a pro golfer is that the difference between a good day and a bad day is just a spin of the ball.

—Kathryn Marshall
LPGA player

I can't control other people. I can only control what I do. I have lived my life by certain standards, both off the golf course and a lot more on it. I have been committed to certain beliefs . . . since I was six years old. Those beliefs have not changed.

—Mark McCumber

There is even as with no other game a fascinating detective literature, a wry commentary on the human comedy, implicit in the book of rules.

—Alistair Cooke

CHAPTER SEVEN

Instruction:
On the Golf Swing, Tee Shots, Putts, and Trouble Shots from Tee to Green

He appears an austere, taciturn man, the 28th president, scrutinizing us through the years from behind his pince-nez spectacles and stiff, high collar. Dogged by world events, he remained a no less passionate and ardent golfer than his Scottish forebears. Woodrow Wilson met his second wife as he was coming off the golf course. They honeymooned at The Homestead in a room overlooking the course, and played each morning. At World War I's nadir, his mental health failing, his personal physician prescribed golf to provide some solace to the war-weary president.

Wilson was described as "fidgety" over his ball. It fits. The game has a knack of exploiting personal quirks of character, unimpressed by rank, wealth or even, in this case, diplomatic skill. Here was a man who could convince warring nations to sit down together. This would prove child's play compared with seeking compromise among the belligerent factions of the swing, a motion that no more lends itself to dissection than the fluidity of a fish moving through water.

What order? The game appears governed by opposites and chaos. Aim left, the ball goes right. The arcs and planes, the slow takeaway, the head at impact, what the right knee is doing . . .?!! What's more, the alchemists who teach golf seem to have a bit of Merlin in them. It often takes the best tutors longer to say hello and procure a bucket of range balls than to pinpoint the source of the affliction.

Yet there's this: Despite taking Man's best punch, the slice shows no more inclination to be eradicated than the common cold. And for this we may ironically rejoice, for had the precise questions of the swing been successfully unraveled by our ancestors, golf may never have emerged from the 1500s.

* * * *

Golf, more than most games, has a number of clichés, often successfully disguised as 'tips.' Watch out.

—KATHY WHITWORTH

Golf tips are like aspirin. One may do you good, but if you swallow the whole bottle you will be lucky to survive.

—HARVEY PENICK

The golf swing is like sex. You can't be thinking about the mechanics of the act while you are performing.

—DAVE HILL

A golf swing is a collection of corrected mistakes.

—CAROL MANN

An efficient golf swing incorporates the fewest moving parts while producing maximum results in terms of direction, distance, and ball flight. These factors add up to control, and to me the ultimate art of golf is in controlling the ball.

—NICK PRICE
FROM *THE SWING: MASTERING THE PRINCIPLES OF THE GAME*

The longer a club is the harder it is to get back to the ball after you've taken the clubhead away. And the more upright you are, the less chance there is of error.

—SANDRA PALMER
1975, IN "SANDRA PALMER CAN HANDLE THE PRESSURE,"
BY SARAH BALLARD, *SPORTS ILLUSTRATED*

His wriggling at the address has been likened to a man squirming his way into a telephone box with a load of parcels in his arms.

—*THE ENCYCLOPEDIA OF GOLF*
DESCRIBING RALPH GULDAHL'S SWING
1975

If you have a good short game you have a powerful ally.

—NICK PRICE

I think I'm the only president whose handicap has gone down while he's been in office. It's only because I've gotten to play with all these pros and other good golfers, and they give me all this good advice.

—PRESIDENT BILL CLINTON
GOLF DIGEST

I don't trust doctors. They are like golfers. Every one has a different answer to your problems.

> —SEVE BALLESTEROS

The most abysmal advice ever given by the ignorant is stupid.

> —TOMMY ARMOUR
> ON KEEPING YOUR EYE ON THE BALL

I'm much better off by myself. When Jack Grout taught me to lay, he taught me to correct myself. Frankly, I've probably had too many teachers. Lately, I'm better off by myself.

> JACK NICKLAUS, 1994

Frank, either you have to get better soon or quit telling people I'm your teacher.

> —DAVE MARR
> TO PRO FOOTBALL HALL OF FAMER FRANK GIFFORD

I've never had a coach in my life. When I find one who can beat me, then I'll listen.

—LEE TREVINO

In no game is the player provided with such a staggering wealth of instruction. There is hardly one stroke in golf which a man cannot play at least a dozen ways, yet remain, according to the information of the masters, correct in method.

—R.C. ROBERTSON-GLASGOW

The reason the pro tells you to keep your head down is so you can't see him laughing.

—PHYLLIS DILLER

The worst advice in golf is, 'Keep your head down.'

—PATTY SHEEHAN

Don't drive at a fellow-creature, so long as there is a reasonable chance of hitting him.

—WILLIAM EDWARD NORRIS

I told him to hit it and run backwards.

—KEN VENTURI
REMEMBERING THE ADVICE HE GAVE TO SOMEONE
WANTING MORE DISTANCE ON HIS DRIVES

Many shots are spoiled at the last instant by efforts to add a few more yards.

—BOBBY JONES

The two mistakes I see most often from amateurs are lifting up and hitting the equator of the ball, sending it into the next country, or taking a divot of sand large enough to bury a cat.

—SAM SNEAD

Golfers are very fond of insisting, and with great justice, that the game is not won by the driver. It is the short game—the approaching and putting —that wins the match. Nevertheless, despite the truth of this, if there were no driving there would be very little golf.

—HORACE HUTCHINSON

You drive for show and putt for dough.

—AL BALDING

The pleasure of the long drive or second shot to the green gives as fine an emotion as is possible for any sinner to receive on this earth.

—R.H. LYTTLETON

It's not just enough to swing at the ball. You've got to loosen your girdle and really let the ball have it.

—BABE ZAHARIAS

Just knock hell out of it with your right hand.

—TOMMY ARMOUR
ON DRIVING

For myself and other serious golfers there is an undeniable beauty in the way a fine player sets his hands on the club.

—BEN HOGAN
FROM *FIVE LESSONS*

———◆———

The point is that it doesn't matter if you look like a beast before or after the hit, as long as you look like a beauty at the moment of impact.

—SEVE BALLESTEROS

———◆———

My swing is so bad I look like a caveman killing his lunch.

—LEE TREVINO

———◆———

I may not swing the prettiest or look the prettiest, and I may do some things kind of funny, but I have a lot of heart.

—TOM LEHMAN

———◆———

Long swing, long career. Short swing, short career.

—JACK BURKE JR.
PGA HALL OF FAMER

I get all kinds of people telling me I have the best swing in the world-it's beautiful, it's effortless. But I know when that isn't true.

—ERNIE ELS
GOLF DIGEST

My swing is faultless.

—IAN WOOSNAM

Give me a man with big hands, big feet, and no brains, and I will make a golfer out of him.

—WALTER HAGEN

Golfers find it a very trying matter to turn at the waist, more particularly if they have a lot of waist to turn.

—HARRY VARDON

The best-stroked putt in a lifetime does not bring the aesthetic satisfaction of a perfectly hit wood or iron shot. There is nothing to match the whoosh and soar, the almost magical flight of a beautifully hit drive or 5-iron.

—AL BARKOW

What goes up must come down. But don't expect it to come down where you can find it.

      —LILY TOMLIN

———•———

Long driving is of prime importance in golf. It need not be long enough to give the golfer some chance against par, and to put him on good terms with himself.

      —TED RAY
         WINNER OF THE 1912 BRITISH OPEN AND THE 1920 US OPEN

———•———

There are three ways of learning golf: by study, which is the most wearisome; by imitation, which is the most fallacious; and by experience, which is the most bitter.

      —ROBERT BROWNING
         WRITER

Being a left-hander is a big advantage. No one knows enough about your game to mess you up with advice.
> —BOB CHARLES

You'll get better results—and often more distance—if you swing at eighty percent effort.
> —ERNIE ELS
> *GOLF DIGEST*

Whether you hit the ball slowly, soft, or hard, everyone needs tempo . . . Tempo is the glue that sticks all elements of the golf swing together.
> —NICK FALDO
> FROM *TRUMP: THE BEST GOLF ADVICE I EVER RECEIVED*

It is always important in golf to realize that there is not just one way of playing a hole and each golfer should decide what will work best.
> —JOHN COMPANIOTTE
> FROM *GOLF RULES AND ETIQUETTE SIMPLIFIED*

Here's the ball and there's the hole, four and a quarter inches in diameter. We're expected to get the ball from here to there in three shots, across all this land and water. And what's more amazing, sometimes we do it in one shot. It boggles the mind to even think of it.

—DAN HALLDORSON

If you expect a miracle, you should expect to pay for one.

—DEREK HARDY
BETH DANIEL'S COACH, WHO CHARGED $1,000
FOR ONE LESSON AND $140 FOR 13 LESSONS

Imagine the ball has little legs, and chop them off.

—HENRY COTTON

If there is one secret to the game, one thing I would tell a beginner to do to become a good player, it's to do as many things as possible with the left hand.

—FRANK WALSH
PGA PRO IN THE 1930s

If you think your hands are more important in your golf swing than your legs, try walking a hole on your hands.
—GARY PLAYER

The ball which arrives at the hole with the proper speed has an infinitely greater chance of falling in the hole from any entrance.
—BEN CRENSHAW
ON PUTTING

Flying the ball, I might have him. Rolling it, he might have me. He doesn't hit it as high as me. On a wet course, I'd take him. On a dry course, he might roll it farther.
—JOHN DALY
ON WHETHER HE'S LONGER OFF THE TEE THAN TIGER WOODS

Sometimes you send the message down to the hands and it stops at the elbows.
—SAM TORRANCE
ON PUTTING

Imagine a short man . . . with a long club placing his feet with meticulous care in regard to line . . . The waggle is careful and restrained; then suddenly all is changed; he seems almost to jump on his toes in the upswing and fairly flings himself into the ball.

—BERNARD DARWIN

If a lot of people gripped a knife and fork the way they do a golf club, they'd starve to death.

—SAM SNEAD

I would be suspicious of anyone who claims there is one way to swing a golf club, because I know it simply is not true.

—GARDNER DICKINSON
A FOUNDER OF THE SENIOR PGA TOUR AND A NOTED
RYDER CUP PLAYER

I have a hook. It nauseated me. I could vomit when I see one. It's like a rattlesnake in your pocket.

—BEN HOGAN

You can't birdie all eighteen holes if you don't birdie the first three.

—NICK FALDO

Walter Hagen never knew where his ball was going and he had to invent six or seven new shots every time he played just to get his ball back into play.

—PETER DOBEREINER

If you're going to miss 'em, miss 'em quick.

—GEORGE DUNCAN
ON PUTTING

I've never been a very technical player. I don't get caught up in swing positions and mechanics. When I work on my swing . . . I'm looking for feels.

—ERNIE ELS
GOLF DIGEST

The most important single move in establishing your tempo and rhythm is your takeaway. It sets the beat for everything that comes later. Strive on every shot to move the club back as *deliberately* as possible, consistent with swinging it [back] rather than taking it [back].

—JACK NICKLAUS

Hitting a golf ball correctly is the most sophisticated and complicated maneuver in all of sports, with the possible exception of eating a hot dog at a ball game without getting mustard on your shirt.

—RAY FITZGERALD
    SPORTSWRITER

Whatever your natural ball flight, you can use it to your advantage, because you can always eliminate one side of the golf course. You can always start a reliable fade down the left side of the fairway . . . A draw works similarly from the right side.

—JIM MCLEAN

The difference between a good golf shot and a bad one is the same as the difference between a beautiful and a plain woman—a matter of millimeters.
— Ian Fleming

The higher the ball sits [on the tee], the more we tend to sweep it away with a somewhat flatter swing. This, in itself, generally squares the clubface a bit sooner in the hitting area.
— John Jacobs

The golfing public has, in the last few decades, been steered away from golf as a game of feel. The emphasis today is on the mechanics of the swing. As you may have already noticed, I think this is the wrong path.
— Jim Flick, 1997
Golf magazine

Make the hard ones look easy and the easy ones look hard.
— Walter Hagen

Man, I can't even point that far.

—GAY BREWER
   WINNER OF THE 1967 MASTERS, ON JOHN DALY'S LENGTH
   OFF THE TEE

———•———

Once you start to deliver the club squarely and solidly to the back of the ball, you may be amazed at the quality of the shots you are able to hit.

—JIM HARDY
   FROM *THE PLANE TRUTH FOR GOLFERS*

———•———

I assume my stance, and take back the club, low, slowly; at the top, my eyes fog over, and my joints dip and swirl like barn swallows, I swing. There is a fruitless commotion of dust and rubber at my feet. 'Smothered it,' I say promptly.

—JOHN UPDIKE
   ON HIS SWING

———•———

You must not begin the downward swing as if you were anxious to get it over. Haste spells disaster and disaster is disheartening. I am always on the look-out against a pupil becoming downhearted.

—ALEXANDER "SANDY" HERD
   BRITISH GOLFER AND INSTRUCTOR

Present day golfers have chopped down their swing action to the barest essentials—go back and come down. This simplification occurred because modern equipment—tailored heads, steel shafts, firmer gripping, better distribution of weight and torque—permits the development of more power with less effort.

      —DOUG FORD
        PGA TOUR PROFESSIONAL

You can take it high in the air and have it land really soft. The ball will stop easier on the green, instead of having it hit and roll off the back of the green, which is what happens with long irons.

      —JIM FURYK

While searching for the perfect swings, I came to the realization that all golf swing techniques, no matter how varied, fell into one of two categories. You either swing your arms in somewhat the same plane as you turn your body, or you don't.

      —JIM HARDY
        FROM *THE PLANE TRUTH FOR GOLFERS*

A physicist can describe the perfect golf swing and write it down in scientific language, but the smart golfer doesn't read it. The smart golfer gives it to his opponent to contemplate.

  —Dr. Fran Pirozollo
   Sports psychologist

The ultimate judge of your swing is the flight of the ball.

  —Ben Hogan

Pavin's swing must be the swing of the future, because I sure as hell haven't seen anything like it in the past.

  —Charles Price
   Criticizing a slumping Corey Pavin in the 1980s

I found that seeing the swing of your body by turning it upon your legge is the largest and strongest motion. Therefor it must begin first and the turning at the small of the back must only second it, and then must follow the motion at the shoulders.

  —Thomas Kincaid, 1687
   From his diary in *The Book of the Old Edinburgh Club*

My ex-wife has never broken 150. I wish she would stop telling people I taught her how to play golf.

—BRUCE LANSKY

Placing the ball in the right position for the next shot is eighty percent of winning golf.

—BEN HOGAN

There are two reasons for making a hole-in-one. The first is that it is immensely labor saving.

—H.I. PHILLIPS
WRITER

A hole-in-one is amazing when you think of the different universes this white mass of molecules has to pass through on its way to the hole.

—MAC O'GRADY

I had a wonderful experience on the golf course today. I had a hole in nothing. Missed the ball and sank the divot.

—DAN ADAMS

The most important shot in golf is the next one.

—BEN HOGAN

It's often necessary to hit a second shot to really appreciate the first one.

—HENRY BEARD
HUMORIST

Play every shot so that the next one will be the easiest that you can give yourself.

—BILLY CASPER

Last week Arnold Palmer told me how I could cut eight strokes off my score. He'd say, 'Skip one of the par 3s.'

—BOB HOPE

Think ahead. Golf is a next-shot game.
— BILLY CASPER

Appreciate the brilliant shots you hit. Give yourself credit. Remember your good shots and make them important—even on the practice tee.
— JIM McLEAN
FROM *THE EIGHT-STEP SWING*

Maybe it's the one way I can get on a video with David Leadbetter instead of Nick Price and Frosty and Faldo.
— MIKE HULBERT
ON HIS ONE-HANDED PUTTING STYLE

Gay Brewer swings the club in a figure eight. If you didn't know better, you'd swear he was trying to kill snakes.
— DAVE HILL

If a man is to get into a hazard let it be a bad one . . . the worse the better. So leave your whins without any pruning or thinning and if the bottom of your sand bunker gets smooth-beaten, howk it up.

—HORACE HUTCHINSON, 1890

When your shot has to carry over a water hazard, you can either hit one more club or two more balls.

—HENRY BEARD
HUMORIST

If you don't have a club-head speed of about 100 mph, it's a waste of time to try to hit long irons.

—DAVID LEADBETTER

The good chip allows you to whistle while you walk in the dark alleys of golf.

—TOMMY BOLT

Dig it out of the ground like I did.

—BEN HOGAN
IN RESPONSE TO SOMEONE'S REQUEST FOR INSTRUCTION

The most important thing in golf is balance. If you are not properly balanced you are under a handicap in one form or another.

—ERNEST JONES
GOLF INSTRUCTOR

Never do anything in the golf swing at the sacrifice of balance.

—GEORGE KNUDSON
CANADIAN PGA PRO

Remember that it is always possible to overgolf yourself. Two rounds a day is enough for any man with a week or more of solid golf in front of him.

—HORACE HUTCHINSON

If you can get the ball in the hole regularly by standing on your head, then keep right on—and don't ever listen to advice from anyone.

> —John Jacobs
> British golf teacher

It is nothing new or original to say that golf is played one stroke at a time. But it took me many years to realize it.

> —Bobby Jones

Golf is a business, and you have to approach it that way. You have to give careful thought to every shot. Every shot sets up what you are going to do next. Every shot has to be placed correctly. Don't ever just hit a shot without thinking it through.

> —Ben Hogan
> From *Five Lessons*

Don't get into the habit of using 'winter rules.' If you do, you'll never learn to be a decent golfer. 'Winter rules' are generally an amusing delusion. They aid neither in the development of the turf nor of the player.

> —Tommy Armour, 1961
> From *How to Play Your Best Golf All The Time*

The secret of golf is to turn three shots into two.

—BOBBY JONES

The secret of golf is to turn three shots into two.

Your golf swing is a work in progress. The work begins the moment you grip your first club and doesn't end until you walk off the eighteenth green after the last round of your life.

—SHAWN HUMPHRIES
FROM *TWO STEPS TO A PERFECT GOLF SWING*

The follow-through is that part of the golf swing that takes place after the ball has been struck, but before the club has been thrown.

—HENRY BEARD
HUMORIST

Dividing the swing into its parts is like dissecting a cat. You'll have blood and guts and bones all over the place. But you won't have a cat.

—ERNEST JONES
GOLF INSTRUCTOR

I don't know enough to take you where you need to be.

> —HARDY LOUDERMILK
> GOLF INSTRUCTOR TO LPGA HALL OF FAMER
> KATHY WHITWORTH AT AGE 17

I was all right teaching kids and beginners because they will listen. It's the 15-handicappers with bad grips who won't. Maybe if I charged them $500 an hour they would, but I couldn't so I told them to bugger off.

> —SIMON HOBDAY
> SENIOR PGA TOUR PLAYER, DESCRIBING WHY HE
> STOPPED BEING A CLUB PROFESSIONAL IN THE 1980S

Just go out and enjoy your golf and to hell with worrying whether it looks right or not.

> —DEREK LAWRENSON
> FROM HIS BOOK *STEP-BY-STEP GOLF TECHNIQUES:*
> *MASTERING THE LONG AND SHORT GAME*

To get an elementary grasp of the game of golf, a human must learn, by endless practice, a continuous and subtle series of highly unnatural movements, involving about sixty-four muscles, that result in a seemingly natural swing, taking all of two seconds to begin and end.

—ALISTAIR COOKE

Build power, store it, and then release it.

—DAVID LEADBETTER
FROM *DAVID LEADBETTER'S LESSONS FROM GOLF GREATS*

I wish to emphasise that there are no secrets to golf.

—ERNEST JONES
GOLF INSTRUCTOR

In using the word rhythm I am not speaking of the swing. The rhythm I have reference to here could also be described as the order of procedure. Walter Hagen was probably the greatest exponent of the kind of rhythm I have in mind to play golf.

—BEN HOGAN, 1948
FROM *POWER GOLF*

The biggest disaster shots in the game are usually tee shots.

    —RAYMOND FLOYD

When you look down at your grip and see wrinkles in your wrists, chances are you are reaching for the ball and not using the club the way it was designed.

    —TOMMY ARMOUR

When teeing off, don't stand too close to the ball after you've hit it.

    —RUSS LEWIS
        CEO OF THE NEW YORK TIMES COMPANY,
        TRUMP: THE BEST GOLF ADVICE I EVER RECEIVED

There is the glorious sensation of making a true hit. This is not only true of the drive. There is a right or wrong way of hitting a yard putt. The right way is bliss, the wrong purgatory.

    —R.H. LYTTLETON

Distance control is critical in pitching. One of the benefits of *light grip pressure* is increased sensitivity in your hands, which in turn provides the intuitive sense for how far the ball will fly on a given pitch.

—COREY PAVIN

The son of a bitch [Bobby Locke] was able to hole a putt over sixty feet of peanut brittle.

—LLOYD MANGRUM

Yes, you're probably right about the left hand, but the fact is that I take my check with the right hand.

—BOBBY LOCKE
SOUTH-AFRICAN GOLFER, ON CRITICISM OF HIS LEFT-HANDED GRIP

Mine was, and remains, almost the antithesis of a 'mechanical' golf swing.

—ARNOLD PALMER, 1999
IN HIS AUTOBIOGRAPHY *A GOLFER'S LIFE*

I think my swing has been on the upright side probably through the years. But these guys who play mechanical means with positions, I don't see how they can even play golf doing that. I have always felt you have to play golf by feel.

>—JACK NICKLAUS, 1991
> *GOLF DIGEST*

It comes and it goes. It's the kind of thing you can't turn loose once you've got it going or it might never come back.

>—CRAIG WOOD
> EXPLAINING THE LACK OF A GROOVED SWING BEFORE 1941

My swing is no uglier than Arnold Palmer's, and it's the same ugly swing every time.

>—NANCY LOPEZ

If your swing was good enough to win one out there, it's good enough to win again. Your problem isn't usually your swing. It's your heart.

>—MARK McCUMBER
> MEMBER OF THE PGA TOUR

Power in golf has become totally out of proportion. This is a game of precision, not strength, and that aspect has become so important to me that I plan my playing program accordingly.

 —JACK NICKLAUS

Always use the club that takes the least out of you.

 —HARRY VARDON

Don't swing the club, let the club swing you.

 —LESLIE NIELSEN
  FROM *BAD GOLF MY WAY*

Let the club swing itself through. Help it on all you can but do not begin to hit with it. Let it do its work itself and it will do it well. Interfere with it, and it will be quite adequately revenged.

 —HORACE HUTCHINSON

If it really made sense to let the club do the work, you'd just say, Driver, wedge to the green, one-putt, and walk to the next tee.

 —THOMAS BOSWELL

When practicing, use the club that gives you the most trouble, and do not waste your time in knocking a ball with a tool that gives you the most satisfaction and with which you rarely make a bad stroke.

> —HARRY VARDON
> FROM *THE COMPLETE GOLFER*

———◆———

It seems to me the more loft there is on a club, the harder it is to play. Why, I don't know.

> —BOBBY JONES

———◆———

To score better, you must replicate on-course conditions as much as possible . . . By moving around, changing clubs and lies, and playing from wherever the shot ends up, you are forced to make the shots necessary to get up-and-down on the course.

> —PIA NILSSON, 1997
> SWEDISH NATIONAL GOLF TEAM COACH, IN *GOLF MAGAZINE*

———◆———

He took a swing like a man with a wasp under his shorts and his pants on fire, trying to impale a butterfly on the end of a scythe.

> —PAUL GALLICO
> SPORTSWRITER, DESCRIBING HIS PLAYING PARTNER

The golfer delivered an instructive lecture on the joys and sorrows of the game, to which the enquirer listened with a quizzical eye—and remarked, 'What a quare lot o' ways of wasting time there is nowadays.'

—W.F. COLLIER, 1890

My swing works for me, so why should I change it? I prefer to have a natural swing and play well rather than a perfect swing and not be able to play good.

—SERGIO GARCIA
TO CRITICS OF HIS SWING

If I'm breathing heavy while walking on a green, I'm going uphill. If I trip, I'm going downhill.

—SPEC GOLDMAN
ON READING GREENS

Feel at ease, lack worry, and no guessing as you hit the ball.

—WALTER HAGEN

I found out that all the important lessons of life are contained in the three rules for achieving a perfect golf swing. 1. Keep your head down. 2. Follow through. 3. Be born with money.

—P.J. O'ROURKE

<hr>

Reverse every natural instinct and do the opposite of what you are inclined to do, and you will probably come very close to having a perfect golf swing.

—BEN HOGAN

<hr>

I don't like mechanics. The best swing is the one with the least mechanics. When you see George Duncan or Harry Vardon or Bobby Jones swing, do you notice any mechanics?

—STEWART MAIDEN
GOLF PRO AND INSTRUCTOR TO SUCH GREATS AS BOBBY JONES

<hr>

Your best shots in golf are your practice swing and the conceded putt. You'll never master the rest.

—LORD ROBERTSON
NATO SECRETARY GENERAL

I told him he was one year away from the Tour and next year he'll be two years away.
—CHI-CHI RODRIGUEZ
ON THE POTENTIAL OF AN AMATEUR

When people ask me where I get my length from, I readily admit that I can't really explain, because it's always been natural for me.
—DAN POHL

The swing is never learned. It's remembered.
—STEVEN PRESSFIELD
FROM *THE LEGEND OF BAGGER VANCE*

The arc of your swing doesn't have a thing to do with the size of your heart.
—CAROL MANN

The Golf Hall of Fame is full of players with unusual-looking swings. Some of the prettiest swings you've ever seen in your life are made on the far end of the public driving range by guys who couldn't break an egg with a baseball bat.

—PETER JACOBSEN

I recommend a rather long and unhurried backswing in putting because it makes the stroke smoother and eliminates the putting yips which sometimes besets golfers who have short, compact backswings.

—BILLY CASPER
PGA HALL OF FAMER

You don't hit anything on the backswing, so why rush it?

—DOUG FORD

You're not going to find a golf swing in a book.

—TONY LEMA

It was a very lonely life. But making a change in a golf swing takes a long time . . . You do it over and over again, and it is so long before you can see the change that you sometimes wonder why you are doing it at all.

—SANDRA PALMER, 1975
IN "SANDRA PALMER: SHE CAN HANDLE THE PRESSURE,"
BY SARAH BALLARD, SPORTS ILLUSTRATED

———◆———

Don't change the arc of your swing unless you are fairly sure you blundered in some way earlier.

—REX LARDNER

———◆———

In the takeaway, key on low, slow and inside, the shoulders and hips turning together and the club an extension of your left arm and shoulders.

—DAN POHL

———◆———

I improve and that is the key to my golf swing . . . I think consistency is the key. That comes from the golf swing. I can hit the ball longer and straighter than I've ever done before, so that's a key factor.

—VIJAY SINGH

Use your authentic swing, the one you were born with.

    —STEVEN PRESSFIELD
        FROM *THE LEGEND OF BAGGER VANCE*

Is there such a thing as a technically perfect swing? . . . I have yet to see it. Certain players are perhaps closer to an ideal than others, and once in a while a player might have found a 'secret' for a string of holes, but none has achieved total perfection.

    —DAVID LEADBETTER
        FROM HIS BOOK *DAVID LEADBETTER'S LESSONS FROM GOLF GREATS*

Miss 'em quick!

    —ALEX SMITH
        SCOTTISH PROFESSIONAL AND WINNER OF THE 1906 AND 1910 U.S.
        OPENS, ON PUTTING

It may have been the greatest four-wood anyone ever hit. It was so much on the flag that I had to lean sideways to follow the flight of the ball.

    —GARY PLAYER
        DESCRIBING A SHOT HE HIT

A good 1-iron shot is about as easy to come by as an understanding wife.

—DAN JENKINS

Love and putting are mysteries for the philosopher to solve. Both subjects are beyond golfers.

—TOMMY ARMOUR

Putting is so individual—so personal—that you must be quite vigilant about the elements that hinder you from being effective and also the elements that help you. Everybody has a different way to putt, and I don't believe there is one golden rule.

—NICK PRICE
FROM *THE SWING: MASTERING THE PRINCIPLES OF THE GAME*
BY NICK PRICE, WITH LORNE RUBENSTEIN

I haven't crouched to read a putt in twenty years because my knees are bad. But I read greens as well as anybody. The only reason golfers go into that crouch is because they see others doing it. Try standing tall when you read putts. I'll bet money it doesn't hurt your putting at all.

—JIM COLBERT
GOLF DIGEST

Short putts are missed because it is not physically possible to make the little ball travel over uncertain ground for three or four feet with any degree of regularity.

—WALTER HAGEN

Putting is probably the most important thing in the game. It's that classic argument you always hear, but it's true. You can hit the ball great, but if you can't make anything, it's so deflating. The psychological aspect is huge. Putting is the source of where you really go in a round.

—NICK PRICE

Twice Open Champion Willie Park coined the slogan: 'The man who can putt is a match for anyone.' To which J.H. Taylor produced the response: 'The man who can approach does not need to putt.'

—MICHAEL HOBBS

I've been squeezing the club so hard the cow is screaming.

—J.C. SNEAD

From the grip we build to the stance and from the stance we graduate to the heart of the game itself, the swing. These are the imperatives. Without them one can't achieve the status of a duffer; with them one has a game. The rest is merely refinement.

  —LOUISE SUGGS
   LPGA HALL OF FAMER

———◆———

Every golfer has a friend who, once in a while, will excitedly make the claim that he has discovered the 'secret' of golf.

  —TED BARRET
   FROM HIS BOOK *THE ULTIMATE ENCYCLOPEDIA OF GOLF*

———◆———

If you're going to be a victim of the first few holes, you don't have a prayer. You're like a puppet. You let the first few holes jerk your strings and tell you how you're going to feel and how you're going to think.

  —DR. BOB ROTELLA
   SPORTS PSYCHOLOGIST

———◆———

My putts looked like rats going in the hole.

  —CHARLIE RYMER
   MEMBER OF THE PGA TOUR, ON SHOOTING 61

The woods are full of long hitters.

—JERRY BARBER

My hands were shaking on the last putt. The only problem with that is you never know which shake is going to hit the putt.

—PATTY SHEEHAN
ON THE WIN THAT QUALIFIED HER FOR THE HALL OF FAME

My agent was yelling: 'Don't move your head!' at me all day. When I move my head before I putt, I get in trouble. On that putt, I looked at the hole too soon.

—COSTANTINO ROCCA
ON A MISSED THREE-FOOTER IN 1993 RYDER CUP SINGLES AGAINST DAVIS LOVE

If a golfer hits his ball to two feet on a par three hole, his companions will all say: 'Good shot.' If he knocks it in the hole, for an ace, they will all say, with equal sincerity: 'You lucky bastard.'

—MARTIN VOUSDEN

You don't need to get your golf swing by going through video cameras and stuff like that. Just kind of go out there and find yourself.

—VIJAY SINGH
FROM *TRUMP: THE BEST GOLF ADVICE I EVER RECEIVED*

———•———

One of the easiest ways to add height to the [sand] shot is to feel like you're sitting down on your right knee at address. You should widen your stance and choke up a little. You should feel as if you're 'under' the ball more and have a wider base.

—BEN CRENSHAW

———•———

Why don't you aim more to the right?

—BEN HOGAN
TO A PLAYER ASKING FOR ADVICE ON WHY HE ALWAYS SHOOTS HIS SHOTS TO THE LEFT

A perfectly straight shot with a big club is a fluke!

—JACK NICKLAUS

Golf is played with the arms.

—SAM SNEAD

On the fairway many golfers have a tendency to try and lift the ball into the air, and in doing so, they lift their body on the downswing as though their arms were going to pick the ball up and send it away.

—JOHNNY FARRELL
FROM *SECRETS OF THE GOLFING GREATS*

The golf swing is among the most stressful and unnatural acts in sports, short of cheering for the Yankees.

—BRAD FAXON
PGA PRO

If you take only one golf lesson in your life, let it deal only with grip, stance, alignment, ball position and developing a routine that enables you to mentally and physically set up every time.

—Dr. Bob Rotella
Sports Psychologist

My point is that there is an ideal grip that will make your life easier, but there is also more than one way to hug your children or hold your glass of wine.

—Nick Price
From *The Swing: Mastering the Principles of the Game*
by Nick Price, with Lorne Rubenstein

Only one golfer in a thousand grips the club lightly enough.

—Johnny Miller

Grip it and rip it. It works for John Daly. It never worked for me. All I did was wear out golf gloves.

—Chuck Stark

Hitting a golf ball and putting have nothing in common. They're two different games. You work all your life to perfect a repeating swing that will get you to the greens, and then you have to try to do something that is totally unrelated.

> —BEN HOGAN

Every good golfer keeps his left hand leading the clubhead through impact.

> —LEE TREVINO

When the old question 'What is the most important part of the game?' is thrown at me, I don't have to think twice. I answer, 'The grip.' Without that, anyone's form is bound to be erratic.

> —LOUISE SUGGS
> LPGA HALL OF FAMER

Flat-footed golf, sir, flat-footed golf.

> —J.H. TAYLOR
> DESCRIBING HIS GOLFING TECHNIQUE

When I'm swinging bad, I need to go to the range. When I'm swinging good, I go to the Cabernet.

—MARK WIEBE

In order to give yourself your best chance of success you must learn to apply all your resources to each and every shot you hit, both in practice and in play.

—T.J. TOMASI
FROM *THE 30-SECOND GOLF SWING*

I think what golfers need to do is play more relaxed, free from tension, with a lot less thought. Obviously, technique is important. But, when you get down to it, a golf swing is a golf swing.

—DAVID LEADBETTER

The ball's got to stop somewhere. It might as well be in the bottom of the hole.

> —LEE TREVINO
> ON HIS AGGRESSIVE PUTTING STROKE

———•———

Keep on hitting it straight until the wee ball goes in the hole.

> —JAMES BRAID

———•———

Hit the ball up to the hole . . . You meet a better class of person there.

> —BEN HOGAN

———•———

Concentrate on hitting the green. The cup will come to you.

> —CARY MIDDLECOFF

A tap-in is a putt that is short enough to be missed one-handed.
>—HENRY BEARD
>   HUMORIST

A man who can putt is a match for anyone.
>—WILLIE PARK

Why didn't I win more? I was the world's worst putter. If I had thought on the putting green the way I did for the rest of the game, none of these guys would have won a tournament. Everybody tried to help me, even some of my enemies.
>—WILLIAM "WILD BILL" MEHLHORN

Ninety percent of putts that are short don't go in.
>—YOGI BERRA

You get no points in style when it comes to putting. It's getting the ball to drop into the cup that counts.
>—LAURIE AUCHTERLONIE

I never really dreamed of making many putts. Maybe that's why I haven't made many.

    —CALVIN PEETE

                  —◆—

The inevitable result of any golf lesson is the instant elimination of the one critical unconscious motion that allowed you to compensate for all your errors.

    —THOMAS MULLIGAN

                  —◆—

Check the diaper; if it's wet you get relief from casual water.

    —BOB MURPHY
        WHEN HIS PLAYING PARTNER'S BALL LANDED IN A BABY CARRIAGE

                  —◆—

Swing the club as though you were driving sixty miles an hour on the freeway. Not too fast, but not deathly slow. Once in a while, if the risk isn't great, you can push your swing to seventy, but never go faster than that.

    —BYRON NELSON

Forget the idea of a three-foot target area around the hole on long putts. Archers and pistol shooters aim for bulls-eyes, not the outer circles. Aim to make the putt.

—DR. BOB ROTELLA
SPORTS PSYCHOLOGIST

I'm putting so badly, I could putt it off a tabletop and leave it short halfway down a leg.

—J.C. SNEAD

The better you putt, the bolder you play.

—DON JANUARY

Gimme: an agreement between two losers who can't putt.

—JIM BISHOP

Hell, I'd putt sitting up in a coffin if I thought I could hole something.

—GARDNER DICKINSON
ON HIS STRANGE PUTTING STANCE

That putt was so good I could hear the baby applaud.

—DONNA HORTON WHITE
AFTER MAKING A 25-FOOT PUTT WHILE SEVEN MONTHS PREGNANT

You've just got one problem. You stand too close to the ball after you've hit it.

—SAM SNEAD
TO A DUFFER

It doesn't take me very long to feel like I am putting the ball pretty well. Frankly, I find that when I lay off, the first thing that comes back is my putter. Not necessarily the attitude of good putting, but certainly my stroke.

—JACK NICKLAUS

I putt so bad I'm gonna eat a can of Alpo.

—LEE TREVINO
IN A TOURNAMENT IN 1975

If I could putt, I'd be a plus-2.
>—JOE BACA
>U.S. CONGRESSMAN

Half of golf is fun; the other half is putting.
>—PETER DOBEREINER

We somehow can't see it. If the putt were shorter, we would ram it in the back if the cup; longer and the break of the green would be obvious. But at this maddening in-between lengths, all systems break down.
>—JOHN UPDIKE
>ON THREE- AND FOUR-FOOTERS

There are many ways of performing the operations successfully. I can claim, however, to be in a position to explain how not to putt. I think I know as well as anybody how not to do it.
>—HARRY VARDON

I play this game waiting for the two weeks a year when I can putt.
>—LARRY NELSON

When all is said and done, and whatever the method and whoever the man, successful putting surely must be a matter more of nerve than technique.

—PAT WARD-THOMAS

Putting is always the great equaliser, because if you are putting well then it takes a lot of pressure off the rest of your game. You can afford to make a few mistakes if you're holing ten- and fifteen-footers for par.

—TOM WATSON
RECALLING HIS WIN AT THE 1975 BRITISH OPEN

Keep close count of your nickels and dimes, stay away from whiskey, and never concede a putt.

—SAM SNEAD

Putting is a game unto itself. If I could putt, I could win.

—TOM WATSON

You can't get too close to a putter, otherwise it will get you.

—GARY MCCORD

It is important to emphasize the necessity for the golfer to use his head as much as his hands; or to make his mental agility match his physical ability.

—H.N. WETHERED
THE ARCHITECTURAL SIDE OF GOLF BY H.N. WETHERED
AND TOM SIMPSON

In my younger and more cavity-prone years, my dentist's wife gave me her golf clubs and some advice to go with them. Here, she said one day as we stood in the waiting room, try to use them more than I did. She had played twice in the past seven years.

—MICHAEL BAMBERGER
FROM *THE GREEN ROAD HOME: ADVENTURES AND MISADVENTURES AS A CADDIE ON THE PGA TOUR*

Bobby Jones told me he used to run back to Stewart Maiden . . . for lessons. He said that when he learned to be able to correct himself on the golf course, control his game and do it himself, that's when he became a good player.

—JACK NICKLAUS, 1991
GOLF DIGEST

It may not be out of place here to say that I never won a major championship until I learned to play golf against something, not somebody. And that something was par.

> —BOBBY JONES

<hr>

Distance, distance, distance. I cannot stress it enough. Know what a forty-yard shot is. Know a twenty-yard shot. A sixty-yard shot. Get that down.

> —ROGER MALTBIE

<hr>

The golfer's left side must be the dominant part of the swing. This is the only way to get maximum power and accuracy. If the right side takes over, there is no golf swing.

> —KATHY WHITWORTH
> LPGA HALL OF FAMER

<hr>

If beginners and club golfers as a whole were to absorb and fully understand four or five basic principles, they would get themselves into a position from which they could hit the ball consistently.

> —GEORGE WILL
> WRITER, FROM *ADVICE FOR MEN AND WOMEN PLAYERS*

Don't play too much golf if you want to get on in the game. Three rounds a day are too much for any man, and if he makes a practice of playing them whenever he has the opportunity, his game will suffer.

—HARRY VARDON

The golf swing is a knack requiring the un-self-consciousness and the confidence with which people bicycle or swim. Such skills are only acquired by associating certain movements with particular effects, and only after innumerable falls and swallowing a considerable amount of water.

—ENID WILSON
BRITISH GOLFER AND JOURNALIST

Every shot in golf should be played as a shot at some clearly defined target. All players realize this when they are playing a shot to the green . . . But what many of them forget is the shot off the tee should also be aimed at the target down the fairway.

—CRAIG WOOD
MASTERS AND U.S. OPEN CHAMPION IN 1921

Don't you wish you could hit the ball like that?

> —BABE ZAHARIAS
> WHILE DEMONSTRATING HOW TO DRIVE AT A GOLF CLINIC

How do I address the ball? I say, 'Hello there, ball. Are you going to go in the hole or not?'

> —FLIP WILSON
> COMEDIAN

I rarely aimed at the flag. I aimed at the spot where I had the best birdie opportunity.

> —BEN HOGAN
> ON HIS FOUR CAREER HOLES-IN-ONE

I went fishing the other day and I missed the lake with my first cast.

> —BEN CRENSHAW
> ON HIS TROUBLE WITH KEEPING SHOTS ON THE FAIRWAY

Whatever amount of controlled turn you can make while feeling as if you have something in reserve is the right backswing length for you.

—BUTCH HARMON

Give me a man with a fast backswing and a fat wallet.

—GOLF HUSTLER'S SAYING

One very simple tip will infinitely improve the timing of most golfers: merely pause briefly at the top of the backswing.

—TOMMY ARMOUR

There are two things you can learn by stopping your backswing at the top and checking the position of your hands: how many hands you have, and which one is wearing a glove.

—THOMAS MULLIGAN

Give me a millionaire with a bad backswing and I can have a very pleasant afternoon.

—GEORGE LOW
ON SURVIVAL IN GOLF

To reach the correct position at the top of the swing it is vital that the first movement should be correct. I can't stress that too strongly.

—DAI REES
SECRETS OF THE GOLFING GREATS

If the average guy hits . . . six greens, that means he must miss at least twelve. Of those, maybe four times he can chip his ball onto the putting surface. Which leaves eight pitch shots. Other than driving or putting, that makes pitching the most important shot in your bag.

—HANK HANEY

We've got a society now looking for answers anywhere. They might go to a car wash to take a lesson.

—JACKIE BURKE JR.
ON PEOPLE'S SEARCH FOR THE PERFECT SWING

You get rewarded at the bottom of the club by what you do at the top end.

—JERRY BARBER

Too many golfers grip the club at address like they were trying to choke a prairie coyote to death.

—CURT WILSON

Every golfer has one ideal ball position in his stance. Take a swing without a ball, and take a divot. The beginning of the divot indicates where the ball should be positioned.

—DAVIS LOVE, JR.

Perfection is achieved not when there is no longer anything to add, but when there is no longer anything to take away.

—ERNEST JONES
ON THE GOLF SWING

Always—and I mean ALWAYS—tee the ball on par-3 holes, or any other time play your opening shot with an iron.

—JACK NICKLAUS

The ideal build for a golfer would be strong hands, big forearms, thin neck, big thighs, and a flat chest. He looks like Popeye.

—GARY PLAYER

All those jokers can putt or they wouldn't be out here. But since I ain't got nothing else to do, I can see when the action goes wrong—and help straighten them out.

—GEORGE LOW

A very fine [drill] for improving your tempo, smoothing out your rhythm, and improving your balance is to swing with your feet together. I mean actually touching . . . This [practice] is a fine way to develop a tempo slower than the one you've been playing with.

—JACK NICKLAUS

I believe the basic principles of the golf swing are rhythm, stance, grip, the takeaway from the ball and the head. Of these, one of the most important is rhythm, and every player must learn for himself what rhythm means to him.

—GEORGE WILL
WRITER, FROM *ADVICE FOR MEN AND WOMEN PLAYERS*

Rhythm is best expressed in any swing directed at a cigar stump or a dandelion head.

—GRANTLAND RICE

If you feel like you're just trying to get the ball into play, it's easier to avoid the urge to swing too hard.

—NEAL LANCASTER

Long drives, if it be not the most deadly, is certainly the most dashing and fascinating part of the game; and of all the others the principal difficulty of the golfer to acquire, and his chief delight when he can manage it.

—H.B. FARNIE, 1857
FROM HIS BOOK *A KEEN HAND*

He didn't know enough about the swing to come back.

—GEORGE FAZIO
ON THE INABILITY OF RALPH GULDHAL TO CHANGE FROM
BEING AN INSTINCTUAL GOLFER

The lofted club is the answer. It is difficult to control a ball with a straight-faced club. Only a few players can do it. The straight-faced club gains distance but it loses accuracy. . . .

—CRAIG WOOD
ON WHY HE DIDN'T USE A DRIVER OFF THE TEE

Learning to play golf is like learning to play the violin. It's not difficult to do, but it's very painful to everyone around you.

—HAL LINDEN
ACTOR

After all, as Benny said when I was speaking to him yesterday, golf teaching is like being a shill in a crap game. You've got to keep the customers coming, you've got to make them feel good and if you don't—no bottle for Buster.

—JOHN P. MARQUAND
FROM *THE WAY THE BALL BOUNCES*

If your adversary is a hole or two down, there is no serious cause for alarm in his complaining of a severely sprained wrist, or an acute pain, resembling lumbago, which checks his swing.

—HORACE HUTCHINSON
FROM *HINTS ON GOLF*

⬥

The hardest shot is a mashie at ninety yards from the green, where the ball has to be played against an oak tree, bounces back into a sand trap, hits a stone, bounces on the green, and then rolls into the cup.

—ZEPPO MARX
COMEDIAN

⬥

Golf demands a complex series of movements to maximize the athlete's latent energy and apply it to the object to be moved.

—JIM MCLEAN
FROM *THE EIGHT-STEP SWING*

⬥

Not every golfer can hit the ball as far as Tiger Woods or as relentlessly straight as Ben Hogan did. But any golfer can hit the ball 40 yards. Learn how to use that wedge.

—ROGER MALTBIE

CHAPTER EIGHT

Caddies, Galleries, Family, and Media

They get the best lines, these peripatetic anachronisms of a feudal apprentice system. Subsisting largely on bemusement, banter, and booze, caddies are equal parts sherpa, cornerman, and Greek chorus. Millions of golfers will, quite happily, never experience one. Others will find the unaccustomed luxury disconcerting, but nevertheless come away won over, carrying forth stories of having had a guide in tow at Prestwick or Turnberry, or anywhere the tradition somehow survives. Sancho Panza to our Don Quixote, Bond had Hawker, Trevino his Herman, Faldo his Fanny. The venerable profession survives, (mostly) respectable, even potentially quite lucrative.

Stolid sentinels of golf morality and manners, the best caddies are dispassionate, sardonic, adept, as the cruel adage holds, at showing, keeping, and shutting up. Little escapes their notice and the accuracy of their powers of observation and insight can be uncanny. The man who reckoned three good ones were needed to reach the green in two was not being clever. He was merely stating a fact.

As for the gallery and the media, from the touring pro's perspective, the less said or heard from the better. They amount to a nuisance, occupational hazards with little relief. The throngs rarely stand still, clapping like Little League parents if a ball gets airborne. The writers ask the same insistent, childish questions. Players know the crowds are really only of any use in deflecting an errant shot back towards the fairway or, better yet, onto the green. Like the loopers, the media too can occasionally get off a good shot. Their presence, however, will be tempered by the underlying truth that few writers could summon a sustained breath, let alone a solid strike, under true tournament conditions.

* * * * *

Without the people, I'd be playing in front of trees for a couple hundred dollars.

—FUZZY ZOELLER

He has a special kind of people in his gallery—the ones who like to sky-dive and walk on hot coals.

—BOB HOPE
ON THE GOLF GAME OF GERALD FORD

I know I'm getting better at golf because I'm hitting fewer spectators.

—PRESIDENT GERALD FORD

I enjoy the 'oohs' and the 'aahs' from the gallery when I hit my drives. But I'm getting pretty tired of the 'awws' and 'uhhs' when I miss the putt.

—JOHN DALY

North from Edina eight furlongs or more
Lies the famed field, on Fortha's surrounding shore . . .
Macdonald and unmatched Dalrymple ply
Their pond'rous weapons and greens defy;
Rattray for skill and Crosse for length renowned,
Stuart and Leslie best the sandy ground.

—THOMAS MATHISON, 1743
FROM *THE GOFF*, ON THE HONORABLE COMPANY
OF EDINBURGH GOLFERS

Right here, Jack.

—SIGNS HELD UP BY ARNIE'S ARMY BEHIND HAZARDS
AT THE 1967 US OPEN

With the huge excited crowd surging all around him, it is only natural that the player should come in for a good deal of buffeting about. It may come as a surprise to many people to know after a big tournament my ankles and shins are black and blue.

—HARRY VARDON

He [Ben Hogan]'s the only player I have ever known to get an ovation from the fans on the practice tee. I've seen him playing practice rounds before a tournament and half the gallery was made up of other professionals.

—TOMMY BOLT

I like it loud, and when you've got people pulling for you like that, you want to play good. The fans have been great everywhere I've gone.

—JOHN DALY

The crowd behaved in the most disgraceful manner, running in before the players and completely blocking up the entrance to the hole. Considerable delay took place before the green was with some difficulty partially cleared.

—BERNARD DARWIN, 1870
REMEMBERING A CLASSIC MATCH BETWEEN
TOM MORRIS AND WILLIE PARK

After all the noise and clamor . . . after the clubs are cleaned and stacked . . . the silence which follows the last round played seems strange, bewildering, yet wonderfully peaceful. However, this silence, to me, often reverberates with the roars and the applause of the fans who followed me for so many years.

—WALTER HAGEN

Another great trick of well-meaning friends in a gallery following your match is that of telling you how you should play your shot . . . That is the worst pest of all because they offer advice, unsolicited as it may be, in such a way that it greatly irritates you.

—FRANCIS OUIMET
WINNER OF THE 1913 US OPEN AND TWO US AMATEURS (1914, 1931)

I have a tough time looking at the fans because of the things I've done. I don't look at myself at being as good enough to talk to them.

—JOHN DALY
ON HIS OFF-THE-COURSE MISDEEDS

Personally, I think the public has seen enough greed out of athletes.

—LANNY WADKINS

I think our galleries enjoy seeing some emotion from the players. I don't think there's anything wrong with showing your temper as long as you don't damage the course or do something to disturb another player. Too many of our players are like robots.

—BETH DANIEL
AFTER BEING FINED FOR CLUB-THROWING

You know I thought our English football [soccer] crowds were bad, but this is worse.

—IAN WOOSNAM
TO PETER JACOBSEN AFTER HEARING OBSCENITIES FROM THE U.S.
OPEN GALLERY AT MEDINAH BECAUSE OF JACOBSEN'S ALLEGIANCE
TO THE PORTLAND TRAILBLAZERS

At least I'm going to get a chance to meet her.

—A SPECTATOR, 1978
AFTER BEING HIT BY AN ERRANT SHOT BY NANCY LOPEZ
IN HER FIRST FULL YEAR ON TOUR

When a man stands alone on the tee, surrounded by galleries . . . in awe because of his talent at the bewildering game of golf and also because of his willingness to risk abject failure right out in the open, he very easily, very naturally sees himself as a hero figure.

—AL BARKOW
IN HIS BOOK *GOLF'S GOLDEN GRIND*

Watching a golf tournament is different from attending other sporting events. For one thing, the drunks are spread out in a larger area.

—DON WADE
AUTHOR

That wee body in the red jack canna play gouf.

—A SPECTATOR
ON ALLAN ROBERTSON'S BAD PLAY IN A MATCH PARTNERED WITH
TOM MORRIS, AGAINST THE DUNN BROTHERS.

It wasn't dangerous enough. I'd rather be in the gallery and get hit by a ball.

—JERRY SEINFELD
ON HIS ONLY ROUND OF GOLF EVER

The gallery becomes almost a part of the course and part of the round, to the experienced competitor, either he can play with a gallery following him or he can't—and if he can't, of course, the gallery doesn't follow him.

—BOBBY JONES

Someone who turns up at the first tee on time and sober.

—ERNIE ELS
DESCRIBING A GOOD CADDIE

It is a game of tradition, one we'd like to maintain. Plus, I don't think their long legs look very good.

—REG MURPHY
USGA PRESIDENT, ON WHY HE DISALLOWED CADDIES TO WEAR SHORTS DURING THE 1994 US OPEN

There were three things in the world that he held in the smallest esteem—slugs, poets, and caddies with hiccups.

—P.G. WODEHOUSE

I was lying ten and had a thirty-five foot putt. I whispered over my shoulder: 'How does this one break?' And my caddy said: 'Who cares?' It's the greatest line from a caddy I've ever heard.

—JACK LEMMON
ACTOR

Very few caddies make good tees. The ball should be just perched on the sand so that none of the latter can be seen.

—HARRY VARDON, 1912
IN *HOW TO PLAY GOLF*, BEFORE MANUFACTURED TEES

Professor, you may have the degrees but you've got to have a head to play golf.

—A CADDIE
TO A COLLEGE PROFESSOR

When you've got a twenty-year-old daughter, you'd like to think she is going to date someone of Justin's quality. But I've been trying to get him out of my house all summer long.

—LENNY WADKINS
ON FELLOW PGA COMPETITOR JUSTIN LEONARD

Remember the basic rule: Make friends with your caddie and the game will make friends with you.

—STEPHEN POTTER

[Bill Clinton] told me that he caddied in the same group with me in the Hot Springs Open. That's why I voted for him, because he was a caddy.

—TOMMY BOLT

The professional [caddie] is a reckless, feckless creature. In the golfing season in Scotland he makes money all day and spends it all the night. His sole loves are golf and whiskey.

—HORACE HUTCHINSON, 1900

I'm doin' the playin' and my caddie's chokin'.

—LEE TREVINO
WHEN HE COULDN'T FIND HIS CADDIE AT THE 1971 US OPEN

If it weren't for golf, I'd probably be a caddie today.

—GEORGE ARCHER

It is not impossible that the caddie knows less about the game than yourself, and . . . his views as to the best thing to do in a particular situation are often regulated by what he has seen the scratch men do at such times. You may not be a scratch man.

—HARRY VARDON
IN HIS BOOK *SOME GENERAL HINTS*

It'll take three good ones to be on in two t'day, sir.
> —A CADDIE

We'd like to get a caddy, said the nurse. Mrs. Mortimer Jones sent us out to play golf, and we don't know how without we get a caddy.
> —F. SCOTT FITZGERALD
> FROM *WINTER DREAMS*

Look here, sir. I'll give you the club, you play the bloody shot.
> —WILLIE BLACK, 1925
> MUIRFIELD CADDIE, TO BOBBY CRUICKSHANK

If a permanent caddie is heroin, if you're going to break out in a cold sweat because you don't have him, then you'd better get one.
> —FRANK BEARD
> SENIOR TOUR PLAYER

There was one fan my caddie used to worry about. He would show up with a grocery bag. He would never come up and say anything to me. My caddie always wondered what they guy had in the bag, but he was harmless.

— JAN STEPHENSON, 1991
IN A *GOLF DIGEST* INTERVIEW

Wee wheels in ya head sir. You've got to forget those bloody wee wheels, sir.

— SANDY MATHESON
A CADDY AT DORNOCH, TO NOTED WRITER RICK REILLY

The only time I talk on a golf course is to my caddie. And then only to complain when he gives me the wrong club.

— SEVE BALLESTEROS

I knew nothing about caddying at first, but it wasn't difficult to learn. The other caddies, though, didn't like to see any new ones, because that might mean they wouldn't get a job sometime.

— BYRON NELSON, 1993
ON HIS CADDYING DAYS, IN *HOW I PLAYED THE GAME*

If a caddie can help you, then you don't know how to play golf.

—DAN JENKINS
IN HIS BOOK *DEAD SOLID PERFECT*

Real golfers, no matter what the provocation, never strike a caddy with the driver. The sand wedge is far more effective.

—HUXTABLE PIPPEY

I know you can be fined for throwing a club, but I want to know if you can get fined for throwing a caddie?

—TOMMY BOLT

You know Deane Beman? When he han' the money out, he look at you like you done stab him in the knee.

—A CADDIE
FROM GEORGE PLIMPTON'S ESSAY "THEY ALSO SERVE"

If your caddie coaches you on the tee, 'Hit it down the left side with a little draw,' ignore him. All you do on the tee is try not to hit the caddie.

—JIM MURRAY

The Royal Hong Kong Club caddies hit the nail on the head; their term for golf: 'Hittee ball, say damn.'

—DICK ANDERSON

Why ask me? You've asked me two times already and paid no attention to what I said. Pick your own club.

—DOW FINSTERWALD'S CADDIE IN THE 1960 US OPEN

The player may experiment about with his swing, his grip, his stance. It is only when he begins asking his caddies' advice that he is getting on dangerous ground.

—SIR WALTER SIMPSON, 1887
IN HIS BOOK *THE ART OF GOLF*

Well, sir, I'd recommend the 4:05 train.

—HARRY VARDON'S CADDIE
RESPONDING TO VARDON'S QUESTION,
"WHAT SHOULD I TAKE HERE?"

Essentially, he has been retired since he was twenty-one.

—JACK NICKLAUS
ON THE WORK HABITS OF HIS LONGTIME CADDIE, ANGELO ARGEA

Little brother, I don't do traps and I don't go into the weeds.

—A CADDIE
TO FUZZY ZOELLER

One time the caddies talked of a strike unless wages were raged. Ross heard of this, walked to the caddie pen, and asked the leader what was going on. Hearing the grievance, he whacked the caddie on the head with his ever-present five-iron and informed him the strike was over.

—ROD INNES
ON GOLF ARCHITECT DONALD ROSS IN EARLY 20TH CENTURY
PINEHURST, FROM *PINEHURST STORIES* (1991) BY LEE PACE

All you've got is your bag carriers now. All they can do is give the golfer a weather report—not the right club.

—ALFIE, TOM WATSON'S CADDIE
AT THE 1977 BRITISH OPEN

It is easy to arrange that your guest opponent shall be deceived into under-tipping his caddie at the end of the morning round, so that the news gets round among the club employees that your opponent is a no good, and the boys will gang up against him.

—STEPHEN POTTER, 1948
"GOLFSMANSHIP," *THE ATLANTIC MONTHLY*

The first bunker lesson I ever got was from my dad, Neels, and it was real simple. He told me to thump the sand behind the ball with the back of my sand wedge and finish my swing.

—ERNIE ELS
GOLF DIGEST

Golf is played by twenty million mature American men whose wives think they are out there having fun.

—JIM BISHOP

I used to love the Tour when it first started because I didn't have to make my own bed. Now I hate living in motels. I want to come home.

—NANCY LOPEZ, 1984
ON HAVING HER FIRST CHILD

Rock-a-bye, baby—till father comes home;

Father's off golfing and mother's alone;

He phoned me this morning—he wanted his cleek;

Perhaps he'll be home again, sometime next week.

—MOTHER GOOSE ON THE LINKS, 1909

She thinks people are crazy to complain about the Tour life. She said, 'You don't have to cook, make beds, or clean houses—it's great.'

—LOREN ROBERTS
ON HIS WIFE'S ATTITUDE TOWARD THE TOUR

When I come back in the next life, I want to come back as a golf pro's wife. She wakes up every morning at the crack of ten and is faced with her first major decision of the day: whether to have breakfast in bed or in the hotel coffee shop.

—SAM SIKES

This is bad for me, my kids, and my ex-wife.

—KEN GREEN
ON MISSING A CUT AT A FLORIDA TOURNAMENT

Of all the fathers of all the athletes I've ever interviewed, none stick to the walls of memory more than Earl Woods. Three gates had to be passed to earn that interview: a cool stare, a cold grunt, a frigid silence. But once you were in . . . Whoa, Nellie!

—GARY SMITH

Playing with your spouse on the golf course runs almost as great a marital risk as getting caught playing with someone else's anywhere else.

—PETER ANDREWS

Shots like that are a little too much for a twenty-four-year-old heart, Dad.

—JACKIE NICKLAUS
TO HIS FATHER, JACK NICKLAUS, AFTER HE NEARLY
SHOT HIS BALL INTO RAE'S CREEK AT THE 1986 MASTERS

I couldn't figure it out. My marriage was fine, my kids were healthy, and everything was good. But I wasn't happy with me. So I went on a low-fat diet and started exercising. I wasn't feeling competitive the previous year; I was just playing golf and that's all.

—NANCY LOPEZ

My wife is flying out here tonight. I haven't seen her in two weeks and I'm horny, so that should help.

—KEN GREEN
ON HIS PROSPECTS FOR THE CANADIAN OPEN

Hopefully my boys will carry on the tradition. But hopefully not too soon.

—SCOTT SPENCE
WHO CARRIES HIS DEAD FATHER'S ASHES IN HIS GOLF BAG

The place of the father in the modern suburban family is a very small one, particularly if he plays golf.

—BERTRAND RUSSELL

It's nice to look down the fairway and see your mother on the left and your father on the right. You know that no matter whether you hook or slice it, somebody is going to be there to kick it back in the fairway.

—LARRY NELSON

A golfer needs a loving wife to whom he can describe the day's play through the long evening.

—P.G. WODEHOUSE

She knows how to hang on to her money. I wish her mom were the same way.

—ORVILLE MOODY
ON HAVING HIS DAUGHTER CADDIE FOR HIM

I motivate myself by thinking of my family . . . If I play well, I feel like I can justify being away from them—it's okay to leave them that week. If I don't play well, then I feel like I've wasted time I could have spent with them.

—NANCY LOPEZ

We'll either hire someone to travel with me or my mom will do it. Just because you've had a baby doesn't mean you can't win tournaments. Nancy Lopez proved that.

—JULIE INKSTER
ON HOW SHE PLANS TO HANDLE COMPETITIVE GOLF AND MOTHERHOOD

It is a sport in which the whole American family can participate—fathers and mothers, sons and daughters alike. It offers healthy respite from daily toil, refreshment of body and mind.

—PRESIDENT DWIGHT D. EISENHOWER

My dad gave me the best golf advice I ever received, which was to have fun. That's the reason why, when I practice, I'm always having fun and enjoying it.

—PHIL MICKELSON

You know at that time you didn't have any managers, so your father was your manager, or at least helped you. My dad was the greatest.

—PATTY BERG, 1986
FROM *GETTING TO THE DANCE FLOOR* BY AL BARKOW

I wonder what they think about women and children. They seem so lonely. Nothing to look forward to, to come home to.

—MURLE MACKENZIE
LPGA PROFESSIONAL, ON THE EARLY LPGA TOUR

There [are] some positives and negatives [to playing at home]. You get to sleep in your own bed, but you might have more responsibilities . . . . Your family is right there and you've got all those people rooting for you and supporting you.

—JIM FURYK

When your forward press is longer than your backswing, you've got to think about giving up the game.

—CHARLIE CRENSHAW
BEN CRENSHAW'S FATHER

Just offer the opportunity. Put the clubs in the corner and give them access to a place to play . . . Anything more . . . and you can run the risk of turning off your children to a game they could enjoy their whole life . . .

—NICK PRICE
ON HOW TO BE A GOLFING FATHER

Dad, I won. I really played well today. Happy Father's Day!

—Nancy Lopez

 Calling home after winning her record fifth consecutive
 LPGA event in 1978, as a rookie.

Do I ever disagree with him on course strategy? Never—unless he's wrong.

—Gary Nicklaus

 Jack Nicklaus' son, on caddying for his father

My wife said to me the other day, 'My God, you may get to sixty-five without ever working a day in your life.'

—John Brodie

 After a career as a football player, announcer,
 and a member of golf's Senior Tour

I know a one-shot finishing hole is not usually well-regarded. But when a player stands on that tee at East Lake, with the match square or dormie—that drive calls for all there is in the delicatessen department.

—Robert Permedus Jones

 Bobby Jones' father on the eighteenth hole
 on East Lake No. 1

My wife told me to quit giving lessons and start taking them.

> —PHIL RODGERS
> ON WORKING AS GREG NORMAN'S INSTRUCTOR

I always thought Tom was a good player and a good man. I don't think it took a Major to make him one.

> —TOM KITE, SR.

I tell him the golf game is a gentleman's game. I point out . . . John McEnroe playing Jimmy Connors in tennis and him cursing and throwing his racket. I tell him not to do it, because it will ruin my reputation as a parent. I will not have a spoiled child.

> —KUTILDA WOODS
> TIGER WOODS' MOTHER, ON TIGER WOODS

I started golf at 8 . . . He [Dad] and Mom sacrificed all the time . . . They would go without, so I could have three new balls or socks. My wonderful parents gave me the opportunity to compete with the best and get the experience I needed to be successful.

> —NANCY LOPEZ

Attending a golf tournament is like trying to watch a 144-ring circus. The game is diffused over four miles of ground where the winning and losing are worked out in no particular corner, and not in a few hours but four days.

—AL BARKOW
IN HIS BOOK *GOLF'S GOLDEN GRIND*

He put his arm around me and said, 'Palsy-walsy, you and I are going to make a lot of money.' I've steered clear of agents since.

—BOB GOALBY

I don't know if he has to talk about me in his press conferences, but I definitely have to talk about him.

—KARRIE WEBB
ON BEING COMPARED TO TIGER WOODS

I don't think television has screwed up my golf. I've pretty much taken care of that on my own.

—CURTIS STRANGE

The men and women who play the game know me, and I know them.

—DICK ENBERG
GOLF DIGEST

———•———

I would have worried if he didn't want a photograph.

—BABE ZAHARIAS
ON AN OVERZEALOUS PHOTOGRAPHER
AT THE BRITISH LADIES' CHAMPIONSHIP

———•———

The worst thing . . . to do is to go into the [Butler] cabin. We've just finished at a high and all of a sudden this deathly silence because we're down in the catacombs. This presentation has always been so sanitized that you can just hear all the sets clicking off.

—FRANK CHIRKINAIN
CBS PRODUCER AND DIRECTOR,
ON THE MASTER'S GREEN JACKET CEREMONY

———•———

I don't resent the media. I get disappointed sometimes. They've got their job to do . . . I've got my job to do. They'll sit back some day in years to come and say, 'Well, geez, I was wrong.' They will. I know they will.

—GREG NORMAN
ON BEING LABELED A CHOKER

I like the press room because you can always get something good to eat and drink there.

> —ROCKY THOMPSON
> ON WHY HE ENJOYED TALKING TO THE MEDIA

———— ◆ ————

Well it just goes to show what we've been saying all along. That all the good-looking golfers are on the ladies' tour.

> —JAN STEPHENSON
> IN RESPONSE TO A *GOLF MAGAZINE* CENTERFOLD
> ON PGA TOUR GOLFERS

———— ◆ ————

At Augusta National 1972, I was having breakfast with Dan Jenkins when Bill MacPhail came up and asked: 'Does anybody know a goddamn limey who speaks halfway decent?' Jenkins said, 'Here's your man.'

> —BEN WRIGHT
> GOLF ANNOUNCER, EXPLAINING HOW HE GOT
> A JOB WITH CBS SPORTS

I have come to understand and appreciate writers much more recently since I started working on a book last fall. Before that, I thought golf writers got up every morning, played a round of golf, had lunch, showed up for our last three holes and then went to dinner.

—PHIL MICKELSON

Bond thought he knew what would be in Goldfinger's mind, what is in most golfers' minds when they smell the first scent of a good lead melting away. Bond wouldn't be surprised to see that grooved quick swing quicken a trifle. It did.

—IAN FLEMING
FROM *GOLDFINGER*

For almost two decades, golf writing had been my home and the life I liked best, and I would even say I loved it because golf had taken me to places I never would have gone, introduced me to the most amazing sorts of people, and forged my deepest friendships.

—JAMES DODSON

I am staying in the house on Tobacco Road that Jeeter Lester moved out of.

—JIM MURRAY
ON HIS ACCOMMODATIONS WHILE COVERING THE MASTERS YEARS AGO

—◦—

If I wanted to know how I had played, I awaited the next day's account in *The Times*. With what was therein written I was content, for here was the truth of things. I want nothing more than to be remembered by posterity in the words of Bernard Darwin.

—J.H. TAYLOR
REGARDING EMINENT WRITER AND GOLF AMATEUR BERNARD DARWIN

—◦—

. . . while with long strokes and short
strokes we tend to the goal,
The pond'rous club upon the ball
Descend
Involved in dust th' exulting orb
Ascends.

—THOMAS MATHISON, 1743
FROM *THE GOFF*, THE FIRST GOLF BOOK EVER WRITTEN

Nick Faldo's victory in the British Open earned him another green jacket.

—DAN PATRICK
ESPN COMMENTATOR, CONFUSING THE MAJORS

* * *

Bumpy greens don't bother me anymore, since I've become an analyst. I don't see the problem.

—DAVID FEHERTY

* * *

The safest place would be in the fairway.

—JOE GARAGIOLA
ANNOUNCER AND TELEVISION HOST, ON THE BEST POSITION
FOR SPECTATORS DURING CELEBRITY GOLF TOURNAMENTS

* * *

Bing Crosby has been in Europe for the last three months dividing his time unequally between making radio tape recordings for America and playing golf. As far as Crosby is concerned, the radio broadcasts are something to do on a rainy day but his golf is not a joking matter.

—ARTHUR BUCHWALD
ON SINGER BING CROSBY, *THE NEW YORK HERALD TRIBUNE*

This year was the first time I've ever been engaged and dating at the same time.

> —TIGER WOODS
> ON ALL THE GOSSIP ABOUT HIM

My dear, did you ever stop to think what a wonderful bunker you would make?

> —WALTER HAGEN
> TO A BUXOM OPERA DIVA

If you didn't know better, six hours of the Masters on CBS could leave you with the feeling that Augusta National Golf Club is a holy land and the winner of the tournament will be passing through a corridor where no mere mortal will ever tread.

> —TOM GILMORE

The Rules of Golf are debated and discussed everywhere the game is played and often are the subject of conversation when the weather prevents the game from being played.

> —JANET SEAGLE
> USGA MUSEUM CURATOR

If I want any sympathy, I have to call up my parents.

—BETH DANIEL
ON WINNING A TOURNAMENT DESPITE A SHOULDER INJURY

It was a great honor to be inducted into the Hall of Fame. I didn't know they had a caddie division.

—BOB HOPE

It was my first glimpse of comedy. When you see grown men near to tears because they've missed hitting a little white ball into a hole from three feet, it makes you laugh.

—BILL MURRAY
RECALLING HIS CADDYING DAYS

An honest and natural slum dialect is more tolerable than the attempt of a phonetically untaught person to imitate the vulgar dialect of the golf club.

—GEORGE BERNARD SHAW
PREFACE TO *PYGMALLION*

You look at Faldo and you have to resist the temptation to look at the back for knobs.

—JIM MURRAY
ON THE ROBOT-LIKE PLAY OF FALDO

Twenty-year-old US Amateur champion Phil Mickelson. He looks like the best player since Jack Nicklaus. Of course, I said the same thing about Bob Dickson, Steve Melnyk and Bobby Clampett.

—FRANK HANNIGAN
FORMER USGA EXECUTIVE DIRECTOR & ABC SPORTS COMMENTATOR

You are entirely right, I can't play golf and I can't lay an egg, but I am a better judge of an egg omelet than any hen you ever saw.

—O.B. KEELER
WRITER

The scores have been lower than Gary McCord's IQ.

—DAVID FEHERTY
ON THE 2001 GOLF SEASON

Lord, I hope this isn't going to be a long interview, or I might lose another stroke.

> —LOU GRAHAM
> BEING INTERVIEWED WHILE TOM WATSON TOOK
> A TWO STROKE LEAD OVER HIM

I tell the lady scorekeepers that if they can hear me cuss, they're standing too close. They've got to realize they're not at a church social.

> —DAVE HILL

TV wants a couple marquee names in the final, but that may not happen. Upsets happen in the NCAA tournament and in tennis all the time. They can happen in match-play, too.

> —SHIGEKI MARAYUMA

Now on the pot, Johnny Tee.

> —LOS ANGELES OPEN ANNOUNCER
> MESSING UP THE INTRODUCTION OF JOHNNY POTT

Had you ever thought of playing the Tour? You could give everyone lessons on how to starve to death.

—FURMAN BISHER
SPORTSWRITER, ON WHAT GOLFERS REALLY THINK WHEN THEY MAKE
ENCOURAGING REMARKS TO AMATEURS

I've got a lot of people rooting for me because there are more poor people than rich people.

—LEE TREVINO

Golfers cannot do their best playing to empty fairways any better than actors can give a fine performance to empty chairs.

—BOB HARLOW, 1929
THE PGA'S FIRST FULL-TIME TOUR DIRECTOR

Arnold Palmer, I think, put his finger on why American golf declined. The American professional tour, he says, makes it too easy for golfers to earn a living. No longer do they play to win, they play to get a good paycheck.

—MARK MCCORMACK
FOUNDER OF INTERNATIONAL MANAGEMENT

I go to sleep when I watch golf on television.

—GEORGE ARCHER

———————

I've always enjoyed the role of being a complementary player, and that's exactly what I'm going to be here. The game is the thing. I'm always appalled at some announcers who think that people tune in to see them and not the event.

—DICK ENBERG
GOLF DIGEST

———————

This [guy] is going to drive over a golf course! Oh, no! If he had drove over the green, I would have had to hang up and get involved with the chase. That would have been just disrespect.

—BILL MURRAY
WHILE WATCHING A POLICE CHASE ON TELEVISION

———————

If you want to take long walks, take long walks. If you want to hit things with a stick, hit things with a stick. But there's no excuse for combining the two and putting the results on TV. Golf is not so much a sport as an assault to lawns.

—*NATIONAL LAMPOON*

The Supreme Court ruled that disabled golfer Casey Martin has a legal right to ride in a golf cart between shots at PGA Tour events. Man, the next thing you know, they're going to have some guy carry his clubs around for him.

—JON STEWART

It would be a boon to a very large number of readers if reports of matches could be made more life-like, showing appreciation of the real turning points of the game and confining themselves less exclusively to a dry chronicling of details.

—HORACE HUTCHINSON, 1890

Whether I'm shooting 10-under or 10-over I have to realize people have come a long way to see me play. I can't be back-handing putts.

—JOHN DALY

Expert golf is an art, not a trade, and unionization of players doesn't work.

—BOB HARLOW
EARLY PGA DIRECTOR, ON THE ORGANIZATION OF PROS

It was in the fall, and when I went into the woods to find a guy's ball, I hung this bag on a branch. I found the ball but lost the bag. I didn't find it until the leaves had fallen. Geez, I thought I was going to be working for this guy for the rest of my life.

—THOMAS P. "TIP" O'NEILL, JR.
LATE SPEAKER OF THE HOUSE OF REPRESENTATIVES,
ON HIS EARLY EXPERIENCE AS A CADDIE IN MASSACHUSETTS

Q: Thirteen? How the hell did you make 13 on a par-5?
Arnold Palmer: Missed a 12-footer for 12.

—ARNOLD PALMER
EXPLAINING HOW HE SHOT A 13 IN THE 1961 LOS ANGELES OPEN

The son of a bitch went in!

—JIMMY DEMARET
COMMENTING ON LEW WORSHAM'S 140-YARD EAGLE APPROACH ON
THE FINAL HOLE OF THE 1953 WORLD CHAMPIONSHIP OF GOLF,
WHICH WON HIM THE TOURNAMENT

I don't think we've ever achieved in golf television—and this may be presumptuous of me—the right balance between audio and video.

  —SANDY TATUM
   OF THE USGA

I feel like I committed a crime—like I was doing something very bad.

  —SEVE BALLESTEROS
   ON THE MEDIA'S CRITICISM FOR HIS BAD PLAY

I refuse to spend an afternoon in April watching Marino and Elway square off on the 18th tee, locked atop the leaders board at 16 over.

  —ED SHIFFER
   WRITER FOR *PRO FOOTBALL WEEKLY*, ON THE PROPOSED
   PRO ATHLETIC GOLF LEAGUE

I'm not saying I could do any better. But if the ratings are down, I understand why.

  —PAUL AZINGER
   ON TV GOLF COMMENTATORS, AFTER SPENDING A YEAR
   WATCHING THEM WHILE RECOVERING FROM ILLNESS

Are you kidding? The only big word I know is delicatessen, and I can't even spell it.

—LLOYD MANGRUM
ON BEING ASKED IF HE WAS INTERESTED IN WRITING

He's hit it fat . . . It will probably be short . . . It just hit the front edge of the green . . . It's got no chance . . . It's rolling, but it will stop . . . It's rolling toward the cup . . . Well, I'll be goddamned, he sank it!

—JIMMY DEMARET
CALLING A 104-YARD EAGLE SHOT

We all shoot better than we score.

—BRIAN SWARBRICK
WRITER

It's gotten to the point where you can't tell race car drivers from professional golfers.

—LEE TREVINO
ON PATCH ADVERTISEMENTS WORN BY GOLFERS

How much money do I have? If I knew I wouldn't have very much, would I?

—JOE JEMSEK
DEPRESSION-ERA CADDIE TURNED GOLF COURSE OWNER

I shot scenes fast and unworried, much like Julius Boros shoots golf: Walk up to the ball, hit it, laugh, and walk on without losing a stride.

—FRANK CAPRA
MOVIE DIRECTOR, DESCRIBING HOW HE MADE THE ACADEMY
AWARD-WINNING FILM *IT HAPPENED ONE NIGHT*

Unless you're able to comprehend the pressures of working for your paycheck each week, I don't know if you can have a true appreciation for the game . . . and how you can go from the top of the mountain to flat on your face.

—DAN PATRICK
ESPN BROADCASTER

I just love to see you guys with long hair, because you can't see. I never saw a hippie playing golf.

—BERT YANCEY
PGA PRO, ADDRESSING THE PRESS IN THE 1970S

Golf is one of the easiest sports to get in a player's face. When I'm done, you have to get through the crowd—to get to the locker room. He runs right out of the locker room. I think it's a little simpler.

—FRED COUPLES
COMPARING HIS EXPERIENCE WITH CROWDS TO MICHAEL JORDAN'S

Fuck . . . Shit . . . these are highly difficult golf terms and you're using them on your first lesson—this is promising.

—RON SHELTON
FROM HIS SCREENPLAY TO THE FILM *TIN CUP*

I think they need to look at their own lives before they use that pen. I'm sure a lot of those guys in the media don't have perfect lives.

—JOHN DALY
ON THE MEDIA

How about Byron Nelson winning the Byron Nelson?

—SKIP BAYLESS

COLUMNIST, ON JACK NICKLAUS, WINNING THE MASTERS AT AGE 46
AND RAY FLOYD WINNING THE US OPEN AT AGE 43

There is one thing in this world that is dumber than playing golf. That is watching someone else play golf. What do you actually get to see? Thirty-seven guys in polyester slacks squinting in the sun. Doesn't that set your blood racing?

—PETER ANDREWS

One of life's great mysteries is just what do golfers think they are playing at. But even more mysterious is what these spectators who traipse around golf courses are looking for.

—MICHAEL PARKINSON

If God wants to produce the ideal golfer then he should create a being with . . . unequal arms and likewise legs . . . knees which hinge sideways and a ribless torso from which emerges, at an angle of forty-five degrees, a stretched neck fitted with one color-blind eye stuck firmly on the left side.

—CHRIS PLUMRIDGE
GOLF WRITER

———•—•———

The Americans respect you more as a player. Australians don't appreciate their own players. They feel like you are a traitor to leave the country and do so well. I think they are jealous.

—JAN STEPHENSON
AUSTRALIAN LPGA PRO, 1991

———•—•———

Better tournament golf scoring was particularly due to the Depression because it induced thousands of urchins who might otherwise have been playing baseball or annoying their parents to earn an honest dollar by caddying.

—NOEL F. BUSH
THE NEW YORKER, 1937

If I had been in the gallery, I'd have gone home.

—JOHNNY MILLER

ON SHOOTING A 39 ON THE FIRST NINE HOLES OF A TOURNAMENT

———————•———————

Guarantee me three million dollars a year and you can scream, yell, or spit on my ball when I'm putting. Because even if I miss, I get paid.

—LEE TREVINO

CHAPTER NINE

Hitting off the Pink Tees:
Women in Golf

We have it on the very best authority. No less than a blue ribbon triumvirate composed of Bob Jones, Ben Hogan and Byron Nelson singled out, respectively, Joyce Wethered and Mary Kathryn Wright as possessing the most fundamentally sound swing—male or female—that ever took a divot. Lady Heathcoat-Amory, as Joyce would later become upon marriage, could hit balls competently to a distance of seventy-five yards gripping a club with just her left hand. (Try it.) A cunning ploy worthy of feminine wiles, she had her skirts tailored to the precise width of her desired stance.

A magnificent ball-striker, Mickey's eighty-two official victories attest to her remarkable consistency. Even more astounding, the number could well have been higher. Like Bobby, Lord Byron and her illustrious English forebear a magnificent ball-striker, she also prematurely eschewed formal competition, hampered by a nagging foot problems and the vagaries of living on the road. With no disrespect to another outstanding champion and human being, Kathy Whitworth, a perusal of the fine print confirms that Kathy's total of eighty-eight wins required over twice the number of years to achieve.

Enough quibbling, the ladies' insights demand our fullest attention. The intrinsic wisdom shared in this section stands tall against all comers: timeless, wry, and knowing. The personalities that have distinguished women's golf at the highest levels have been underappreciated. The Babe, Joanne 'Big Mama' Carner, Nancy Lopez, for starters, cast Ruthian shadows as they exploded the tired myths. Larger than life, populist figures, their exuberance for golf and competition was infectious. Their games, prodigious for their times, elicited cheers and gasps from naysayers as their personal warmth and candor drew smiles.

* * * * *

Look like a woman but play like a man.

    —JAN STEPHENSON

I thought you had to be dead to win that.

    —JoANNE CARNER
       ON WINNING THE BOBBY JONES AWARD FOR SPORTSMANSHIP

I've got no objection to women coming into our game if they are good enough.

    —IAN WOOSNAM

The most important advice I'd give any woman just starting to play is: get the fundamentals correct. It's a bad mistake simply to pick up a club and start swinging.

    —LOUISE SUGGS
       LPGA HALL OF FAMER

I've seen it happen that one girl will help another who's having trouble with her swing, knowing that next week she may go out and beat her because of it.

—BOB HAGGE, 1961

When we complain about conditions, we're just bitches. But when the men complain, people think, 'Well, it really must be hard.'

—BETSY KING
ON GOLF'S DOUBLE STANDARD

Rosa Parks was told to go to the back of the bus. I was thrown off the bus.

—MILLIE RECH
ON BEING EJECTED FROM HER COUNTRY CLUB WHEN
SHE WAS DIVORCED

People have said that the Babe was a little crude once in a while, but I didn't see that in her. No, I saw a wonderful athlete and someone with a lot of class . . . She gave everybody hope.

—PATTY BERG
LPGA TOUR PIONEER AND HALL OF FAMER,
REMEMBERING BABE ZAHARIAS

In my fifty-seven years of golf, this hole in one is my first ever. To think how many balls I have hit in my life—I was running out of time.

—LOUISE SUGGS

All I was thinking was that I didn't have anything to wear the next day. I thought I was going to have to do laundry that night, especially after Helen [Alfredsson] hit her shot at 18. She nearly flew it into the hole.

—LAURIE MERTEN
HER FINAL THOUGHTS IN THE FINAL ROUND OF THE 1993
WOMEN'S OPEN, EXPECTING A PLAYOFF

I'm terrible! No one could be two up on the 16th and lose.

—PAMELA BARTON
AFTER LOSING TO HOLLIS STACY IN THE 1971 US GIRLS' JUNIOR

Q: Are you a golfer?
Hurd: I don't think so, but I believe that they will want me inside to receive the championship cup.

—DOROTHY HURD
RESPONSE TO AN OFFICIAL BLOCKING HER WAY TO THE
AWARDS CEREMONY AFTER SHE WON THE 1909 BRITISH
LADIES' CHAMPIONSHIP

After all, golf is only a game, said Millicent. Women say these things without thinking. It does not mean that there is a kink in their character. They simply don't realize what they are saying.

—P.G. WODEHOUSE
FROM *ORDER BY GOLF*, 1922

We played all our competitions off men's tees. We played country matches off men's tees, we played our county championship off men's tees, we played our championships off of men's tees. What do they do now? They play from the up women's tees.

—ENID WILSON

Daddy, am I ready to beat the ladies?

—NANCY LOPEZ
AT AGE 11, JUST BEFORE WINNING THREE CONSECUTIVE
NEW MEXICO AMATEUR TITLES

There's hope for us old farts yet.

—DALE EGGELING
AFTER WINNING FOR HER FIRST TIME IN FIFTEEN YEARS

We were always taught to swing slow with good tempo. But you have to have some acceleration throughout the swing. I think that's where a lot of women go wrong. They should try to whack it a few times and see what happens

—HELEN ALFREDSSON

There must be nothing in sport quite like a golf match involving girls.

—FRANK HANNIGAN
GOLF JOURNALIST, ON THE 1963 US WOMEN'S AMATEUR

There are no more set standards in golf. You don't have to be twenty-five to turn pro. You just have to feel like I do, have a burning inside for the game.

—CHRISTIE KERR
ON WHY SHE TURNED DOWN A SCHOLARSHIP TO STANFORD
TO TURN PRO

You've got a free shot. You can always pitch out of the woods.

—JOANNE CARNER
ON HER "ATTACKING" APPROACH TO GOLF

Well, they're southern people, and if they know you are working at home, they think nothing of walking right in for coffee. But they wouldn't dream of interrupting you at golf.

—HARPER LEE
ON WHY CREATIVE THINKING COMES BEST TO
HER WHILE ON THE GOLF COURSE

When you step on the first tee it doesn't matter what you look like. Being pretty, ugly, or semi-ugly has no effect on the golf ball. It doesn't hurt your five-iron if you're pretty.

—LAURA BAUGH
ON HER GOOD LOOKS

I may not be the prettiest girl in the world, but I'd like to see Bo Derek look like a 10 after playing 18 holes of golf in 100-degree weather.

—JAN STEPHENSON

I like the thought of playing for money instead of silverware. I never did like to polish.

—PATTY SHEEHAN
ON TURNING PRO

To anyone . . . perhaps the fact that I had beaten Cecil Leitch was unimportant—an off-day for the champion. To me it was the beginning of a successful career. I had gained confidence I needed so badly. My nerves became steadier, my shot bolder. No opponent held any terror for me.

—GLENNA COLLETT
AFTER BEATING CECIL LEAITCH IN THE
BERTHELLY CUP MATCHES IN 1921

This is not the Ice Capades. You don't fall on a double axel and get up and smile and everything's OK, you know.

—DOTTIE MOCHRIE
LPGA PRO, ON HER GRIM DEMEANOR ON THE COURSE

I think I have a real good stroke . . . but . . . I'm the queen of the lip-out and the rim-out. The ball comes out and looks up at me and grins, as if to say 'Too bad, you missed again.' I just don't know how to die the ball into the cup.

—PAT BRADLEY
LPGA PLAYER

A spectator said, 'I don't think you understand. You have to hit the hole, not the car.'

—MARY DWYER
    AFTER HITTING THE CAR THAT WOULD BE AWARDED TO ANY
    PLAYER IN THE TOURNAMENT WHO SHOT A HOLE IN ONE

Maybe it helps to have a very controlled logical sort of mind to play golf . . . Of course you also have to play a lot when you are young.

—BETSY RAWLS
    LPGA HALL OF FAMER

I don't like the idea of golf widows. I was raised to believe I could do anything a man can do.

—JANE SEYMOUR
    ACTRESS, 34 HANDICAP

Nobody wants to work for anything. We have a deal for juniors at my club. You caddie, you get free golf. Nobody comes . . . They'd rather play Nintendo. When I earned a golf scholarship you had to shoot in the 70s. Now they are giving them to kids who shoot 80.

—JULIE INKSTER
    LPGA HALL OF FAMER

JoAnne has a swing like Babe [Zaharias] did. JoAnne has the power that Babe had and the same sort of three-quarter swing. She also had the Babe's communication with her galleries.

—Marilyn Smith
on JoAnne Carner's swing

Women should rely upon their woods more, without fear of being criticized. We're after results and whatever club will put us where we want to be is the club to use.

—Mickey Wright

How on earth any of us managed to hit a ball, in the outrageous garments which fashion decreed we should wear, is one of the great unsolved mysteries.

—Mabel Stringer
pioneer British women's golfer and former LPGA player

I used to think pressure was standing over a four-foot putt knowing I had to make it. I learned that real pressure was sixty-five people waiting for their food with only thirty minutes left on their lunch break.

—Amy Alcott
on working as a waitress

I am not talking about ladies' golf because strictly speaking, there is no such thing as ladies' golf—only good or bad golf played by a member of either sex.

—JOYCE WETHERED
WINNER OF THIRTY-THREE SUCCEEDING MATCHES,
INCLUDING FIVE ENGLISH LADIES' TITLES (1920–1924)

When I hit iron, I say good-bye to ball.

—AYAKO OKAMOTO
ON HAVING TROUBLE WITH HER IRONS

I simply swing at the ball with the one idea of hitting it . . . The old idea was to hit the ball—few attempts were made at theorizing—and I'm not too sure it wasn't a blessed good idea.

—DOROTHY HURD

It was one of the greatest thrills of my life. I remember she was wearing tennis shoes and outdistancing the other ladies by twenty yards.

—PAUL AZINGER
ON THE TIME HE CADDIED FOR MICKEY WRIGHT

Paul Azinger wins a tournament and his wife is there on the 18th green with hugs and kisses. Could you imagine me hugging and kissing my woman lover at the conclusion of my last tournament win? Well, that's what you'll see at my next one.

—MUFFIN SPENCER-DEVLIN

The only thing I like about that number is that it's a good score to turn in for nine holes.

—LISELOTTE NEUMANN
MEMBER OF THE LPGA TOUR, ON TURNING 30

The early golf swing was more or less just a swing. Babe [Zaharias] brought the swing and a hit to the game. She got people, especially women, power-minded.

—PATTY BERG

They thought I was somebody just walking, hanging out in the rough.

—HELEN ALFREDSSON
ON HOW A MARSHAL THOUGHT SHE WAS A SPECTATOR

I'm not a heavy bettor. I bet for Cokes and stuff. I choke when I play for five dollars.

—NANCY LOPEZ

Imagine having a three-foot putt for $4 million on the final hole of the 1985 J & B Pro-Am after winning the other three tournaments. I think that I'd finally find my choking price.

—JOANNE CARNER
ON PRIZE MONEY OF $4 MILLION TO THE LPGA WINNER
OF THE DINAH SHORE, THE J & B SCOTCH PRO-AM,
AND TWO OTHER TOURNAMENTS FOR TWO
YEARS IN A ROW

If I could go back in time and you asked me whether I took it for granted, the answer would be, 'No.' But deep down, I always thought I would play that good my whole career without any road bumps.

—KARRIE WEBB

Once last year after I'd won four events, someone asked me, 'What kind of year are you having?' Ever hear of a pitcher with a 20-4 record asked what kind of year he's having?

    —BETSY KING

Are you sure you played all the holes, Christy?

    —HENRY COTTON
        TO CHRISTY O'CONNOR WHEN SHE SHOT 64 IN 1985 TO BREAK
        COTTON'S COURSE RECORD SET FIFTY-ONE YEARS EARLIER

For a long while, my son thought only women played golf.

    —JUDY RANKIN
        ON HER SON, WALTER, WHO TRAVELED AROUND
        WITH HER ON THE PRO TOUR

I kept seeing her ass all day bending over to pick her ball out of the hole.

    —HOLLIS STACY
        ON SALLY LITTLE SHOOTING A LAST-ROUND 64 TO WIN
        THE DINAH SHORE

Most difficult of all is trying to be a 'good sport.' You are compelled to do many things you don't give two hoots about. To go to parties when you just long to be in bed, to be nice to all sorts of people, ask all sorts of favors.

—GLENNA COLLET VARE

It is my belief that this attitude of aggressiveness is far more prevalent in competitive golf today than it used to be. It creates poor sportsmanship and spoils the joy of the game for the players and the pleasures of watching a shot-making game for the gallery.

—VIRGINIA VAN WIE
ON WOMEN'S COMPETITIVE GOLF, *THE AMERICAN GOLFER MAGAZINE*

My headstone will read, 'Here lies Amy Alcott, winner of twenty-nine tour titles, but not a member of the Hall of Fame.'

—AMY ALCOTT
ON THE RULE OF HAVING TO WIN THIRTY TOURNAMENTS
TO QUALIFY FOR THE LPGA HALL OF FAME

The only area where I have ever experienced discrimination is athletics. Growing up, I couldn't play Little League baseball or be on the high school golf team simply because I was a girl. But that's changing.

—BETSY KING

I cannot find a job that pays me $700,000 a year, so until I do, I'll be right here.

—PAT BRADLEY
ASKED IF SHE WOULD RETIRE AFTER HER AUTOMATIC
ENTRANCE INTO THE LPGA HALL OF FAME

Let us examine the proposition that women golfers are people. It requires an effort to adjust to this idea, for, ever since the beheading of the first woman golfer, Mary Queen of Scots, the golf world has openly regretted that the practice didn't start a trend.

—PETER DOBEREINER

I'm kind of in between a goody-goody and a rebel. I'm not bad, but I'm not good either. I'm a little crazy.

—MICHELLE WIE

More than once I visualized myself, gray-haired and stooped, wearily trudging over the windswept fairways of an English course seeking that elusive title.

—GLENNA COLLETT
ON HER INABILITY TO WIN THE BRITISH LADIES AMATEUR

In 1587, golf's first famous woman player [Mary Queen of Scots] was convicted and beheaded. Women's golf went into something of a decline after that.

—RHONDA GLENN

When women in America first began to play golf, they were allowed at many of the big clubs to use the links only at certain hours on certain days when it was thought their presence would not incommode the Lords of Creation.

—GENEVIEVE HECKER
AUTHOR OF GOLF FOR WOMEN (1904) AND WINNER OF 4
METROPOLITAN GOLF CHAMPIONSHIPS (1900, 1901, 1905, 1906)
AND THE UNITED STATES WOMEN'S AMATEUR GOLF
CHAMPIONSHIP (1901)

No one could expect a married women with young children to win a championship. It would be enough grounds for a divorce.

—SIR ERNEST HOLDERNESS
1931 FORMER BRITISH AMATEUR CHAMPION ON PLANS FOR MATCHES
BETWEEN THE LADIES GOLF UNION AND AMERICAN GOLFERS

———◆———

Why do men have the right to feel superior? I think women are far superior to men, or at any rate, we're all equal. I don't see why I can't have the same rights as a man.

—MARY ANDERSON
CHAIR OF THE LADIES' GOLF UNION, IN RESPONSE TO DISCRIMINATION
AGAINST WOMEN GOLFERS IN ENGLAND IN 1991

———◆———

Not only did our presence there indicate that any prejudices against women's intrusion on men's rights had been overcome, but the subsequent happenings of the week clearly showed that we had justified our rights to play over the ground where other women had played three hundred years before.

—MABEL STRINGER
ON THE 1908 BRITISH LADIES AMATEUR BEING PLAYED
ON THE OLD COURSE AT ST. ANDREWS

By Gad! cried Mr. T.A. Hedrick, they ought to put some of these crazy women off the course. It's getting to be outrageous.

—F. SCOTT FITZGERALD
FROM *WINTER DREAMS*

So far as our home-bred golfers are concerned, she [Beatrix Hoyt] is not only in a class by herself, but also superior in the quality of her game to any of our men.

—*NEW YORK SUN*
1898

We had to wear long skirts . . . and they were rather a nuisance. You took care they were not wider than they needed to be or they would swirl in the wind. And we didn't want them narrower than necessary because they would be too constricting.

—JOYCE WETHERED
DESCRIBING WOMEN'S ATTIRE IN HER ERA

I'll take a two-shot penalty, but I'll be damned if I'm going to play the ball where it lies.

—ELAINE JOHNSON
AFTER HER SHOT HIT A TREE AND REBOUNDED INTO HER BRA

If ah didn't have these ah'd hit it twenty yards further.
>   —BABE ZAHARIAS
>   EXPLAINING HOW HER BREASTS IMPEDED HER GOLF SWING

If it weren't for golf, I'd be waiting on this table instead of sitting at it.
>   —JUDY RANKIN

After a tournament, we'd always sit around together and have a party. Usually the winner would buy the drinks because she was the only one who had any money.
>   —KATHY WHITWORTH
>   REMEMBERING HER EARLY TOUR YEARS

I have not played golf with anyone, man or woman, amateur or professional, who made me feel so utterly outclassed.
>   —BOBBY JONES
>   ON JOYCE WETHERED

CHAPTER TEN

Equipment:
The Importance and Evolution
of the Clubs in Your Bag

It's reassuring to see club names still have a place, especially with putters, which deserve them. There's no way of knowing, but were the 14-club limit rescinded, it's conceivable the additions would promote closer relations with those cherished clubs that do listen. Much improved though equipment may be, the consistency has come at a cost. Clubs are more sterile, the attachment less romantic. Reaching for your *Strate-a-way*, your *Dang Buster*, and your *Little Lassie* just sounds so much more inviting than the more clinical, numerical next-generation tags in vogue today, leaving us to dance with, say, our R7, MP-33s, and XG.

No matter what they're called, progress obscures several irrefutable truths. Sandra Palmer's assertion, for instance, that the longer the club the harder it is to return squarely to the ball has only been true for about forever. It does seem that the mysteries of equipment have been enhanced not only by the golfing public's gullibility but by our active disinterest in why they're better. Few golfers have any earthly idea of a club's swingweight, loft, bounce, or other technical properties, let alone whether their irons are perimeter-weighted or cavity-backed. (And, no, it has nothing to do with Fluoride or brushing between meals.) Akin to the various parts underneath the hood, all we really care about is whether the thing works, not why or how—not even how much. We know the tools invariably perform better, sometimes much, much better, for others than they do for us. It's just one more object in our reflective blind spot, another episode in a doomed, one-sided relationship. The thrill, we know, will be gone, yet another depressing reminder that the fault rests with the Indian and not the arrow.

* * * * *

The best wood in most amateurs' bags is the pencil.

—CHI-CHI RODRIGUEZ

Although golf was originally restricted to wealthy, overweight Protestants, today it's open to anybody who owns hideous clothing.

—DAVE BARRY

If you think it's hard to meet new people, try picking up the wrong golf ball.

—JACK LEMMON

Selecting a putter is like selecting a wife. To each his own.

—BEN HOGAN

All golfers fear the one-iron. It has no angle, no loft. The one-iron is a confidence-crusher, a fear trip, an almost guarantee of shame, failure, dumbness, and humiliation if you ever use it in public.

—HUNTER S. THOMPSON

Of course some new inventions are good, but it is usually best to wait a little while to see whether any considerable section of the golfing public approves of them before rushing to order one.

—HARRY VARDON

I've lost balls in every hazard on every course I've tried. But when I lose a ball in the ball washer, it's time to take stock.

—MILTON GROSS

I've been playing with a white golf ball for twenty years, and I'll keep playing it unless somebody comes up with the right numbers. For $50,000, I'd paint my driver pink.

—ANDY BEAN
PGA PRO

Being slave to the game is one thing. Being a cringing captive to one warped club is something else.

—GRANTLAND RICE

This golf cart has opened the eyes of Americans to the need for more truly universal design that not only improves the lives of people with disabilities, but the lives of us all.

—PRESIDENT GEORGE H.W. BUSH

The gutta-percha ball made all the difference to golf because the game would have dried out if a cheaper ball hadn't come in. The feather ball cost three to five shillings, which made it more expensive than the club. A man could only make three of them a day.

—BOBBY BURNET
CLUB LIBRARIAN OF THE ROYAL & ANCIENT ON GOLF TECHNOLOGY

I may be the only golfer never to have broken a single putter, if you don't count the one I twisted into a loop and threw into a bush.

—THOMAS BOSWELL

I've thrown or broken a few clubs in my day. In fact, I guess at one time or another I probably held distance records for every club in the bag.

—TOMMY BOLT

To many, Bolt's putter has spend more time in the air than Lindbergh.

  —JIMMY DEMARET
   ON TOMMY BOLT'S CLUB-THROWING HABITS

—•—

Bolt (to caddie): Why are you handing me a 3-iron for a shot of less than 100 yards?
Caddie (nervously): Because it's the only club left.

  —TOMMY BOLT

—•—

Why am I using a new putter? Because the last one didn't float too well.

  —CRAIG STADLER

—•—

There are many ways to punish a putter, such as burning, rusting and drowning, but the most torturous is to drag it along pavement out of the door of a fast-moving vehicle.

  —DAN JENKINS
   WHILE DEMONSTRATING ONE OF HIS *TEN BASIC RULES*
   FOR HAPPY PUTTING

It's about the same as mine, except it's got about forty-eight less cart-path grooves on the bottom and twenty less spike marks on the face.

—CRAIG STADLER
COMPARING HIS AND BEN CRENSHAW'S PUTTERS

When the going is good and the putts are dropping, you love your putter. When it's going bad, it's like it has betrayed you and you want to throw the sucker in a lake.

—KEN GREEN

Murphy's first law of golf: You can't lose an old ball!

—JOHN WILLIS

If you ask me, I don't think anything should be illegal . . . golf equipment, that is.

—JOHN DALY

The sound of a golf ball on a skull is remarkably like that of two blocks of wood being knocked together.

—JOHN UPDIKE
THE GOLF BOOK

Some virtue went out of the game with the advent of the rubber-core . . .
it made for a pleasanter and easier game.

> —BERNARD DARWIN
> COMMENTING ON HOW GOLF CHANGED WITH THE ADVENT
> OF THE HASKELL BALL OVER THE GUTTA-PERCHA

The modern player has grown so accustomed to having a special club for
every conceivable stroke, that he fails to realize how much of his vaunted
skill is due to the science of the club-maker.

> —ROBERT BROWNING
> WRITER

If it was good enough for Hogan, it's good enough for me.

> —STEVE ELKINGTON
> ON WHY HE STILL USED METAL SPIKES

Nice clods, Stadler. Did you get those at a Bustler Brown fire sale?

> —FUZZY ZOELLER
> TEASING CRAIG STADLER ABOUT HIS SHOES

'Play it as it lies' is one of the fundamental dictates of golf. The other is: 'Wear it if it clashes.'

—HENRY BEARD
HUMORIST

———•———

Claude Harmon not only taught me most of what I know about the golf swing, he took me out of Argyle socks.

—DAVE MARR

———•———

Fashions come and go in golf clubs as they do in clothes and often what is hailed as the latest thing is only a revival of what was all the rage fifty years ago.

—HENRY LONGHURST

———•———

The most important item was the plus fours, a kind of knickers that had to hang exactly right if they were to make the wearer look like Gene Sarazen or Walter Hagen, not the guy who put on his mother's bloomers by mistake.

—RICHARD ARMOUR, 1962
IN HIS BOOK *GOLF IS A FOUR LETTER WORD*

He dresses like a gardener and usually plays like one.

> —HENRY COTTON
> ON 1935 OPEN CHAMPION ALF PERRY

If you don't send me a couple hundred pounds a week, I'm going to start wearing your clothes.

> —SIMON HOBDAY
> IN REPLY TO A QUESTION ABOUT WHAT THIS FAMOUSLY
> UNFASHIONABLE MAN WROTE IN A LETTER TO THE
> MANUFACTURER OF MUNSINGWEAR, A LINE OF CLOTHES
> ENDORSED BY MANY EUROPEAN GOLFERS

Baffling late-life discovery: Golfers wear those awful clothes on purpose.

> —HERB CAEN
> COLUMNIST

I'd give up golf if I didn't have so many sweaters.

> —BOB HOPE

Winning is only part of the thing. I wanted people to enjoy seeing me, and I figured if I had fun, they'd have fun.

> —JIMMY DEMARET
> ON HIS COLORFUL WARDROBE

Here's a simple way to abolish golf's elitist and exclusionary image and make it a truly all-American sport: ditch that fifties-Republican-martini-drinker's green Brooks Brothers-style sport jacket and make the winner of the Masters slip on something in, say, black leather with plenty of metal studs.

> —BRUCE MCCALL
> THE CASE AGAINST GOLF, FROM ESQUIRE

I'll have to go shopping. I don't think I have any more clean shirts.

> —MARK MCCUMBER
> ON MAKING HIS FIRST PGA TOUR CUT IN TWO YEARS

They talked me out of polyester golf slacks.

> —DAVE STOCKTON
> ON THE IMPACT HIS SONS' INTEREST IN GOLF HAD ON HIM

No power on earth will deter men from using a ball that will add to the length of their drive.

—*GOLF ILLUSTRATED*, 1902

Had the gutta-percha golf ball not been invented, it is likely enough that golf itself would be in the catalogue of virtually extinct games, only locally surviving, as stool-ball and knurr spell.

—HORACE HUTCHINSON, 1899

When you're down to four or five balls, put the driver away and try for two good shots with a wedge. Once you've hit your two, pick the other balls up and go home.

—TOM PAXSON

By the time a man can afford to lose a golf ball, he can't hit it that far.

—LEWIS GRIZZARD
AMERICAN HUMORIST

You better use a putter cover, because you can put a dent in the face just by breathing on it.

—BOBBY GRACE
GOLF CLUB DESIGNER, DISCUSSING HIS "FAT LADY SWINGS"
SOFT-FACED PUTTER

———◆———

Sports gear purchases are about all that's keeping the fragile US economy alive, and you'd have to get into America's Cup yachting or cross-country airplane racing to find a sport that needs more gear than golf.

—P.J. O'ROURKE

———◆———

Nobody needs fourteen clubs. The reduction would have zero effect on scoring, would make the game a touch less expensive and might diminish the importance of riding by encouraging more golfers to carry or pull their clubs. Francis Ouimet won the 1913 U.S. Open with a set of seven clubs.

—FRANK HANNIGAN
FORMER USGA EXECUTIVE DIRECTOR; ABC SPORTS COMMENTATOR

———◆———

Some people say it's a 3-iron/4-iron, but I say it's the secret to a happy life.

—DAN JENKINS
IN RESPONSE TO BEING ASKED WHAT A 7-WOOD IS,
GOLF WITH THE BOSS

I think they should ban all drivers. Just use irons.

—JOSE MARIA OLAZABAL

The only thing a golfer needs is more daylight.

—BEN HOGAN
ON NEW EQUIPMENT

The sport isn't like any other where a player can take out all that is eating him on an opponent. In golf, it's strictly you against your clubs.

—BOBBY ROSBURG

[Scottish golf] is a more public game, more reasonably priced, they play faster. It isn't cart golf. The only reason resorts force you into carts is for the money. They are selling off the soul of the game for a few dollars.

—DAN KING

The niblick, with its heavy head of iron, is a capital club for knocking down solicitors.

—ANONYMOUS

Golf is played with a number of striking implements more intricate in shape than those used in any form of recreation except dentistry.

—E.V. KNOX
AUTHOR

———— • ————

Some people think the new metal shafts are a great improvement over the old wooden ones. I have tried both and I would do just as well with a rhubarb or asparagus.

—RUBE GOLDBERG
FROM *LEFT-HANDED GOLF COURSES: OUR GREATEST NEED*

———— • ————

I still hit balls with my old wooden driver once in awhile, because swinging a club with such a small sweet spot helps me focus on solid contact.

—ERNIE ELS

———— • ————

You know the old rule: He who has the fastest cart never has to play a bad lie.

—MICKEY MANTLE

I never like to use the same putter for too long. When I play a tournament, I go into the pro shop and select a putter off the rack, take it out, use it, then take it back . . . As long as it's got a shaft and a grip, it'll putt.

—GARY McCORD

It's a marriage. If I had to choose between my wife and my putter, well, I'd miss her.

—GARY PLAYER

You have to put your putter out to pasture every so often, let it eat and get fat so it can get more birdies.

—GREG NORMAN

I curse the day the head of my putter fell off. It's kind of like losing one of your best friends.

—NICK PRICE

The fact is all golfers are equipment junkies and professional golfers are the worst of the lot. They'll do anything to find the perfect putter even though they'll insist no such instrument exists.

—DAVE MARR

The finale in freak putters has apparently not yet come, for after nearly every shape of iron, wood and aluminum had been exhausted . . . a Chicago professional has come to the front with a putter made of gaspipe.

—*THE NEW YORK TIMES*, 1922

But during the last quarter century, as we all know, greens have become more difficult to putt. The main reason, of course, is related to the solunar tables and the gradual warming of the earth's atmosphere. Then of course, there's the new multi-dimpled golf ball.

—GEORGE PEPER
AUTHOR AND EDITOR OF *GOLF MAGAZINE*

With wooden shafts you could stay on the ball longer. The club face stayed with the ball longer that is, the ball did not leave it so quickly. You retained the feel longer. The ball didn't spring away from you.

—JOYCE WETHERED

I don't like number 4 balls. And I don't like fives, sixes or sevens on my scorecard.

—GEORGE ARCHER
WHEN ASKED ABOUT SUPERSTITIONS

Titleist has offered me a big contract not to play its balls.

—BOB HOPE

The winds were blowing 50 mph and gusting to seventy. I hit a par-3 with my hat.

—CHI-CHI RODRIGUEZ

I don't like the way most people dress on the golf course. I think it's pretty bland, pretty boring.

—IAN POULTER

Why do I wear a red sport shirt on Sundays? Well, if I play bad on the last round of a tournament and cut my throat, it blends.

—LEE TREVINO

In the USA a number of first-class golfers take as long to choose a wife as a club. Sometimes they make the wrong choice in each case.

> —DAI REES

The cart doesn't hit the ball. The golfer does.

> —DAVE ANDERSON
> *THE NEW YORK TIMES*

I'm sure this looks like I'm all over the charts, but it's what works out best for me. I test each club to find my personal preference, so there's a little bit of trial and error involved.

> —LOREN ROBERTS
> ON WHY HE USES CLUBS FROM SEVERAL MANUFACTURERS

The last thing you want to do is shoot 80 wearing tartan trousers.

> —IAN POULTER

I played nine holes with the new short-distance ball. Playing a match with it is like two boxers fighting with pillows.

> —SAM SNEAD

Look at those spoiled bastards. They don't know the value of a dollar.
>—GENE SARAZEN
>CRITICIZING TOUR PROS WHO DROP BALLS INSTEAD OF
>SEARCHING FOR THE SHOTS THEY HIT IN THE ROUGH

They interested us immensely by bringing with them huge quantities of clubs and balls—the latter for practice purposes—which were carted about the countryside in the most awe-inspiring voluminous leather caddie bags.
>—ENID WILSON
>ON THE AMERICAN TEAM'S PREPARATION FOR AN
>INFORMAL MATCH AGAINST THE BRITISH IN 1930

We're in America, aren't we? If people want to buy a Chevy or Cadillac, they should be able to buy one. If you can build a better golf club, you should build it.
>—KARSTEN SOLHEIM
>FOUNDER OF PING

Do not be tempted to invest in a sample of each golfing invention as soon as it makes its appearance. If you do, you will only complicate and spoil your game—and encumber your locker with useless rubbish.

—HARRY VARDON

———•—•———

You begin to get the idea that maybe golf manufacturers are out of control when you find out they are making clubs and balls out of components used in nuclear weapons and bulletproof vests.

—E.M. SWIFT
SPORTSWRITER

———•—•———

I feel calm in calm colors. I don't want people to watch the way I dress. I want people to watch the way I play.

—SEVE BALLESTEROS

———•—•———

Nobody else is that stupid.

—ROCKY THOMPSON
ON HOW HE KNEW THAT HE WAS THE ONLY PLAYER
USING A 54-INCH DRIVER

When I used to gamble, I looked for players with head covers on their irons. Those guys I could beat.

—CHI-CHI RODRIQUEZ

Real golfers don't use animal club covers.

—SHANNON SULLIVAN

Golf is not a good walk spoiled. It is becoming a good walk prohibited. Show me the common sense in this and I promise I will relent. But there is no common sense at all in the prohibition of walking.

—LORNE RUBENSTEIN
ON COMPULSORY GOLF CARTS

Man, this is one of them airport drivers. That's right. You hit this thing for two days, miss the cut, and go to the airport.

—LEE TREVINO
COMMENTING ON A FELLOW SENIOR'S OLD CLUB

Always use a clean ball, and carry a sponge to keep it clean. It detracts from the pleasure of a game more than you may imagine if your ball is always dirty and cannot be seen from a distance.

—HARRY VARDON
THE COMPLETE GOLFER

The game of golf would lose a great deal if croquet mallets and billiard cues were allowed on the putting green.

—ERNEST HEMINGWAY

I think most of the guys are happy with their personal barbers. I don't want any part of John's barber—not that it doesn't look good on John.

—LANNY WADKINS
RESPONDING TO JOHN DALY'S OFFER TO SHAVE
THE HEADS OF THE US RYDER CUP TEAM

There is little fun to be had in playing from a set of tees that doesn't allow a golfer to score well on almost any hole. Play from tees that allow you to enjoy the game.

—JOHN COMPANIOTTE
FROM *GOLF RULES AND ETIQUETTE SIMPLIFIED*

I hold the firm opinion that from this date the essential attitude towards accuracy was completely lost sight of. This was the start of the craze for length and still more length.

> —HARRY VARDON
> ON THE ADVENT OF THE RUBBER BALL

No one would ever believe that any man ever played with that club in an international match.

> —JOHN WARD
> EX-PROFESSIONAL BASEBALL PLAYER AND 1922 WALKER CUP
> UMPIRE COMMENTING ON BERNARD DARWIN'S SPOON-LIKE
> BRASSIE AT THE FIRST WALKER CUP CONTEST

Always keep in mind that if God didn't want a man to have mulligans, golf balls wouldn't come three to a sleeve.

> —DAN JENKINS

There's an old saying, 'It's a poor craftsman who blames his tools.' It's usually the player who misses those three-footers, not the putter.

> —KATHY WHITWORTH
> DESCRIBING THE DIFFERENT BETWEEN STEEL-SHAFTED
> AND HICKORY SHAFTED CLUBS

There's an amazing golf ball that comes equipped with beeps and lights so that it simply can't be lost.

    —LEE TREVINO

I think golf carts take a little piece of golf's quality away. The tradition of the game is being passed by because revenue is the number one consideration. There's money in carts.

    —RICHARD ZOKOL

Armed with ignorance, golfers shell out hundreds, sometimes thousands of dollars on new clubs, believing that their investment is going to help them play better. You can spend a million dollars; if your clubs don't fit, you're not going to play good golf.

    —JONATHAN ABRAHAMS

The trouble that most of us find with the modern matched sets of clubs is that they don't really seem to know any more about the game than the old ones did.

    —ROBERT BROWNING

Properly fitted clubs are the only part of improved golf that anyone can buy.

—TOMMY ARMOUR

———— • ————

How could I have intimidated the hitters if I looked like a goddamn golf pro?

—AL HRABOSKY
FORMER MAJOR LEAGUE RELIEF PITCHER WHO WAS
FORCED TO SHAVE HIS MENACING BEARD

———— • ————

A golf ball simply cannot find the hole by itself. Even if it could, the ball would never do so willingly, after the hatred and hammering you've heaped on it to get it to the green.

—DICK BROOKS

———— • ————

The advent of the rubber ball was instrumental in creating an entirely different method of striking objects. The solid ball required to be hit for carry, whereas it was quickly apparent that the Haskell lent itself to an enormous run.

—HARRY VARDON

If I were you, I would give your driver to your worst enemy.
> —JOHN JACOBS

Back in the old days, they didn't call it a driver. They referred to it as a 'play club.' In other words, it was a club you used to put the ball in play—maybe *keep* the ball in play.
> —NEAL LANCASTER

The yard-consuming club which more than any other has made a mockery of par.
> —ROBERT TRENT JONES
> ON DRIVERS

I'm wearing an Arnold Palmer hat made in Japan. These are Johnny Miller slacks, but I've taken the tag out.
> —CHI-CHI RODRIGUEZ,
> ON HIS OUTFIT IN THE U.S. OPEN

He does it to all his clubs all the time. The man's got magic in there and always changes them.

> —MIKE SOUCHAK
> ON ARNOLD PALMER'S TENDENCY TO FIDDLE WITH HIS GOLF CLUBS

Maybe the number of clubs we carry is less important than the selection. Five clubs may truly be all I need—as long as none of the five is a driver, a long iron, or the elusive Unhittable Club of the Day, which moves unpredictably around my bag.

> —DAVID OWEN

One never realized what a stubborn, inert thing a gutty is until the Haskell came on the scene.

> —GOLF ILLUSTRATED
> 1902

The other day I broke 70. That's a lot of clubs.

> —ANONYMOUS

Not orange. That's tangerine.

—DOUG SANDERS

TO A SPECTATOR COMMENTING ON HIS ORANGE OUTFIT

I found very little difference in the length of drive between the Haskell and gutta balls; perhaps they run further, but certainly don't carry as far. They are also more difficult to stop when approaching and on the putting green are very liable to jump out of the hole.

—JAMES BRAID

CHAPTER ELEVEN

Practice and Preparation: On the Importance of Working on One's Game

The drive home was a somber affair. Dave Marr had not played well. His mother, Grace, imbued with an incisive wit, herself once a scratch golfer, would not hear any excuses. "I don't know what you're complaining about," she chided. "You never practice." Countered the former PGA Champion and Ryder Cup captain: "When you've got a Rolls Royce, you don't have to warm it up."

"You do when you've got a Volkswagen under the hood!" shot back Mom. The silence returned. We can be assured the steering wheel received far tighter a grip than conventionally recommended for a club.

Practice always presents a conundrum. Should we continue once having attained a measure of proficiency with one club, the better to hone our skill? (What might be termed The Hogan Approach.) Or does our apparent success suggest the time would be better spent moving on to some other facet? That, in fact, continuing to hit good shots with the same club is not only ineffectual but detrimental? (The Bobby Jones Approach.)

It doesn't help that the riddle has two right answers. Each of the aforementioned illustrious practitioners early on found the solution that worked best for him, best suiting his temperament. Since most of us can hardly steal away the time and, when we do practice, do so inefficiently, inexpertly, or in haste before racing to the tee, perhaps it's a moot point. Apart from its function, the range remains a source of vicarious, even fiendish, pleasure. How easily we forget that there is always someone better *and* worse. A good swing stands out like a ripe raspberry on the vine, and nowhere is this more evident than on pro-am day. No starker contrast to the efficacy of practice can be found than on the driving range: on one side the swings fluid and balanced contrasted with those on the other seemingly caught between the pause and fast-forward settings on the remote.

* * * * *

The most valuable time to practice is right after your round, when your mistakes are fresh in your mind.

  —TOM WATSON

I decided I'm either going to work my ass off or just be an average guy on this Tour. I don't want to be average.

  —JOHN DALY

Knowledge, like a sharpened razor, shaves those hardest-to-get strokes and smoothes the rough edges of your game.

  —SHAWN HUMPHRIES
   FROM *TWO STEPS TO A PERFECT GOLF SWING*

There is no movement in the golf swing so difficult that it cannot be made even more difficult by careful study and diligent practice.

  —THOMAS BOSWELL

You see the practice ground out there? It is an evil place. It's full of so-called coaches waiting to pounce on young guys or players who have lost their form. They just hope they can make money out of them.

—ERNIE ELS

For practice to have full value, make each swing with the care of a stroke from a tee on medal day.

—JAMES BRAID
FIVE-TIME BRITISH OPEN CHAMPION

They might be able to beat me, but they can't out-practice me.

—JERRY BARBER
JOURNEYMAN PGA TOUR PROFESSIONAL

When you're prepared, you're more confident. When you have a strategy, you're more comfortable.

—FRED COUPLES

It is strange how few bunkers one gets into during the pre-tournament rounds, but in the competition proper they have a habit of almost springing up in the night. So bunker shot practice is very important to test the texture and depth of the sand.

—BILL COX
"SIX POINTERS TO BETTER GOLF" IN *SECRETS OF THE GOLFING GREATS*

Very few times in my life I laid off two to three days. It seemed like it took me a month to three months to get back those three days when I took a rest. It's a tough situation. I had to practice all the time.

—BEN HOGAN

Swinging at daisies is like playing electric guitar with a tennis racket: if it were that easy, we could all be Jerry Garcia. The ball changes everything.

—MICHAEL BAMBERGER

It is the constant and undying hope for improvement that makes golf so exquisitely worth the playing.

—BERNARD DARWIN

Overall I hope I can still improve.
—DAVID DUVAL
AFTER SHOOTING A 59 AT THE 1999 BOB HOPE CLASSIC

There's no secret to taking your game to the next level. I did it by getting back to basics.
—ERNIE ELS

A four-hour round of golf can certainly be preceded by ten or fifteen minutes on the practice tee. By simply hitting a dozen balls you have eliminated three or four bad holes from your system.
—JACK BURKE, JR.

What can you do? You're not going to kill yourself. You're just going to keep working on it and hopefully one of these years I'll have a good Sunday.
—SERGIO GARCIA

The average golfer claims he hasn't the time to warm up, when the truth is he won't make or take the time.

—JACK BURKE, JR.

A driving range is the place where golfers go to get all the good shots out of their system.

—HENRY BEARD
HUMORIST

I worked as hard to perfect my golf game as any other fellow would work in his brokerage office, in his job as a mechanic in a garage, as a lawyer or as a traveling salesman.

—WALTER HAGEN
FROM HIS AUTOBIOGRAPHY *THE WALTER HAGEN STORY*

You must work very hard to become a natural golfer.

—GARY PLAYER

It's a funny thing, the more I practice the luckier I get.

—GARY PLAYER

That's the hard thing, the time it takes to keep yourself prepared. That I still have the discipline and the desire to get out there day after day, beat balls and putt and chip, do my hour of stretching and exercise. I really don't understand why I keep doing that.

—RAYMOND FLOYD
1994 GOLF DIGEST INTERVIEW

I used to go to the driving range to practice driving without slicing. Now I go to the driving range to practice slicing without swearing.

—BRUCE LANSKY
AUTHOR

You hear stories about me beating my brains out practicing, but . . . I was enjoying myself. I couldn't wait to get up in the morning, so I could hit balls. When I'm hitting the ball where I want, hard and crisply, it's a joy that very few people experience.

—BEN HOGAN

My dad always told me, 'Don't lift weights, you will lose your feel and your touch.' David and Tiger have proven that you can keep your swing and keep your touch, and they are better, stronger, golfers for it.

—DAVIS LOVE III, 2000
ON THE CONDITIONING OF TIGER WOODS AND DAVID DUVAL

What a shame to waste those great shots on the practice tee. I'd be afraid of finding out what I was doing wrong.

—WALTER HAGEN
ON PRACTICE

First thing you have to do is get a room with blackout curtains. Start with full wedge shots. The window won't break. You can pretty much go through your short irons and not break the window.

—ANDREW MAGEE
DESCRIBING HOW TO PRACTICE IN MOTEL ROOMS

If you are only practicing those things that will be successful for you, then you cannot fail to improve.

—JIM HARDY
FROM *THE PLANE TRUTH FOR GOLFERS*

I am still trying to understand this game . . . I am still learning how to play golf. There are a lot of shots I still don't know. I am still trying to learn, and I think that's a good attitude to have.

  —HALE IRWIN

The real road to improvement lies in gaining a working understanding of the correct swing in general, and of his own swing in particular. When he has done this, there will be something on which to hang his concentration.

  —BOBBY JONES

When I grew up there was always a wager. It was just part of the fabric of the game. We'd play for nickels, dimes, and quarters on the putting green . . . It made me work that much harder.

  —RAYMOND FLOYD
  GOLF DIGEST, 1994

I never practice golf. All it does is louse up my game.

  —ORVILLE MOODY

Work puts a negative connotation on practicing.

—TOM KITE

There's so much to learn and always constant practice in golf. I never worked this hard playing baseball.

—KEN HARRELSON
FORMER MAJOR LEAGUE BALLPLAYER

I'm not very good at practice. But if you tell yourself you love the hole and love hitting it on the fairway, it's a big difference.

—BARRY LANE
ENGLISH PROFESSIONAL GOLFER

Practice is necessary, but it is not sufficient. Smart practice is what golfers need to do to improve.

—DAVE PELZ

What a farce is this business of length! Golf is surely the only game, either in the United States or Britain, whose whole character has been changed solely by so-called 'improvements' in the instruments with which it is played.

—HENRY LONGHURST
ROUND IN SIXTY-EIGHT

If you play poorly one day, forget it. If you play poorly the next time out, review your fundamentals of grip, stance, aim and ball position. Most mistakes are made before the club is swung. If you play poorly for a third time in a row, go see your professional.

—HARVEY PENICK
HARVEY PENICK'S LITTLE RED BOOK
WITH BUD SHRAKE

The strengths of my game were developed in the States . . . I wasn't born with this ability. I had to work bloody hard to become the player I am today.

—COLIN MONTGOMERIE

No matter how good you get you can always get better and that's the exciting part.

— TIGER WOODS

<hr>

Around the clubhouse they'll tell you even God has to practice his putting. In fact, even Nicklaus does.

— JIM MURRAY

<hr>

I have never been a heavy practicer from the standpoint of just hitting balls. I thought hitting balls in preparation for playing and finding out how your swing was working, was practice.

— JACK NICKLAUS, 1991
GOLF DIGEST

<hr>

I love practicing in Texas. You can find anything. You can practice rain, you can practice wind, you can practice on hardpan, you can practice on lush gold courses, you can find all the conditions you will ever encounter, in Texas.

— TOM KITE

You can be the greatest iron player in the world or the greatest putter, but if you can't get the ball in position to use your greatness, you can't win.

—BEN HOGAN

There is no such thing as a natural touch. Touch is something you create by hitting millions of golf balls.

—LEE TREVINO

They say 'practice makes perfect.' Of course, it doesn't. For the vast majority of golfers it merely consolidates imperfection.

—HENRY LONGHURST

'Trusting it' is the goal of every swing coach, every sports psychologist, and every touring professional. With enough practice, you can patent any motion and let nature take its course.

—KELLY TILGHMAN
ANCHOR/REPORTER, THE GOLF CHANNEL,
TRUMP: THE BEST GOLF ADVICE I EVER RECEIVED

If you want to score, the most important 'game' to improve is your short game.

—DAVE PELZ
FROM *DAVE PELZ'S SHORT GAME BIBLE*

* * *

To play winning golf, you have to have your personal life in order so that you can be focused on the course.

—FUZZY ZOELLER
FROM *GRIP IT AND RIP IT* BY JOHN DALY AND JOHN ANDRISANI

* * *

Make the basic shot-making decision early, clearly and firmly, and then ritualize all the necessary acts of preparation.

—SAM SNEAD

* * *

Never try a shot you haven't practiced.

—HARVEY PENICK
GOLF TEACHER AND AUTHOR OF *HARVEY PENICK'S LITTLE RED BOOK*

The proper score for a businessman golfer is 90. If he is better than that he is neglecting his business. If he's worse, he's neglecting his golf.

—St. Andrews Rotary Club Member

Thank God! Now I'll never have to practice again.

—Dorothy Germain Porter, 1977
After winning the US Senior Women's Amateur

Confidence is the most important single factor in this game, and no matter how great your natural talent, there is only one way to obtain and sustain it: work.

—Jack Nicklaus

You know guys like me and Fuzzy [Zoeller], you spend three hours on the range out here, but you know what happens—you spend two-and-a-half of that [socializing], and you wind up practicing for twenty-five minutes.

—Craig Stadler

Once you play in a tournament, you really get hooked on practice.

—Betsy Rawls

But golf is fluid. It's always evolving, changing, you are never there. That's the beauty of it—waking up tomorrow trying to become a better player. I enjoy that.

—TIGER WOODS

Train yourself to accept the fact that as a human being you are prone to mistakes. Take pride in being emotionally resilient and mentally tough.

—DR. BOB ROTELLA
SPORTS PSYCHOLOGIST

I open the driving range and I close it. I thought you ought to know that I work hard. I like practicing. I enjoy it. If I did not enjoy it I would not do it.

—VIJAY SINGH

The formula for success is simple: practice and concentration, then more practice and more concentration.

—BABE ZAHARIAS

I guess about fifteen yards.

—GARY PLAYER
IN RESPONSE TO SOMEONE ASKING HOW MUCH EXTRA LENGTH
HIS FITNESS ROUTINES HAVE AWARDED HIM.

I mean, at the time I would rather come here and sit on the lake than go practice and work on my golf game. Today I have a different philosophy.

—PAYNE STEWART
COMPARING HIS 1994 SEASON TO HIS 1999

The only natural golfer is a kid at five years old. Everyone else has to adjust their swings. Otherwise, we would go to the moon on a catapult if we didn't make any changes.

—NICK FALDO

I don't know if you're ever finished trying to improve. As soon as you feel like you are finished, then I guess you are finished, because you've already put a limit on your ability and what you can attain. I don't think that's right.

—TIGER WOODS

Why do we work so hard to feel so terrible?

> —HOLLIS STACY

Most people want to spend all their time on the golf course, but if they want to be good players they're wasting their time. You've got to hit balls every day.

> —LEE TREVINO

The best place to refine your swing is, of course, on the practice range. You will have an opportunity to make the same mistakes over and over again so that you no longer have to think about them, and they become part of your game.

> —STEPHEN BAKER

My theory is this: if you perfect your golf shots, your opponent will need more than an unfriendly attitude to defeat you.

> —VIRGINIA VAN WIE, 1934
> LEADING AMERICAN AMATEUR GOLFER

They say golf came easy to me because I was a good athlete, but there's not any girl on the LPGA Tour who worked near as hard as I did in golf. It is the toughest game I ever tackled.

—BABE ZAHARIAS

There is, and always will be, room for improvement.

—TIGER WOODS
FROM *HOW I PLAY GOLF*

To give yourself the best possible chance of playing to your potential, you must prepare for every eventuality. That means practice.

—SEVE BALLESTEROS

It is very rare that tension is observed in a practice swing, and this is so because the player, not feeling the necessity of being entirely correct, comes closer to assuming a natural posture. Let him take this naturalness into the actual shot.

—BOBBY JONES

A golfer has to train his swing on the practice tee, then trust it on the course.

—Dr. Bob Rotella
Sports Psychologist

I tell 'em to take one hundred chip shots and when they make one hundred in a row, we go on to putting.

—Jackie Burke
On giving golf lessons

I don't know why you're practicing so hard to finish second.

—Babe Zaharias
To players practicing before a tournament

I realized that achieving my goal of being number one was not a matter of improving my swing; it was about me improving as a total player—and as a person. Every shot must have a purpose.

—Annika Sörenstam

I want to win every week. I go to the driving range and bop 'til I drop.
—ROCKY THOMPSON

No golfer can ever become too good to practice.
—MAY HEZLET

When I was a schoolgirl my idea of good golf was a good drive. What happens afterwards did not matter . . . Fortunately, I revised my ideas fairly quickly and settled down to practicing the various kinds of approach play, determined to master all of them.
—PAMELA BARTON
BRITISH LADIES' AND US WOMEN'S AMATEURS CHAMPION IN 1936

My whole life is focused toward studying this game, understanding it, and teaching it. Listen, I don't care how smart you are, experience matters.
—DAVE PELZ

Go find some stimulating, fulfilling, challenging human endeavor that, unlike golf, does not require a commitment of time and effort to realize maximum enjoyment. And call me when you find it.

—JIM FLICK

Golf is my job and that motivates me. I have a talent. I want to develop it. Every year I learn a different shot. That's what great about golf. It's a very complex game, very challenging. You never stop learning.

—BETSY KING

I believe scoring and self-improvement are what the game is all about. The challenge to each golfer's ability to post a score is the very essence of the game.

—DAVE PELZ
FROM DAVE PELZ'S SHORT GAME BIBLE

He was the most dedicated practitioner of all time. His tenacity had no equal.

—PAUL RUNYAN
ON BEN HOGAN

CHAPTER TWELVE

Stardom:
From Jones to Hogan
to Nicklaus to Woods

Seating at the head table is strictly reserved. Only those Olympians whose standing in the greater sporting conscience is conveyed by the mere mention of their first name are welcome. A short list. Jack, Tiger, Arnold, Bobby, Byron, Ben.

Working the door at Club Stardom then gets interesting. We could accommodate a worthy collection of notables distinguished by their festive, if often obscure, nicknames. These would have to include: Old and Young Tom (Morris), Sir Walter (Hagen), the Squire (Gene Sarazen), the Human One Iron (Jim Barnes), Slammin' Sammy (Snead), the Ganton Greyhound (Harry Vardon) and the Silver Scot (Tommy Armour). Some of these fanciful monikers were likely creations of enterprising publicists and sports editors seeking a little sizzle back when everyone couldn't just be—to pick two more golf examples—Jock Hutchison or Dick Metz. They had to be Jumping Jock or Dashing Dick. Pulling an ancillary guest list depends upon the age of the considerer, with candidates like Freddie (Couples) and the Walrus (Craig Stadler), the Merry Mex (Lee Trevino), or the Big Easy (Ernie Els).

Calling the No Last Name Club to order presents a handy litmus test in selecting qualified candidates for membership. Figure that if you have to ask whether someone belongs that they probably don't. That's not to say the criteria never changes. The dues may be raised. Arguments pitting one generation's stars against another can get heated. It's hopeless, ultimately inconclusive, but can we agree that the true stars are lead pipe locks?

Having witnessed many of the greats, including Tiger playing some of his most superlative golf, the distinguished essayist Herbert Warren Wind, then 88, was asked who he thought was the best.

"You can't do that," he challenged. "You have to think of what clubs they used, what balls, what the courses were like. You have to take different people at different times."

His comments won't quell the debate but perhaps for the moment he can have the last word.

* * * * *

I'll sign everything. But please don't shove stuff at me, especially pens. I ruin about three hundred and sixty-five shirts a year from pens.

—ARNOLD PALMER

———◆———

I swear Arnold would sign an autograph at a red light. If a guy pulled up to Arnold in a car and asked him for an autograph, Arnold probably would pull over if he could read his lips.

—LEE TREVINO
ON PALMER'S REPUTATION AS A NICE PERSON

———◆———

Arnold [Palmer] said to the waitress: 'You shouldn't use this kind of ketchup; Heinz is better.' After she left, I asked him: 'What's with the ketchup?' He said: 'I have a ketchup contract.'

—RAY CAVE

———◆———

It's hard being the father of a famous son.

—JACK NICKLAUS
AFTER JACK NICKLAUS II WON AN AMATEUR TOURNAMENT

I asked my wife, Gill, if she wanted a Versace dress, diamonds, or pearls as a present and she said no. When I asked her what she did want, she said: 'A divorce,' but I told her I wasn't planning to spend that much.
— NICK FALDO

Somebody asked me once, Who's better? Jack Nicklaus or Ben Hogan? Well, my answer was, I saw Nicklaus watch Hogan practice. But I never saw Hogan watch Nicklaus.
— TOMMY BOLT

I didn't have to deal with that kind of subjectivity [e.g. Baseball Hall of Fame balloting]. I was Pat Bradley, Hall-of-Famer, the moment I won my thirtieth.
— PAT BRADLEY
ON HOW SHE PLAYED HER WAY INTO THE LPGA
HALL OF FAMER WITH THIRTY WINS

I . . . don't think they have a sense for how much golf talent is out there and what it really means to be great at golf. How good these guys are, even the guys whose names they don't know, how really good and special those players are.
— TOM COYNE
ON THE PUBLIC

I don't like to be honored by anything. I don't see why anybody makes a big deal out of a poor little Mexican guy that hits a golf ball better than most people.

— LEE TREVINO

Who's caught up with Tiger? Who is this person? I haven't met him yet. All it looks like to me is Tiger is catching up with God.

— PAUL GOYDOS,
ON TIGER WOODS

I never wanted to be a millionaire. I just wanted to live like one.

— WALTER HAGEN

I don't think any of us ever thought we'd be getting the attention we do now ... You look at my dad, he was maybe the greatest teacher ever, and he never got this notoriety. It just shows you how much golf has taken off and the game has changed.

— BUTCH HARMON
GOLF TEACHER

Nobody's seen me. I haven't been on television. I've been going off the 10th tee early in the morning. I've been playing, literally, in front of tens and tens of people.

—TOM KITE
ON HIS BAD 1995 SEASON

When I finally quit, for the first time in my life I am going to unpack everything, get all of my clothes pressed, and put them on hangers.

—NANCY LOPEZ, 1984
ON BEING CATERED TO ON THE TOUR

Louise, we've got to hide this $600 before we hit the road. Since we're rich, we're bound to get robbed. But if we hide it, maybe they won't get it all.

—BYRON NELSON
TO HIS WIFE AFTER WINNING HIS FIRST BIG CHECK

All you got to do to write a book is win one tournament. All of a sudden, you're telling everybody where the Vs ought to point. And them that don't win, they're haberdashers. They sell sweaters and slacks and call themselves pros.

—GEORGE LOW

I really like the attention. I guess I'm sort of a ham.

> —CAROL MANN
> ON HER HEIGHT AND THE ATTENTION IT BRINGS HER

I seem to be a target for everything. I must walk around with a dart board on my back.

> —GREG NORMAN
> ON CRITICISM

I signed Lee Buck Trevino Pit Barbecue, Albuquerque, New Mexico.

> —LEE TREVINO
> ON AN ATTRACTIVE WOMAN WHO ASKED TREVINO
> TO AUTOGRAPH HER BODY

Nowadays, wherever I go, people say, 'That's the man who got the double eagle.' Actually, it was just a piece of luck. They forget the championships I won.

> —GENE SARAZEN

I opened my locker and there were a dozen new shirts, boxes of balls and two pair of golf shoes. Now that I can afford them, they give them to me.

—PAUL AZINGER

I did envisage being this successful as a player, but not all the hysteria around it off the golf course.

—TIGER WOODS

I love what people say about me now. I have never received as many accolades as I am receiving now. I would like people to say, Oh, Byron was a pretty good player, but he is a nice man.

—BYRON NELSON
WHEN ASKED HOW WE WANTS TO BE REMEMBERED, *GOLF DIGEST*

I wish my name was Tom Kite.

—IAN BAKER-FINCH
ON SIGNING AUTOGRAPHS

You listen to all my jokes, and then you go and follow Arnie.

—CHI-CHI RODRIGUEZ
KIDDING WITH THE GALLERY AT A SENIOR TOUR EVENT

I think I just played with the next God.

—CURTIS STRANGE
ON ERNIE ELS

I played the Tour in 1967 and told jokes and nobody laughed. Then I won the Open the next year, told the same jokes, and everybody laughed like hell.

—LEE TREVINO

I just love American girls. That is a big attraction for me over here. The girls have class and are incredibly beautiful. There are nice girls in Europe, but not too many of them get to golf events.

—SERGIO GARCIA

What I want is to be obscure and happy.

—Ian Baker-Finch

Playing golf is not hot work. Cutting sugar cane for a dollar a day—that's hot work. Hotter than my first wrist watch.

—Chi-Chi Rodriguez

I wouldn't know him if he came up and bit me.

—Payne Stewart
On his 1993 Ryder Cup opponent, Joakim Haeggman

I learned you can't drink whiskey and play golf.

—John Daly

I don't like the glamour. I just like the game.

—Ben Hogan

The players themselves can be classified into two groups—the attractions and the entry fees.

—JIMMY DEMARET

Someday I'll tell my grandkids I played in the same tournament as Tiger Woods. We are witnessing a phenomenon here that the game may never, ever see again.

—TOM WATSON

I suspect that the Jones humor has been what really got him through all those trying years of being a celebrity in our country.

—PAUL GALLICO

A big-name winner like Palmer is a modern King Midas. Everything he drinks, smokes, wears, or drives can turn to gold. All he has to do is testify, yes, that's what I put on my hair, smoke, drink, wear, drive, swing and hit.

—TONY LEMA

That little man is the only one in golf I've ever been afraid of.
>—LLOYD MANGRUM
>ON BEN HOGAN

God said to Faldo, as He once said to Nicklaus: 'You will have the skills like no other.' Then he whispered to Ballesteros, as he whispered to Palmer, 'But they will love you more.'
>—TOM CALLAHAN

Sorry, I don't play golf while on vacation.
>—BEN HOGAN
>WHEN ASKED IF HE WAS WILLING TO PLAY A ROUND OF
>GOLF WITH THE KING OF BELGIUM

Perhaps if I dyed my hair peroxide blonde and called myself 'The Great White Tadpole,' people would take more notice of me.
>—IAN WOOSNAM, SOUNDING A LITTLE JEALOUS OF GOLFER
>GREG NORMAN, "THE GREAT WHITE SHARK"

I played a practice round with Hubert [Green] the other day, and when we got to the ninth green, I heard a fan say, 'Why does Hubert have two caddies?'

    —KEN GREEN
      ON HIS OBSCURITY

You can make a lot of money in this game. Just ask my ex-wives. Both of them are so rich that neither of their husbands work.

    —LEE TREVINO

To be truthful, I think golfers are overpaid. It's unreal, and I have trouble dealing with the guilt sometime.

    —COLIN MONTGOMERIE

More people show up to watch Lee Trevino change shoes than watch me tee off.

    —ORVILLE MOODY

Since I don't understand English, I thought they were for me.

—ISAO AOKI
ON CHEERS FOR JACK NICKLAUS, WITH WHOM HE PLAYED
IN THE 1980 US OPEN

Showmanship was needed and happily I possessed a flair for that, too, and I used it. In fact some fellows sort of believed I invented the kind of showmanship which, in those early days, began to put golf on a big-time money basis.

—WALTER HAGEN

I was so far away I thought I was in Massachusetts.

—JUSTIN LEONARD
1997 BRITISH OPEN CHAMPION
ON HIS ROOKIE YEAR, AFTER A PARKING LOT ATTENDANT FORCED HIM
TO PARK IN THE SPECTATOR'S PARKING LOT BECAUSE THE ATTENDANT
DIDN'T BELIEVE HE WAS A COMPETITOR

Seve [Ballesteros] owns Spain and Greg [Norman] just bought a house at Bay Hill and a $73,000 Ferrari, and here I am worrying about making my next rent payment.

—MIKE NICOLETTE
AFTER BEATING NORMAN IN A PLAYOFF, WITH
SEVE BALLESTEROS IN CONTENTION

I don't answer the phone. I get the feeling whenever I do that there will be someone on the other end.

—FRED COUPLES

If I ever find the SOB who came up with these cards, I'm going to shoot him.

—LEE TREVINO
HIS REACTION TO FANS TRYING TO GET HIM AUTOGRAPH
HIS GOLF SPORTS CARD

I got my name in the record books and for every golf ball I hit I got to know someone . . . caddies, kings, golf fans, and even a few phonies.

—WALTER HAGEN

Hagen was at home with all classes of society, far more than Dempsey or Ruth, the other great champions of the twenties, whom he resembled in the blackness of his hair, his amazing magnetism, his love of admiring crowds, and his rise from humble beginnings.

—GENE SARAZEN
FROM HIS BOOK *THIRTY YEARS OF CHAMPIONSHIP GOLF*

Nobody cares if John Daly shoots 80. They just want to see him hit a ball.

—GENE SARAZEN

How long does John Daly drive a golf ball? When I was a kid, I didn't go that far on vacation.

—CHI-CHI RODRIGUEZ

CHAPTER THIRTEEN

Courses:

From St. Andrews to Pebble Beach

It's enough for most of us to hit our ball, find it, and hit it again. There are few additional obligations with the green fee. The etiquette must be mastered along with something of the language. A recognition of the importance of attitude and preferably some restraint will come in handy but certainly, Lord knows, are not required. With any luck, having survived the dicey and pricey questions of equipment, finding the time for golf and becoming inured to embarrassing oneself in public, the newcomer may forge a measure of basic competency among friends.

The rest is pretty much gravy. Literally millions of dollars are poured into the ground on our behalf to create an aesthetically pleasing and challenging environment. It would be a shame not to take much notice. The golfer who stops to consider what makes a "good" course is on his way to a deeper contentment. Appreciation for the landscape and detail of design opens new doors of understanding. Our experts know this and reserve some of their most trenchant, warm and meaningful insights for the subtleties of the course that, as the good doctor MacKenzie observes, may defy even the strongest first impressions.

It's true Oakmont and Augusta National are gated communities. Then again, the likelihood of our taking the field in Yankee Stadium or playing a set at Wimbledon is laughable. The historic venues of golf's oldest championship nevertheless remain open. Even without our clubs, merely attending a tournament to acquaint ourselves with a great course can be enriching.

Every round played offers a live, three-dimensional presentation on the architect's intellect and imagination, the course an expression of his judgment, skill and, quite possibly, his sense of whimsy and bias. The consuming interest in our ball also makes it easy to overlook that our search, though far removed, is reminiscent of a quest that Man has been making since he first stood upright.

* * * * *

Golf architecture is the art and science of designing and building golf courses, and it involves much knowledge of landscape, soils, grasses, water drainage, engineering, and sometimes—I feel—black magic.

—ALISTAIR COOKE
FROM *WORKERS, ARISE! SHOUT FORE*

In discussing the need for simplicity of design, the chief object of every golf course architect worth his salt is to imitate the beauties of nature so closely as to make his work indistinguishable from nature itself.

—ALISTER MACKENZIE
FROM HIS BOOK *GOLF ARCHITECTURE*

Twenty years ago people weren't aware of [golf] as a profession . . . Now the first question in the marketing is, 'Who designed this course?'

—TOM DOAK

A good golf course makes you want to play so badly that you hardly have the time to change your shoes.

—BEN CRENSHAW

Crooked Stick is so long I had to take the curvature of the Earth into consideration.

—DAVID FEHERTY
ON CROOKED STICK GOLF CLUB

I cleaned all the rough and all the branches on the course. I'm sure the members at Oakland Hills won't be losing any golf balls this week.

—SEVE BALLESTEROS
AFTER ONLY HITTING THREE FAIRWAYS IN HIS THREE
1995 RYDER CUP MATCHES

It was a morning when all nature shouted Fore! The breeze, as it blew gently up from the valley, seemed to bring a message of hope and cheer . . . The fairway, as yet unscarred by the irons of a hundred dubs, smiled greenly up at the azure sky.

—P.G. WODEHOUSE
IN HIS BOOK *HEART OF A GOOF*

I'm not going back to a place where they never rake the goddamn bunkers.

       —BEN HOGAN
           AFTER HIS BRITISH OPEN VICTORY AT CARNOUSTIE, 1953

           ———•———

It would look great in my obituary, I said. He was a member of Shinnecock Hills.

       —DAVE ANDERSON

           ———•———

There's no such thing as a green with too much slope.

       —TOM DOAK
        GOLF DIGEST

           ———•———

And I've been a proponent of this for a long time, that if somebody has come out intentionally and puts sand in these divots, then they're trying to repair part of the golf course. So a freshly sanded divot constitutes ground under repair.

       —PAYNE STEWART

If you try to fight the course, it will beat you.

—LOU GRAHAM

The ardent golfer would play Mount Everest if somebody put a flagstick on top.

—PETE DYE

About this toun are the fairest and largest of any pairt in Scotland, fitt for Archery, Goffing, Ryding, and all other exercises; they doe surpasse the fields of Montrose or St. Andrews.

—SIR ROBERT GORDON, 1630

Would you like to see a city given over soul and body to a tyrannizing game? If you would, there's little need to rove, for St. Andrews is the abject city's name.

—R.F. MURRAY, 1885
AMERICAN STUDENT AT ST. ANDREWS UNIVERSITY

From what has been said as to the changes in the links, the balls, and the clubs, it is obvious that the round ought to be done in much fewer strokes now . . . How many fewer it is not easy . . . to determine. Some say twenty. I incline to think fifteen or sixteen . . .

  —JAMES BALFOUR, 1887
   ON THE OLD COURSE AT ST. ANDREWS

———•———

St. Andrews? I feel like I'm back visiting an old grandmother. She's crotchety and eccentric but also elegant. Anyone who doesn't fall in love with her has no imagination.

  —TONY LEMA

———•———

Maybe we Americans should come look at [St. Andrews], considering the crap we are building today.

  —CURTIS STRANGE

———•———

This is the origin of the game, golf in its purest form, and it's still played that way on a course seemingly untouched by time. Every time I play here, it reminds me that this is still a game.

  —ARNOLD PALMER
   ON THE OLD COURSE AT ST. ANDREWS

Game plan? St. Andrews is the only course in the world where the only thing you try to do is miss all the bunkers. That's the game plan.

—STEVE ELKINGTON

St. Andrews is drenched in golf. It reminds me of a Spanish town when bull-fighting is afoot. Every man, woman, and child seems to have a stake in the game. The butcher, the baker, and the candlestick-maker but finish their day's work to be off to the links.

—PETER LAWLESS

There's nothing wrong with the Old Course at St. Andrews that a hundred bulldozers couldn't put right.

—ED FURGOL

The reason the Road hole at St. Andrews is the most difficult par 4 in the world is that it was designed as a par 6.

—BEN CRENSHAW

They are the same people who knock the pyramids because they don't have elevators.

—JIM FERREE, MEMBER OF THE PGA AND CHAMPIONS TOUR
ON PLAYERS WHO COMPLAIN ABOUT ST. ANDREWS

The worst piece of mess I've ever played. I think they had some sheep and goats there that died and they just covered them up.

—SCOTT HOCH
AFTER PLAYING THE OLD COURSE AT ST. ANDREWS

St. Andrews never impressed me at all. I wondered how it got such a reputation. The only reason could be on account of its age.

—BILL MEHLHORN

The more I studied the Old Course, the more I loved it; and the more I loved it, the more I studied it.

—BOBBY JONES
ON ST. ANDREWS

Until you play it, St. Andrews looks like the sort of real estate you couldn't give away.

—SAM SNEAD

They don't build courses for people. They build monuments to themselves.

—GEORGE ARCHER
ON GOLF ARCHITECTS

You know you're in for a challenge when the rough comes up over your shoes.

—ERNIE ELS
GOLF DIGEST

The name Pebble Beach might suggest a seaside course in the manner of the links of Britain. But it is far from that. I can think of no approximate parallel.

—PAT WARD-THOMAS

The best architects feel it to be their duty to make the path to the hole as free as possible from annoying difficulties for the less skillful golfers, while at the same time presenting to the scratch players a route calling for the best shots at their command.

    —ROBERT HUNTER

Ma God! It's like playing up a spout.

    —JAMIE ANDERSON
        WINNER OF THREE CONSECUTIVE BRITISH OPENS (1877–1879),
        AFTER STRIKING FIVE BALLS OUT OF PLAY ON THE FIRST
        HOLE AT HOYLAKE

Good greens have done nothing but give the golfer a split personality. First, he is a violent, physical athlete who tries to slash enormous divots out of the fairways . . . But when on the green, the golfer becomes . . . a solemn, timid, prayerful soul who wants only to peck tenderly at the ball.

    —DAN JENKINS
        AUTHOR

At Jinja there is both hotel and golf course. The latter is, I believe, the only course in the world which posts a special rule that the player may remove his ball from hippopotamus footprints.

—EVELYN WAUGH

Rough open ground; especially, a tract of low-lying seaside land on the east coast of the lowlands held by a town as a common . . . Such land is characteristically sandy, treeless, undulating, or hummocky, often with dunes and typical ground cover is bent grass with gorse bushes.

—PETER DAVIES, 1992
ON THE NATURE OF EARLY SCOTTISH LINKSLAND GOLF COURSES,
"DESIGNED BY GOD" IN HIS *THE HISTORICAL DICTIONARY OF GOLF*

I lost a ball in your rough today. I dropped another ball over my shoulder and lost it too—and while looking for that one, I lost a caddie.

—JOCK HUTCHINSON
COMPLAINING TO AN OFFICIAL ABOUT THE
1926 US OPEN COURSE CONDITIONS

How do you read mud?

—TOMMY BOLT
COMMENTING ON BAD COURSE CONDITIONS

The reformers are trying to reform the game from the wrong end. The thing that needs changing is not the golf ball or the golf club or the golf trousers. It is the golf course.

—RUBE GOLDBERG
FROM *LEFT-HANDED GOLF COURSES: OUR GREATEST NEED*

Every time you see a piece of land you almost immediately see a great hole, but if it doesn't fit in with the flow and rhythm of the rest, it has to be discarded. Most good architects end up abandoning their favorite child.

—DAVID MCLAY KIDD
GOLF COURSE DESIGNER

I think I'll go cold turkey in the end and build golf courses. I'll torture other people.

—DAVID FEHERTY

We live with bad conditions. We should be able to cope with them better than Americans.

—BERNHARD LANGER
ON EUROPEAN COURSES

If we all played golf like Macdonald Smith, the National Open Championship could be played on one course every day in the year and never a divot mark would scar the beautiful fairway. He treats the grass of a golf course as though it were an altar cloth.

—TOMMY ARMOUR

It doesn't matter what golf course you're on, you still got to hit the shots.

—RETIEF GOOSEN

If there's a golf course in heaven, I hope it's like Augusta National. I just don't want an early tee time.

—GARY PLAYER

I vowed that I would bring this monster to its knees.

—BEN HOGAN
ON OAKLAND HILLS AFTER HE DEFENDED
HIS US OPEN TITLE THERE IN 1951

The old style courses were designed to make a player hit a variety of shots high, low, draw, fade, bump and run, floating chips. Now with a lot of the new courses, our only choice is to hit it high and soft.

—COREY PAVIN

A golf course should be a bit wild, at least in some corners. A weed now and again would be a great relief.

—PETER THOMSON
PRO GOLFER AND MEMBER OF THE WORLD GOLF HALL OF FAME

The biggest problem we have in golf is course conditions.

—SEVE BALLESTEROS
ON THE CONDITION OF COURSES ON THE EUROPEAN TOUR

The trick for the developer, as devised through his architect, is to build something that is photogenically stunning, however impractical, extravagant or absurd. Never mind the golfer, that most gullible of all citizens.

—PETER THOMSON
PRO GOLFER AND MEMBER OF THE WORLD GOLF HALL OF FAME

Golf architects can't play golf themselves and make damn sure that no one else can.

—ANONYMOUS

Saw a course you'd really like, Trent. On the first tee you drop the ball over your left shoulder.

—JIMMY DEMARET
TO COURSE DESIGNER ROBERT TRENT JONES. SR.

When the ducks are walking, you know it is too windy to be playing golf.

—DAVE STOCKTON

A ball will always come to rest halfway down a hill, unless there is sand or water at the bottom.

—HENRY BEARD
HUMORIST

It's a longish hole. We start on the first tree here and hole out in the doorway of the Hotel Astor in Times Square. A distance, I imagine, of about sixteen miles.

      —P.G. WODEHOUSE
        FROM *THE LONG HOLE*

Golf is not a fair game, so why build a course fair?

      —PETE DYE
        GOLF COURSE ARCHITECT

I like going there for golf. America's one vast golf course these days.

      —EDWARD VIII
        DUKE OF WINDSOR

This is another thing I like about golf, the exclusiveness. Of course most country clubs exclude the wrong kinds of people, such as me. But I hold out the hope that somewhere there's a club that bans first wives.

      —P.J. O'ROURKE

Columbus went around the world in 1492. That isn't a lot of strokes when you consider the course.

—LEE TREVINO

The golfer is always irrational about the place in which he first falls in love. Ask anyone. For me, it was a public golf course in Bellport, New York.

—MICHAEL BAMBERGER
FROM *THIS GOLFING LIFE*

Sixty-one million dollars. It's the most expensive golf hole of all time. We moved more than a million yards of earth on that hole alone. Unprecedented! Moving that much to build a whole course would be massive.

—DONALD TRUMP
ON A GOLF HOLE ON HIS COURSE

By all means screw their women and drink their booze, but never write one word about their bloody awful golf courses.

—HENRY LONGHURST
TO A FELLOW JOURNALIST BEING PRESSED TO MAKE
A TRIP TO A NEW EXPENSIVE GOLF DEVELOPMENT

Every game of golf that has ever been played—whether the medal was 68 of 168—has taken place on a golf course that measured eight inches or less. I arrived at the dimensions . . . by taking a ruler and measuring my own head from back to front.

> —EDDIE LOOS
> AMERICAN GOLF PROFESSIONAL AND TEACHER

No other game combines the wonder of nature with the discipline of sport in such carefully planned ways. A great golf course both frees and challenges a golfer's mind.

> —TOM WATSON

I just do not want to play those long, dull, wide-open turf nursery courses any more. Where is the challenge in just beating at the ball? Length is only one factor.

> —JACK NICKLAUS

Great golf courses seem to have an uncanny way of producing wonderful golf tournaments, with unforgettable shots and world-class champions.

> —GARY PLAYER
> FROM GARY PLAYER'S *TOP GOLF COURSES OF THE WORLD*

A hole should always give one the impression that it owes its existence to its own intrinsic merits, to its individuality and character, and not, as too often happens, to the fact that it had to be there because, forsooth, there was no other place to put it.

—GARDEN G. SMITH, 1898
FROM *THE WORLD OF GOLF*

Bunkers have long been steeped in mystique and the best of them are the stuff of legend.

—DEREK LAWRENSON
FROM *STEP-BY-STEP GOLF TECHNIQUES:*
MASTERING THE LONG AND SHORT GAME

Never call a Scottish bunker a sand trap, at least not in the presence of your Scottish host . . . They are designed to penalize you for making a stupid shot rather than frame a pretty green fairway or provide a soft white cushion for your 6-iron shot to the green.

—JAMES DODSON, 1997
FROM *GOLF IN THE HOMELAND*

The behavior etiquette for greenside bunkers should go into reverse. Players should be forbidden to smooth them in any way. The bunker should be the fearful place it once was, not the perfect surface from which a pro expects to float his ball out stone dead.

> —Michael Halls

The object of the bunker or trap is not only to punish a physical mistake, to punish a lack of control, but also to punish pride and egotism.

> —Charles Blair Macdonald
> Noted golf course designer and the so-called
> "father of American golf architecture"

If some hole does not possess striking individuality through some gift of nature, it must be given as much as possible artificially, and the artifice must be introduced in so subtle a manner as to make it seem natural.

> —A.W. Tillinghast

Even in defeat, the scenic surroundings at Pebble Beach were absolutely dazzling, the dream of an artist who had been drinking gin and sobering up on absinthe. It is too extravagantly decorated not to be a painting.

—O.B. KEELER
FROM *THE BOBBY JONES STORY*

A golf course is the epitome of all that is purely transitory in the universe, a space not to dwell in, but to get over as quickly as possible.

—JEAN GIRAUDOUX

There are one hundred and eighteen golf holes here. All I have to do is eliminate one hundred.

—PERRY MAXWELL
ON DESIGNING PRAIRIE DUNES

Pine Valley is an examination in golf.

—BERNARD DARWIN
APPRAISAL OF ONE OF THE WORLD'S BEST
AND MOST DIFFICULT TESTS OF GOLF

Foursomes have left the first tee there and have never been seen again. They just find their shoelaces and bags.

—Bob Hope
EVALUATING PINE VALLEY

———•———

Nowhere [but Pine Valley] is the brave and beautiful shot rewarded so splendidly in comparison to the weak and faltering; nowhere is there such a terrible contrast between reward and punishment, and yet the examination is just.

—Pat Ward-Thomas
ON THE PINE VALLEY GOLF COURSE

———•———

Always count your blessings. Be thankful you are able to be out on a beautiful course. Most people in the world don't have that opportunity.

—Fred Couples

———•———

Palm Springs is an inland sandbar man has wrested from rodents and the Indians to provide a day camp for over-privileged adults.

—Jim Murray
ON THE SELF-PROCLAIMED GOLF CAPITAL OF THE WORLD

A golf course is an outdoor insane asylum peopled with madmen suffering from the delusion that they will finally master the game.
—ROBERT H. DAVIS

If I ever reach a par 5 in two, they change it to a par 4.
—FRED FUNK

There is a saying around Georgia that the Augusta National Golf Club is the closest thing to heaven for a golfer and it's just as hard to get into.
—JOE GESHWILER
JOURNALIST

Frankly, I was overwhelmed by the exciting possibilities of a golf course set in the midst of such a nursery.
—BOBBY JONES
OBSERVING THE THREE HUNDRED AND SIXTY-FIVE-ACRE FRUITLANDS
NURSERY THAT WOULD BECOME AUGUSTA NATIONAL

We could make the greens so slick we'd have to furnish ice skates on the first tee.

—HORD HARDIN
MASTERS CHAIRMAN

While I have never met Pete Dye, I know him well. He is five hundred years old and has absorbed the wisdom of the ages. He has a pointed hat and a flowing robe embroidered with occult symbols . . .

—PETER DOBEREINER
ON GOLF COURSE ARCHITECT PETE DYE, WHOSE COURSES
ARE OFTEN CONSIDERED MAGICALLY HARD

Golfers just love punishment. And that's where I come in.

—PETE DYE
GOLF COURSE ARCHITECT

Don't give me the excuse that you weren't standing there, and you approved it. I don't want to listen to your alibis, let's just fix the hole.

—ALICE DYE
AMATEUR GOLF CHAMPION, TO HER HUSBAND PETE DYE,
ON A GOLF COURSE CONSTRUCTION SITE

Faith, sir, she looks like the Old Course.

—TOM MORRIS

LOOKING THROUGH A NINETEENTH-CENTURY TELESCOPE AT THE MOON

Old Tom Morris was popular and consistently successful at endearing himself to the owners of the land for a new course by remarking on his arrival that surely providence had intended this for a golf links.

—DAVID HAMILTON

AUTHOR

Broadly speaking, the penal school follows more or less the methods of Tom Morris and the brothers Dunn, in scattering plenty of bunkers in places most likely to catch inaccurate shots.

—TOM SIMPSON, 1931

GOLF COURSE ARCHITECT, IN HIS BOOK *THE GAME OF GOLF*

I'd like to see the fairways more narrow. Then everybody would have to play from the rough, not just me.

—SEVE BALLESTEROS

This is easily the finest course in the world . . . I am glad it is difficult to get here and I am not going to tell anyone about Dornoch. I want to keep it for myself, the way it is, and come back every year until I die.

—AN AMERICAN GOLF ARCHITECT

This is the essence of strategic architecture: to encourage initiative, reward a well-played stroke, and yet to insist that there must be planning and honest self-appraisal behind the daring.

—ROBERT TRENT JONES, 1954
COURSE DESIGNER, ON STRATEGIC DESIGN

Americans are less mystical about what produced their inland or meadow courses; they are the product of the bulldozer, rotary ploughs, mowers, sprinkler systems and alarmingly generous wads of folding money.

—ALISTAIR COOKE

It is today an accepted principle of golfing architecture that the tiger should be teased and trapped and tested, while the rabbit should be left to peace, since he can make his own hell for himself.

—BERNARD DARWIN
ON HOW COURSE ARCHITECTURE AFFECTS THE
LOW AND MIDDLE TO HIGH HANDICAPPERS

No matter how skillfully one may lay out the holes and diversify them, nevertheless one must get the thrill of nature. The puny strivings of the architect do not quench our thirst for the ultimate.

—George Thomas

At most golf courses, eagles of the feathered and golfing variety are very rare indeed . . . but not nearly so rare as the sight of an albatross, either in the air or on a par five.

—Derek Lawrenson
FROM *STEP-BY-STEP GOLF TECHNIQUES:*
MASTERING THE LONG AND SHORT GAME

The last mile or so runs down the side of the links and the first exciting glimpse of St. Andrews is caught. All too soon the train carries us ahead, wreathing the seventeenth tee in its smoke as it chugs into the gloom of the station.

—Joyce Wethered, 1933
FROM HER ESSAY *THE ESSENCE OF SCOTTISH GOLF*

The object of inventors is to reduce the skill required for golf. If it were not for the counterskill of architects, the game would be emasculated.

—John L. Low
A FOUNDER OF THE OXFORD AND CAMBRIDGE
GOLFING SOCIETY IN 1897

Mediocre players are just out there messing up the sand traps.

—Lloyd Mangrum

Hey, I won three times and I never even got an outhouse.

—Jimmy Demaret
ON THE BRIDGES BUILT IN HONOR OF GENE SARAZEN
AND BYRON NELSON AT AUGUSTA NATIONAL

[Grand Cypress] is like one of those hot-air hand dryers in toilets. It's a great idea and everybody uses it once, but never again. It takes too long.

—David Feherty

Water holes are sacrificial waters where you make a steady gift of your pride and high-priced golf balls.

—TOMMY BOLT

Putting on Winged Foot greens is like playing miniature golf without the boards.

—HALE IRWIN

Fairways are bottlenecked where most of us would hit the driver. That's the narrower part, and it's a little unfair. I feel the fairways should be the same width for everyone.

—NICK PRICE
ON THE CUT OF THE ROUGH AND OTHER HAZARDS

If you birdie the 18th [at Sawgrass], do you get a free game?

—JOHN MAHAFFEY

When I do a course that is in the trees and hills, it has to evolve. But any time we get a flat piece of property, I'll just take a piece of paper and sketch it.

—JACK NICKLAUS, 1991

———•———

Most of the courses today, the guys shoot twenty under par and think they've accomplished something . . . Golf was meant to be a great game of skill, not just strength. You get around here, you have to have some skills.

—CHI-CHI RODRIGUEZ
EVALUATING PGA WEST

———•———

Dream golf is simply golf played on another course. We chip from glass tables onto moving stairways; we swing in a straitjacket, through masses of cobweb, and awaken not with any sense of unjust hazard but only with a regret that the round can never be completed.

—JOHN UPDIKE

Now this whole safety business on golf courses is chimerical. There can never be serious safety standards of any consequence connected with golf any more than there can be with baseball.

—DESMOND MUIRHEAD
GOLF COURSE ARCHITECT

Rail-splitting produced an immortal president in Abraham Lincoln; but golf, with 29,000 courses, hasn't produced even a good A-Number-1 congressman.

—WILL ROGERS

I've never seen Augusta so beautiful. If heaven is this pretty, I'd go there tomorrow.

—GENE SARAZEN

I just happened to be hitting the right sort of ball for the day.

—JOHN BALL
EXPLAINING HOW HE WON A MEDAL COMPETITION
IN THE WIND AT HOYLAKE

I had never seen or heard of a bent grass before. I had played on sand greens and Bermuda, but these were frightening, slick and fast. I three-putted everything.

 —BYRON NELSON
  RECALLING HIS FIRST ENCOUNTER WITH BENT GRASS
  GREENS IN THE 1934 US AMATEUR

Golf courses are not the countryside—they're outdoors for people who wish the countryside had wipe clean surfaces.

 —LINDA SMITH

I believe in leaving a way open for a player who can only drive one hundred yards, if he can keep the drive straight.

 —CHARLES BLAIR MACDONALD
  NOTED GOLF COURSE DESIGNER AND THE SO-CALLED "FATHER OF
  AMERICAN GOLF ARCHITECTURE," ON HIS BALANCED COURSES

To learn golf architecture one must know golf itself, its companionship, its joys, its sorrows, its battles—one must play golf and love it.

 —GEORGE THOMAS
  GOLF COURSE ARCHITECT

The mystique of Muirfield lingers on. So does the memory of Carnoustie's foreboding. So does the scenic wonder of Turnberry, and the haunting incredibility of Prestwick, and the pleasant deception of Troon. But put them all together and St. Andrews can play their low ball for atmosphere.

—Dan Jenkins

Players don't get relief from divots in fairways or footprints in bunkers. Why should they get relief from spike marks on greens?

—Jeff Hall
USGA official

Sir Guy Campbell's classic account of the formation of the links . . . suggests that such notable features of our planet as dinosaurs, the prairies, the Himalayas, the seagull, the female of the species herself, were accidental by-products of the Almighty's preoccupation with the creation of the Old Course at St. Andrews.

—Alistair Cooke

Lord only knows what the colorful and gruff [Alister] Mackenzie would have made of the lava flows of Mauna Kea, or the island green 17th hole at the Tournament Players Club at Sawgrass.

—TOM DOAK
ON MODERN GOLF COURSES

I fell violently in love with Cypress Point. But I was furious because I was so besotted with the beauty of it that I just couldn't hit a golf ball.

—ENID WILSON

When a tourist drives through Switzerland, he is staggered by its prodigal beauty; around the corner from the most wondrous view he has ever beheld he comes upon a view that surpasses it—and on and on, endless. Ballybunion is something like that. One stirring hole followed by another and another.

—HERBERT WARREN WIND
ON THE BALLYBUNION GOLF COURSE, *THE NEW YORKER*

Where are the windmills and animals?

—FUZZY ZOELLER
ON PETE DYE'S TPC STADIUM COURSE AT SAWGRASS

A good golf course is like good music. It does not necessarily appeal the first time one plays it.

—ALISTER MACKENZIE

A golf course is nothing but a poolroom moved outdoors.

—BARRY FITZGERALD

Bunkers are not placed on a course haphazard, but they are made at particular places to catch particular kinds of defective shots.

—JAMES BRAID

At St. Andrews you can hit pretty good shots and get shafted because the fairways are hard. The ball keeps rolling and ends up in a fairway bunker. You can also hit bad shots and finish perfect.

—SCOTT HOCH

The golf course is made for playing a game! So go there and *play* golf.
　　—CHUCK HOGAN

Golf courses are like children. I have no favorite.
　　—ROBERT TRENT JONES, SR.

The average golfer is inclined to become emotional when talking about golf course architecture.
　　—RICHARD S. TUFTS
　　GOLF DIGEST, 1968

A golf course is a field of maneuver and action, employing the military and engineering side of the game. It opens up a series of tactical and stratetgical opportunities, the implications of which it would be well for every golfer to grasp.
　　—H.N. WETHERED
　　THE ARCHITECTURAL SIDE OF GOLF BY H.N. WETHERED
　　AND TOM SIMPSON

Until the days of Allan Robertson in the second quarter of the nineteenth century and his successor Old Tom Morris who lived in the twentieth, man did not change existing land to create golfing grounds.

—GEOFFREY S. CORNISH
GOLF ARCHITECT AND WRITER

————◆————

They've done $500 worth of renovations on the greens, but I'll bet in the books it's $700,000. A good husband on a weekend could have done it.

—LEE TREVINO
ON THE GROUNDS REPAIR DONE AT THE MASTERS

————◆————

Every hole should be a difficult par and a comfortable bogey.

—ROBERT TRENT JONES

————◆————

Because you pray after you play.

—FUZZY ZOELLER
WHEN ASKED HOW AMEN CORNER AT AUGUSTA
NATIONAL GOT ITS NAME

While PGA touring professionals have been brought up on manicured courses since junior golf, the foreign contingent have been raised on bad lies and rough weather requiring mental toughness.

>—PETE DYE
>ON WHY INTERNATIONAL GOLFERS HAVE SURPASSED THE AMERICANS

Fifty percent of the fairways we play on today are better than ninety percent of the greens we played on thirty years ago.

>—JIM FERREE

It is quite certain that, had the ground on which ordinary inland golf is played today been the only available ground for the purpose, the game would never have been invented at all.

>—GARDEN G. SMITH
>1898 *THE WORLD OF GOLF*

The more you study the course, the more you appreciate what a great test it is.

>—PHIL MICKELSON

The USGA doesn't want to recognize the fact that today's players are better than ever. They seem willing to do anything to prevent us from shooting scores that would make us appear better than the great names of the past.

—HALE IRWIN
ON THE COURSE SET-UP FOR THE US OPEN

Golf courses are beautiful. Many people think mature men have no appreciation for beauty except in immature women. This isn't true, and anyway, we'd rather be playing golf.

—P.J. O'ROURKE

It can be asserted with total confidence that one of the most important reasons why we golfers believe golf to be the finest of all games is that it is played in beautiful surroundings.

—PETER DOBEREINER

I'd rather be on a golf course than eat. If I couldn't go and dig some dirt, you might as well put me in a box.

—PETE DYE
GOLF COURSE ARCHITECT

In Britain, you skip the ball, hop it, bump it, run it, hit under it, on top of it, and then hope for the right bounce.

  —DOUG SANDERS

I don't think there's any way to Tiger-proof any golf course these days, short of pulling out the flagsticks.

  —KEITH REESE
   VALHALLA GOLF COURSE HEAD PRO

I think Darth Vader is actually a USGA official.

  —JOHNNY MILLER
   ON THE COURSE PREPARATIONS FOR MAJOR CHAMPIONSHIPS

Anyone who criticizes a golf course is like a person invited to a house for dinner who, on leaving, tells the host that the food was lousy.

  —GARY PLAYER

CHAPTER FOURTEEN

The Future of Golf:
Where is Our Game Headed?

We must have faith that whatever further emasculation awaits, Mr. Willie Park's apothegm of Far and Sure will never become passé. Nor can we expect an abatement anytime soon in the deadly golfing sins of greed, pomposity, and ego that can detonate a decent round with a single, delusional, thought. Two other constants unlikely to change: the emotional bedrock required to win, and the spirit of enterprise that replaced feathers with gutta-percha and the gutty with the hardcore, ad infinitum. One also presumes that the ancient dictum to "is it 'arder'" will be sound as long as something resembling golf is played.

Let the imagination run wild over The Golf of Tomorrow. Moving cart paths? Fifteen-hundred yard par-fives? On-course traffic signals, automated bunker rakes, four-wheel drive carts, putters capable of reading the green? Misdemeanor criminal charges for slow play? (One can dream.)

What lies ahead has always been an avid topic of conversation among golf's stewards. "I believe that what we have today in the game is the best that has survived," was how Howard Whitney, a U.S.G.A. president, put it in 1922. Old school, perhaps, but the same could be said today. Several years before his passing, Gene Sarazen, whose life spanned Vardon to Woods, was asked to share his concerns for the future. He didn't hesitate. More public courses and cheaper equipment, he said, an answer that we can expect will be true far onto the horizon, for, whatever else can be said about the future, it is only as certain as the next shot. Above all, we can keep our fingers crossed that uncertainty and luck will remain.

* * * * *

In thirty years, we're going to be in our nineties. We're going to play three-hole tournaments for $900,000 and the one who remembers his score wins.

—BOB BRUCE
SENIOR PGA TOUR MEMBER

In playing golf for more than fifty years, I don't believe there ever was a round in which I used more than six clubs . . . Today there's a stick in the sack for every shot . . . Golfers used to be made on the golf course. Now they are made in the machine shops.

—DONALD ROSS

That's what we need, some guys that have done well at their level. I tell them they're far more advanced at their age than I was. I couldn't play like they could when I was in my early twenties.

—MIKE WEIR

I'm not smart enough to figure out if it's good for the game or not.

—FRED COUPLES
ON THE PROPOSED WORLD TOUR

I think it is wrong. I think the idea of paying players to play or reducing the field is ludicrous. I think when you start paying players and reducing fields that is the beginning of the end.

—PETER JACOBSEN

Golf twenty years from now will continue to be the most civil of all popular competitive sports. There will be no trash talking, no attempts to circumvent rules, no physical threatening of competitors, no arguing with officials. For those reasons alone we can be proud as we look ahead.

—GARY WIREN
FROM "I TOLD YOU SO: TWO DECADES AFTER HIS PREDICTIONS
FOR 2001 CAME TRUE, OUR SWAMI FORECASTS WHERE GOLF
IS HEADED IN THE NEXT TWENTY YEARS," *GOLF DIGEST*

I used to go to the bar when I finished a round. The kids today go back and practice.

—LEE TREVINO

How do they learn to play? Courses are so busy and many of them are restrictive for kids. I worry about this.

—Bill Ogden
Ex-club professional, North Shore Country Club
on kids not being allowed to play at country clubs

———◆———

The best thing we can do is fifty years from now look back on our lives and say: 'We're good fathers.' I don't care how many tournaments we win and how much money we make. If we aren't a good dad, we leave the world a bad place.

—Brad Bryant

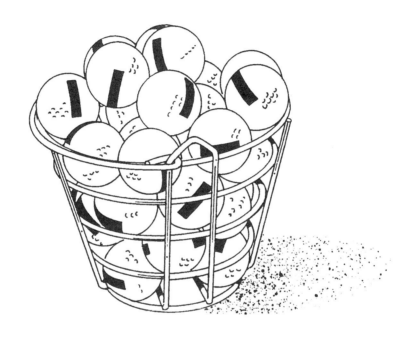

CHAPTER FIFTEEN

The Big Picture:
On Golf's Impact on
the World at Large

Let the detractors get in their cheap shots, they always do. Mystifying to small minds golf has always been an easy target, tending to its own affairs, oblivious to the caterwauling.

The game may be true to its Calvinist roots, as Mr. Reston implies, but we remorseless penitents return happily, broodingly, willingly. For the simplest of reasons, the ranks continue to grow. This comes as no surprise to the faithful. The cynic merely scratches his head.

Consider: In this turbulent nano-second of human history, we find the game has again entertained nascent attempts in outer space. There are hijab-wearing women flocking to play in the Iranian Republic as a multi billion-dollar Persian Gulf course and island resort nears completion. Should anyone really be surprised to see the Muslim world embrace golf, as one headline writer wryly noted, a burgeoning Axis of Eagle? And golf has been, albeit not without controversy, added to the list of course requirements at a major Chinese university for all management, law, economics and software engineering majors. Rightly so, for those entering the corporate cross-cultural world will find golf a social and professional adjunct of the global economy, a capitalist tool.

Could the critics only look past the argyle socks and Egyptian cotton in colors nature never intended. They would see that civility remains golf's most precious export. The backdrop of scandal in sports and beyond is now so routine as to hardly furrow a brow: senseless violence, blatant attempts at cheating, comical if not for their tragic outcomes, the crass commercialism, investigations, lawsuits, probes. By contrast, golf occupies a moral and ethical high ground that it is unlikely to cede, a standard bearer for sportsmanship, as out of step from the mainstream as that may sometimes be.

Golf's other significant bequest to the world, and its principal draw, is no less than its success in providing an outstanding means of escape from the onerous, incessant demands of our age. One may give up the game, curse it, forsake it, question it, but a world without golf? Ridiculous!

* * * * *

There are now more golf clubs in the world than Gideon Bibles, more golf balls than missionaries, and, if every golfer in the world, male and female, were laid end to end, I, for one, would leave them there.

—MICHAEL PARKINSON
   PRESIDENT OF THE ANTI-GOLF SOCIETY

The best thing about Eisenhower's Presidency was his Jeffersonian conviction that there should be as little government and as much golf as possible.

—ALISTAIR COOKE

You can, legally, possibly hit and kill a fellow golfer with a ball, and there will not be a lot of trouble because the other golfers will refuse to stop and be witnesses because they will want to keep playing.

—DAVE BARRY

Golf is, obviously, more in the forefront now, largely because of Tiger Woods, than it has been in America, but it doesn't yet, and probably never will, capture the imagination of America as a whole the way baseball, football and basketball have.

—BOB COSTAS
   ON *LARRY KING LIVE*

I don't consider myself a great black hope. I'm just a golfer who happens to be black and Asian.

—TIGER WOODS

A lot of kids watch football and basketball, and that's fine . . . If they don't see any other African-Americans playing golf, then you don't want to do it, either.

—JIM DENT

My God, you can get starting times in six different languages.

—THOMAS P. "TIP" O'NEILL, JR.
ON THE CAMBRIDGE, MASSACHUSETTS COURSE
RENAMED IN HIS HONOR

Involving minorities in the game of golf has financial, political and social implications. But the bottom line is simple: the more people who play the game, the fewer problems we'll have in the world. Because the game itself teaches people so much about themselves and others.

—EARL WOODS

You'd think I'd never done anything else but hit that shot. In the Orient for a while I became known as Mr. Double Eagle, which non-golfers probably took to mean that I was an Indian chief.

> —GENE SARAZEN
> ON THE SHOT THAT WON THE MASTERS

Cheap golf, it is accepted, is the Scotsman's birthright.

> —PETER DOBEREINER

You don't expect to be hit by a small white ball while walking through a meadow in Russia.

> —PROFESSOR ALEXY NIKOLOV
> BEFORE PERESTROIKA, COMMENTING ON HOW
> FEWER THAN THREE HUNDRED RUSSIANS PLAY GOLF

Did you know you have to demonstrate a minimum competence just to get on the course? You need a 'green card.'

> —JESPER PARNEVIK
> ON THE PROTOCOL OF SWEDISH GOLF

Only in America can you explain a man working three days and making $52,000.

—CHI-CHI RODRIGUEZ

I'm not opposed to the World Tour but you can't crap on the people who supported you all these years, who put you where you are to begin with. This has to be done right.

—LANNY WADKINS
ON THE WORLD TOUR

The Englishman is at his best on the links and at his worst in the Cabinet.

—GEORGE BERNARD SHAW

If you think about it, the golf ball doesn't know which country you're in.

—ANNIKA SÖRENSTAM

What a joy it is to jump into the train in the evening at a London terminus, with one's clubs on the rack overhead, and to wake the next morning to the sounds of Edinburgh and then the strange hum of the train rumbling over the Firth Bridge.

> —JOYCE WETHERED, 1933
> FROM HER ESSAY *THE ESSENCE OF SCOTTISH GOLF*

What earthly good is golf? Life is stern and life is earnest. We live in a practical age. All around us we see foreign competition making itself unpleasant. And we spend our time playing golf! What do we get out of it? Is golf any *use*?

> —P.G. WODEHOUSE
> *THE CLICKING OF CUTHBERT*

We've lost our national way. We are a society of chip Becks laying up intelligently.

> —TOM CALLAHAN
> COMMENTING ON GOLF IN 1995

I remember [country singer] Charlie Pride and he said: 'Always pass the buck down. Don't keep it all in your pocket' . . . For us golfers, our main focus is giving.

—JIM DENT

* * *

Tiger has already transcended the game of golf. The next step is for him to be someone on the world scale who makes an impact on humanity, and that is what he is going to be doing.

—EARL WOODS
GOLF DIGEST

* * *

It all comes back to the all-exempt Tour. It ruined the game . . . If you miss a cut and have to qualify to play next week, it's a whole different ball game. Half of them making more than $100,000 a year would be back home.

—BOB DRUM

* * *

I think a career is complete when you finish it.

—TOM KITE
WHEN ASKED IF HE THOUGHT HIS CAREER WOULD BE
COMPLETE SHOULD HE WIN A MAJOR

As you walk down the fairway of life you must smell the roses, for you only get to play one round.

—BEN HOGAN

About three days before Jones's death . . . he said to his family, 'If this is all there is to it, it sure is peaceful.' That is good to know. We were lucky we had Jones so long, for he had a rare gift for passing ideas and ideals on to other people.

—HERBERT WARREN WIND
ON BOBBY JONES

Golf's reliance and regard for personal responsibility also outdistances other sports; perhaps that carries over off the course.

—JIM APFELBAUM

It is not a matter of life and death. It is not that important. But it is a reflection of life, and so the game is an enigma wrapped in a mystery impaled on a conundrum.

—PETER ALLISS

Men trifle with their business and their politics but never trifle with their games. It brings truth home to them. They cannot pretend they have won when they have lost nor that they had a magnificent drive when they foozled it.

—GEORGE BERNARD SHAW

One of the most fascinating things about golf is how it reflects the cycle of life. No matter what you shoot, the next day you have to go back to the first tee and begin all over again and make yourself into something.

—PETER JACOBSEN

And the wind shall say: Here were decent godless people. Their only monument the asphalt road. And a thousand lost golf balls.

—T.S. ELIOT
FAMOUS POET, DRAMATIST AND LITERARY CRITIC

There's more to life than flying all over to hit a golf ball.

—NICK PRICE
GOLF DIGEST

Professional golf isn't big enough to hold the conversation that must be had about Tiger Woods now because he's dominating a sport that has never been dominated, not by the great Bobby Jones, not by Arnold Palmer and not even by Nicklaus.

> —MICHAEL WILBON
> "TIGER FINDS WAY TO EXCLUSIVE CLUB," *WASHINGTON POST*

I would like to think of myself as an athlete first, but I don't want to do a disservice to the real ones.

> —DAVID DUVAL

The number eighteen is symbolically meaningful because it is the numerical equivalent of the Hebrew word *chai*, which means life.

> —MICHAEL BAMBERGER
> FROM *TO THE LINKSLAND*
> ON THE NUMBER OF HOLES ON A GOLF COURSE

Golf is used by people of every color, race, creed, and temperament, in every climate. No recreation, apart from the simple contests of the river and field, has been so universal since the world began.

—HENRY LEACH

He's the bridge between the East and the West . . . He is the chosen one. He'll have the power to impact nations. Not people. Nations.

—EARL WOODS
ON HIS SON, TIGER

Tiger Woods is the only person I know who can change the focus in golf from yesterday to today and tomorrow.

—JOHN MERCHANT
USGA EXECUTIVE COMMITTEE MEMBER

The pat on the back, the arm around the shoulder, the praise for what was done right and the sympathetic nod for what wasn't are as much a part of golf as life itself.

—PRESIDENT GERALD FORD

CHAPTER SIXTEEN

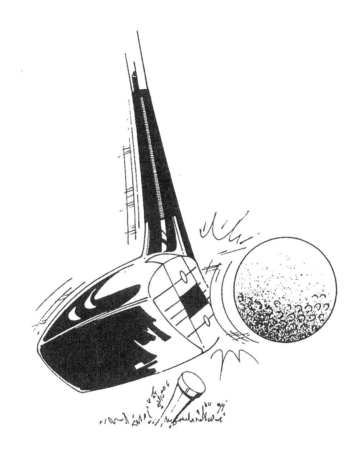

Golf Jokes:
A Priest, a Rabbi, and a Minister are Standing at the First Tee . . .

The reality is that you're unlikely to hear any good football jokes, and the next good basketball joke that bounces off the ball rack will be the first. Not that sports can't be a source of amusement; indeed, most have an inherent absurdity. Any number of reasons explain the surfeit of sports jokes, the obvious one being that there just isn't time. In the time it takes to either think of a good joke, set it up, or deliver the punch line —the score may have repeatedly changed. In the case of football, the quarterback finds himself otherwise distracted, routinely flat on his back under a pile of human ballast, unable to recall his mother's maiden name without the application of smelling salts, let alone what it was that Butkus once said to Unitas.

By contrast, golf humor can be sharp as a niblick. At its best, it's self-deprecating and playful, and often wise. Hours spent walking in Nature has always proved inspirational to the muse. In most cases, no one is actively pursuing us with the intent of inflicting bodily harm. No horse-hide is deliberately thrown at our chin. There is no clock, no whistle, no screams from the bench or sideline. No maniacal fans bang inflatable sticks attempting to interrupt our train of thought; just a pleasant game, played in pleasant surroundings by mostly pleasant people.

Above all, golf offers a rich vein of ineffable pathos, the foundation of all legitimate comedy. The mighty scrape that carves a pelt from the turf that outdistances the drive, the pured wedge that has the ball strike the pin only to carom back into the hazard, the putt that so perfectly hits the bottom of the cup that it pops back out, the skulled ricochet that trans-forms into an ace. Golf has a million of them, a perpetual bubbling spring of A material. There are stinkers, true, but it would be presumptuous to play favorites though we all certainly have them. The sad fact of the matter remains that—whatever the joke—"it" will always be funnier if "it" happened to someone else.

* * * * *

A couple has played golf every day for fifty years. One day the wife says, "Honey, to celebrate five decades of golf and marriage, let's start off with a clean slate and confess all our past wrongs."

"OK," the husband says. "Do you remember that blond secretary who worked for me twenty years ago? Well, I had an affair with her."

And the wife says, "That's nothing. Before we met, I had a sex change."

And the husband says, "Why, you dang cheat! All this time you've been hitting from the red tees!"

—WILLIE NELSON

Golfer: The doctor says I can't play golf.
Caddie: Oh, he's played with you, too, huh?

—ANONYMOUS

I don't want to say Colin Montgomerie and Darren Clarke are big, but if you took a picture of them together from behind, it would look like one of these double greens.

—STEVE ELKINGTON

579

Let's see, I think right now I'm third in money-winning and first in money-spending.

—TONY LEMA

"I'd move heaven and earth to be able to break 100 on this course," sighed Mac the golfer.

"Try heaven," advised the caddie. "You've already moved most of the earth."

—ANONYMOUS

"That can't be my ball, caddie. It looks far too old," said the player looking at a ball deep in the trees. The caddie replied, "It's a long time since we started, sir."

—ANONYMOUS

A golfer hits a huge slice off the first tee. The ball soars over a fence and onto a highway, where it hits a car, which promptly crashes into a tree.

The stunned golfer rushes into the golf shop and shouts, "Help! Help! I just hit a terrible slice off the first tee and hit a car and it crashed. What should I do?"

And the pro says, "Try a slightly stronger grip."

—ANONYMOUS

A group of golfers were putting on the green when suddenly a ball dropped in their midst.

One of the party winked at the others and kicked the ball into the hole. Seconds later, a very fat player puffed on to the green quite out of breath and red of face.

He looked round distractedly and asked: "Seen my ball?"

"Yeah, it went in the hole," the joker answered with a straight face. The fat one looked at him unbelievingly. Then he walked to the hole, looked in, reached down and picked up his ball. His astonishment was plain to see. Then he turned, ran down the fairway and as he neared his partner the group on the green heard him shout:

"Hey, Sam, I got an eleven."

—ANONYMOUS

He could do mankind a wonderful service, I suggested, if he signed into law the death penalty for slow-playing golfers.

—DAN JENKINS
ON PRESIDENT GEORGE H. BUSH
GOLF WITH THE BOSS

———

A hack golfer spends a day at a plush country club, playing golf and enjoying the luxury of a complimentary caddie. Being a hack golfer, he plays poorly all day. Round about the 18th hole, he spots a lake off to the left of the fairway. He looks at the caddie and says, "I've played so poorly all day, I think I'm going to go drown myself in that lake."

The caddie looks back at him and says, "I don't think you could keep your head down that long."

—ANONYMOUS

———

Lee Trevino doesn't want to talk about his back operation. That's all behind him.

—DON CRIQUI
SPORTSCASTER

Ever since my wife found it in the glove compartment.

—LEE TREVINO
ASKED WHEN HE STARTED WEARING A CORSET FOR HIS BAD BACK

———•———

A married man was having an affair with his secretary. One day, their passions overcame them and they took off for her house, where they made passionate love all afternoon. Exhausted from the wild sex, they fell asleep and awoke at around 8 p.m. As the man threw on his clothes, he told the woman to take his shoes outside and rub them through the grass and dirt. Mystified, she nonetheless complied and he slipped into his shoes and drove home.

"Where have you been?" demanded his wife when he entered the house.

"Darling," replied the man, "I can't lie to you. I've been having an affair with my secretary and we've been having sex all afternoon. I fell asleep and didn't wake up until eight o'clock."

The wife glanced down at his shoes and said, "You lying bastard! You've been playing golf!"

—ANONYMOUS

After a series of disastrous holes, the strictly amateur golfer in an effort to smother his rage laughed hollowly and said to his caddie:

"This golf is a funny game."

"It's not supposed to be," said the caddie gravely.

—ANONYMOUS

After coming from a long round of golf, his wife kissed him and kissed their son who came in a few moments later.

"Where's he been?" the husband asked.

"He's been caddieing for you all afternoon," the wife replied.

"No wonder he looks so familiar!"

—ANONYMOUS

Golfer: Caddiemaster, that boy isn't even eight years old.
Caddiemaster: Better that way, sir. He probably can't count past ten.

—ANONYMOUS

Golfer: Do you think I can get there with a 5 iron?
Caddie: Eventually.

—ANONYMOUS

A wife asks her husband, "If I were to die, would you get married again and share our bed with your new wife?"

He responds, "I guess I might."

"What about my car?" she asks. "Would you give that to her?"

She says, "Perhaps."

"Would you give my golf clubs to her, too?" his wife asks.

"No."

"Why not?" asks the wife.

"She's left-handed."

—GEORGE ARCHER

Golfer: Notice any improvement today, Jimmy?

Caddie: Yes, ma'am. You've had your hair done.

—ANONYMOUS

Golfer: This is the worst golf course I've ever played on!

Caddie: This isn't the golf course, sir! We left that an hour ago!

—ANONYMOUS

Golfer: Well Caddie, how do you like my game?

Caddie: Very good, Sir! But personally I prefer Golf.

—ANONYMOUS

Golfer: Caddie, do you think it is a sin to play golf on Sunday?

Caddie: The way you play, Sir, it's a crime any day of the week!

—ANONYMOUS

Golfer: Caddie, do you think my game is improving?

Caddie: Oh yes, Sir! You miss the ball much closer than you used to.

—ANONYMOUS

Golfer: Notice any improvement since last year?

Caddie: Polished your clubs, didn't you?

—ANONYMOUS

Golfer: Please stop checking your watch all the time, caddie. It's distracting!

Caddie: This isn't a watch, Sir, it's a compass!

—ANONYMOUS

Golfer: Caddie, why didn't you see where that ball went?

Caddie: Well, it doesn't usually go anywhere, Mr. Smith. You caught me off guard.

—ANONYMOUS

Golfer: Well, I have never played this badly before!

Caddie: I didn't realize you had played before, Sir.

—ANONYMOUS

On the phone with a golf buddy who has asked him to play, a guy says: "I am the master of my home and can play golf whenever I want. But hold on a minute while I find out if I want to."

—ANONYMOUS

The game of choice for unemployed people or maintenance level workers is basketball.

The game of choice for frontline workers is football.

The game of choice for middle management is tennis.

The game of choice for CEOs and executives is golf.

Conclusion: The higher up on the corporate ladder you are, the smaller your balls are.

—ANONYMOUS

Two guys are golfing on a course that is right next to a cemetery. After they tee off, one of the golfers notices that there is a funeral procession passing by. So he takes off his hat, and places it over his heart. When the funeral is over, the other golfer looks at the guy and asks, "Why did you do that?"

The man replies, "Well, we were married for almost forty years. It's the least I could do."

—ANONYMOUS

Why do women like making love to Greg Norman, the Australian golfer?

Because he always finishes second!

—ANONYMOUS

"Bad day at the course," a guy tells his wife. "Charlie had a heart attack on the third hole."

"That's terrible!" she says.

"You're telling me. All day long, it was hit the ball, drag Charlie."

—ANONYMOUS

"I play golf in the low eighties," the old man was telling one of the youngsters at his club.

"Wow," said the young man, "that's pretty impressive."

"Not really," said the old man, "Any hotter and I'd probably have a stroke."

—ANONYMOUS

"Mildred, shut up," cried the golfer at his nagging wife. "Shut up or you'll drive me out of my mind."

"That," snapped Mildred, "wouldn't be a drive . . . that would be a gimme putt."

—ANONYMOUS

"Your trouble is that you're not addressing the ball correctly."

"Yeah, well I've been polite to the bloody thing for long enough."

—Anonymous

A foursome of elderly gentlemen went to the bar after a round of golf. At the bar, the new Pro asked them, "How did your game go today?" The first said he had a good round with twenty-five riders. The second said he did OK with sixteen riders. The third said not too bad since I had ten riders. The fourth was disappointed and said that he played badly and had only two riders.

The Pro was confounded by the term "rider" but, not wanting to show his ignorance, just smiled and wished them better golf the next time.

He then approached Jerry the bartender and asked, "Can you tell me what the term 'riders' means?"

Jerry smiled and explained that a "rider" is when you have hit a shot long enough to take a ride on a golf cart.

—Anonymous

A foursome of senior golfers hit the course with waning enthusiasm. "These hills are getting steeper as the years go by," one complained.

"These fairways seem to be getting longer too," said one of the others.

"The sand traps seem to be bigger than I remember them too," said the third senior.

After hearing enough from his senior buddies, the oldest and wisest of the four of them, at eighty-seven years old, piped up and said, "Just be thankful we're still on the right side of the grass!"

—ANONYMOUS

A genie appears and offers a golfer three wishes:

"The only catch," says the genie, "is that whatever you wish for, your wife will receive ten times over."

"OK," the guy says. "I want to be the best golfer in the world." The genie blinks and suddenly the guy can feel a new golf swing—the grip, the takeaway, the power.

"You can now crush every golfer in the world," the genie says, "except your wife, who's gonna beat you like a drum." The guy is a little bummed about that, so for his second wish he asks to be the world's richest man.

"It's done," says the genie. "But don't forget that your wife can now buy and sell you ten times over. One wish left."

"OK," the guy says. "For my last wish, I'd like to have a mild heart attack."

—ANONYMOUS

A golfer comes home to find his wife waiting on the front porch with steam coming out of her ears.

"Where the hell were you?" she demands. "Our guests came over, but the yard wasn't mowed, there was no barbecue and you were missing. I've never been so humiliated!"

"I'm sorry," the husband says. "Let me explain. We played golf this morning, but on the way back to town we stopped at a strip joint. I met one of the dancers, and she was so beautiful, and one thing led to another, so I took her to a hotel room for several hours of wild passion. Then I had a quick shower and rushed straight home."

"Don't you lie to me," his wife says. "You played another 18, didn't you?"

—ANONYMOUS

A golfer hit his ball into a ravine. His buddies heard "whack, whack, whack" on and on, until finally he got the ball out. His buddy asked, "How many strokes did it take you to get out of there?"

The golfer said, "Three."

His buddy replied, "I heard seven."

"Four of them were echoes."

—ANONYMOUS

A golfer hits a big slice on the first hole, and his ball ends up behind a small shed.

"Wait! I'll open the window and the door, then you can hit a 3-wood right through the shed," the caddie says, as he's about to chip out. After the caddie opens the escape route, the golfer makes a big swing. The ball nearly makes it, but hits the windowsill, then bounces back and hits the golfer in the head. The next thing the golfer knows, he's standing at the Pearly Gates. Saint Peter sees him with his 3-wood in hand and says, "I guess you think you're a pretty good golfer."

The guy says, "Hey, I got here in two, didn't I?"

—ANONYMOUS

I swear that ball saw more lip than Bianca Jagger on her wedding night. But the kiss never came.

—PETER JACOBSEN
ON A MISSED PUTT

There are two things that guys on Tour do not like: playing in the wind and me dating their sister.

—GARY MCCORD

A guy goes golfing with his girlfriend. As he tees off, she steps into ladies' teebox and gets hit in the head with his drive. She is pronounced D.O.A. and taken to the morgue. The coroner calls him in and says, "She definitely died from a blow to the head caused by the golf ball. But the only thing we can't understand is why there was a golf ball in her rectum."

"Oh," he replies, "that must have been my mulligan."

—ANONYMOUS

A guy stood over his tee shot for what seemed an eternity, looking up, looking down, measuring the distance, figuring the wind direction and speed. He was driving his partner nuts. Finally his exasperated partner says, "What the heck is taking so long? Hit the ball!"

The guy answers, "My wife is up there watching me from the club-house. I want to make this a perfect shot." His partner ponders this for a moment, and then replies:

"Forget it man, you don't stand a snowball's chance in hell of hitting her from here!"

—ANONYMOUS

Have you ever noticed what golf spells backwards?

—AL BOLISKA

A husband and wife were playing on the ninth green when she collapsed from a heart attack.

"Please dear, I need help," she said. The husband ran off, saying, "I'll go get some help." A little while later he returned, picked up his putter and began to line up his shot. His wife, on the ground, raised up her head and said, "I may be dying and you're putting?"

"Don't worry, dear. I found a doctor on the second hole who said he'd come and help you."

"The second hole? When is he coming?"

"Hey! I told you not to worry," he said, stroking his putter. "Everyone has already agreed to let him play through."

—ANONYMOUS

That's the trouble with Nick [Faldo]. The only time he opens his mouth is to change feet.

—DAVID FEHERTY

A murder has been committed. Police are called to an apartment and find a man standing, holding a 5 iron in his hands, looking at the lifeless body of a woman on the floor. The detective asks, "Sir, is that your wife?"

"Yes."

"Did you hit her with that golf club?"

"Yes, yes, I did." The man stifles a sob, drops the club, and puts his hands on his head.

"How many times did you hit her?"

"I don't know. Five, six, seven . . . Put me down for a five."

—ANONYMOUS

Years ago we discovered the exact point, the dead center of middle age. It occurs when you are too young to take up golf and too old to rush to the net.

—FRANKLIN ADAMS
AMERICAN JOURNALIST

A pastor, a doctor and an engineer were waiting one morning for a particularly slow group of golfers. The engineer fumed, "What's with these guys? We must have been waiting for fifteen minutes!"

The pastor said, "Hey, here comes the greens keeper. Let's have a word with him." There was a dramatic pause.

"Hi George. Say, what's with that group ahead of us? They're rather slow aren't they?"

The greens keeper replied, "Oh, yes, that's a group of blind firefighters. They lost their sight saving our clubhouse from a fire last year, so we always let them play for free anytime." The group was silent for a moment.

The pastor said, "That's so sad I think I will say a special prayer for them tonight."

The doctor said, "Good idea. And I'm going to contact my ophthalmologist buddy and see if there's anything he can do for them."

The engineer said, "Why can't these guys play at night?"

—ANONYMOUS

———•———

Golf's three ugliest words: still your shot.

—DAVE MARR

A priest on Easter sneaks out to play a round of solo golf, and makes an ace.

"How could you possibly reward him for playing golf on such a holy day?" an angel asks God. God responds, "Who's he gonna tell?"

—ANONYMOUS

A priest rushed from church one day to keep a golf date. He was halfway down the first fairway, waiting to hit his second shot, when he heard "Fore!" and a ball slammed into his back. Soon, the golfer who had made the drive was on the scene to offer his apologies. When the priest assured him that he was all right, the man smiled.

"Thank goodness, Father!" he exclaimed. "I've been playing this game for forty years, and now I can finally tell my friends that I've hit my first holy one!"

—ANONYMOUS

If a guy says it's against his religion, tell him to get another religion.

—LANNY WADKINS

ON GAMBLING IN PRACTICE ROUNDS BEFORE TOURNAMENTS

I am among those who firmly believe that a round of golf should not take more than three-and-a-half hours, four at most. Anything longer than that is not a round of golf, it's life in Albania.

—DAN JENKINS
ON SLOW PLAY

There is not the slightest doubt in my own mind that golf as played in the United States is the slowest in the world.

—HENRY LONGHURST

Don January's playing with all the passion and verve of a meter reader.

—VIN SCULLY
ON JANUARY'S SLOW PLAY

A little boy came up to me and asked for my autograph. He had a broken arm in a cast. I signed it and asked him what happened. "Someone catch you teeing it up in the rough?"

—LEE TREVINO

No, Trevino speaks Mexican.

—SEVE BALLESTEROS
ASKED IF HE AND TREVINO SPEAK SPANISH WHEN THEY CONVERSE

I haven't seen them at the family reunion yet.

—CHRIS PATTON
WHEN ASKED IF HE WAS RELATED TO GENERAL GEORGE PATTON OR
GOLFER BILLY JOE PATTON

A retiree was given a set of golf clubs by his co-workers. Thinking he'd try the game, he asked the local pro for lessons, explaining that he knew nothing whatever of the game. The pro showed him the stance and swing, then said, "Just hit the ball toward the flag on the first green." The novice teed up and smacked the ball straight down the fairway and onto the green, where it stopped inches from the hole.

"Now what?" the fellow asked the speechless pro.

"Uh . . . you're supposed to hit the ball into the cup," the pro finally said, after he was able to speak again.

"Oh great! Now you tell me," said the beginner in a disgusted tone.

—ANONYMOUS

After being reassured that his eighty-year-old caddie has perfect eyesight, the golfer hits his first tee shot deep in the right rough.

"Did you see it?" the golfer asks as they walk off the tee.

"Yep!" Old Eagle Eye replies with confidence.

"Well, where is it?"

"I can't remember."

—ANONYMOUS

An alien spaceship hovered over a golf course and two aliens watched a solitary golfer in amazement. The golfer duffed his tee shot, shanked his second into the rough, took three to get out of the rough onto the fairway, sliced the next shot into the bushes, and then took a putter to get it out on the fairway again.

Meanwhile, one alien told the other that he must be playing some sort of weird game and they continued to observe the golfer. The golfer then skulled a shot into a bunker by the green. He then took several shots to get out of the bunker and finally on to the green. He putted several times until he finally got into the hole. At this point, the other alien told his partner, "Wow, now he is in serious trouble!"

—ANONYMOUS

An amateur was talking to his golf pro. The amateur asked, "How do you get so much backspin?"

"Before I answer that, tell me, how far do you hit a 5 iron?" the pro responded.

"About 130."

"Then why in the world would you want the ball to spin back?"

—ANONYMOUS

An American businessman is on a business trip in Japan and hires a hooker. The whole night, the Japanese hooker keeps screaming: "Hoshimota! Hoshimota!" He can't quite remember what the word means, but he's sure he's pleased the hooker to best of his ability. The next morning, he goes to play a game of golf with his Japanese business partner when he makes a hole-in-one. Everyone is congratulating him in Japanese and he can't think anything to say but "HOSHIMOTA!" Concerned, his partner turns to him.

"What do you mean it's in the wrong hole?"

—ANONYMOUS

Being out in the woods is fun, but this pays better.

—ROBERT LANDERS

WHEN ASKED IF HE WOULD RATHER CUT WOOD OR GOLF

An American went to Scotland and played golf with a newly acquainted Scottish golfer. After a bad tee shot, he played an extremely good mulligan. He then asked the Scottish golfer, "What do you call a Mulligan in Scotland?"

"We call it 3."

—ANONYMOUS

What else is there to do over there? Wear a skirt?

—GEORGE LOW

ON HIS NEED TO PLAY GOLF IN HIS FATHER'S NATIVE SCOTLAND

Be funny on a golf course? Do I kid my best friend's mother about her heart condition?

—PHIL SILVERS

Did you know that O.J. Simpson, Monica Lewinsky, Ted Kennedy, and President Bill Clinton are all avid golfers? O.J.'s a slicer, Monica's a hooker, Ted Kennedy can't drive over water, and Clinton can't seem to hit the right hole!

—ANONYMOUS

For most of the round the golfer had argued with his caddie about club selection, but the caddie always prevailed. Finally on the 17th hole, a 185-yard par three into the wind, the caddie handed the golfer a 4-wood.

"I think it's a 3-iron," said the golfer.

"No, sir it's a 4-wood," said the caddie.

"Nope, it's definitely a 3-iron." So the golfer set up, took the 3-iron back slowly, and struck the ball perfectly. It tore through the wind, hit softly on the front of the green, and rolled up two feet short of the pin.

"See," said the caddie. "I told you it wasn't enough club."

—ANONYMOUS

The uglier a man's legs are, the better he plays golf. It's almost a law.

—H.G. WELLS
BEALBY

Sure I went to college. I delivered Christmas trees to SMU.

—LEE TREVINO
WHEN ASKED IF HE WENT TO COLLEGE

Golf.

—DOUG SANDERS
WHEN ASKED HIS MAJOR IN COLLEGE

I was on the golf team for two semesters and in school for five minutes.

—JOHN HUSTON
ON HIS COLLEGE YEARS AT AUBURN UNIVERSITY

I probably would have taken it. Except they wanted me to rent cross-country skis during the winter.

—TOM LEHMAN
ON BEING OFFERED THE JOB AS THE GOLF COACH
AT THE UNIVERSITY OF MINNESOTA

Golf is what you play when you're too out of shape to play softball.

—ANONYMOUS

"How many strokes d'ye have, laddie?" the Scot asked his guest after the first hole.

"Seven."

"I took six. Ma hole." They played the second hole and once again he asked: "How many strokes?"

"Oh no sir!" said the guest. "It's my turn to ask."

—ANONYMOUS

"I want you to know that this is not the game I usually play," snapped an irate golfer to his caddie.

"I should hope not, sir. But tell me," inquired the caddie, "What game do you usually play?"

—ANONYMOUS

I was playing golf. I swung, missed the ball, and got a big chunk of dirt. I swung again, missed the ball, and got another big chunk of dirt. Just then, two ants climbed on the ball saying "Let's get up here before we get killed!"

—ANONYMOUS

Golfers who carry ball retrievers are gatherers, not hunters . . . Their dreams are no longer of conquest, but only of salvage.

—DAVID OWEN

———◆———

It was a sunny Saturday morning on the course and I was beginning my pre-shot routine, visualizing my upcoming shot, when a voice came over the clubhouse loudspeaker.

"Would the gentleman on the woman's tee back up to the men's tee please!" I was still deep in my routine, seemingly impervious to the interruption. Again the announcement, "Would the MAN on the WOMEN'S tee kindly back up to the men's tee." I simply ignored the guy and kept concentrating, when once more, the voice yelled: "Would the man on the woman's tee back up to the men's tee, PLEASE!

I finally stopped, turned, looked through the clubhouse window directly at the person with the mic and shouted back, "Would the person in the clubhouse kindly shut up and let me play my second shot?"

—ANONYMOUS

———◆———

When you're having trouble and topping the ball, it means the ground is moving on you.

—CHI-CHI RODRIGUEZ

Judge: Do you understand the nature of an oath?

Boy: Do I? I'm your caddie, remember!

———— • ————

There are two things that won't last long in this world, and that's dogs chasing cars and pros putting for pars.

—LEE TREVINO

———— • ————

"Now," said the golf pro, "suppose you just go through the motions without driving the ball."

"But that's precisely the difficulty I'm trying to overcome," said his pupil.

—ANONYMOUS

———— • ————

One golfer asked his friend, "Why are you so late in arriving for your tee time?"

His friend replied, "It's Sunday. I had to toss a coin between going to church or playing golf."

"Yes," continued the friend, "but that still doesn't tell me why you are so late."

"Well," said the fellow, "It took over twenty-five tosses to get it right!"

—ANONYMOUS

When the average golfer takes out his driver he calls for all our faith, when he tees up the ball he calls for all our hope, and when he drives, for all our charity.

—TED OSBORNE

One golfer tells another: "Hey, guess what! I got a set of golf clubs for my wife!"

The other replies: "That's a great trade!"

—ANONYMOUS

Never bet with anyone you meet on the first tee who has a deep sunburn, a one-iron in his bag, and squinty eyes.

—DAVE MARR

Q: Where can you find one hundred doctors all at the same place on any given day?

A: A golf course!

—ANONYMOUS

There's an old saying, "Beware of the ailing golfer. And whenever he's complaining, we know we're in trouble."

—PHIL MICKELSON

Q: Why do golfers wear two pairs of socks?
A: In case they get a hole in one.

—ANONYMOUS

THE 10 COMMANDMENTS OF GOLF:
THOU SHALT NOT covet thy neighbors putter.
THOU SHALT NOT pick up lost balls before they stop rolling.
THOU SHALT NOT wager with those who carry a one-iron.
THOU SHALT NOT play "inside the leather" with a 52" putter.
THOU SHALT NOT build thy house of handicap with sand bags.
THOU SHALT NOT worship St. Mulligan, except on the 1st tee.
THOU SHALT NOT imitate a stunt driver in a golf cart.
THOU SHALL yell "Fore!" before the body hits the ground.
THOU SHALL restrict profanity on the course to three putting or worse.
THOU SHALL throw thy clubs in non-lethal directions.

—ANONYMOUS

Two long time golfers are standing overlooking a river. One golfer turns to the other and says, "Look at those idiots fishin' in the rain."

      —ANONYMOUS

Q: What's the difference between a Ford and a golf ball?
A: You can drive a golf ball two hundred yards.

      —ANONYMOUS

Nothing goes down slower than a golf handicap.

      —BOBBY NICHOLS

Q: What's the difference between a golfer and a sky diver?
A: A golfer goes, whack! ... "Damn!" And a sky diver goes, "Damn!" ... whack!

      —ANONYMOUS

You know it's too wet to play golf when your cart capsizes.

      —ANONYMOUS

I have three-putted in forty countries.

—FRED CORCORAN

You know how most golfers look . . . They look in poor light like your brother-in-law. Plumbers have to be in better shape.

—JIM MURRAY

Two women were put together as partners in the club tournament and met on the putting green for the first time. After introductions, the first golfer asked, "What is your handicap?"

"Oh, I am a scratch golfer," the other replied.

"Really!" exclaimed the first woman, suitably impressed that she was paired up with her.

"Yes, I write down all my good scores and scratch out the bad ones!"

—ANONYMOUS

It may be popular, but it will never be cool.

—JOE QUEENAN
ON GOLF

My opponent said he'd give me a stroke on 14 if I'd give him a free throw. That sounded pretty good until we got to the green, and he picked up my ball and threw it into the pond.

—BOB HOPE

Two balls in the water. By God, I've got a good mind to jump in and make it four.

—SIMON HOBDAY
WINNER OF THE 1994 USGA SENIOR CHAMPIONSHIP

It was a hole-in-one contest and I had three.

—ABE LEMONS
DESCRIBING HOW HE MISSED WINNING A CAR
IN A TOURNAMENT BY TWO STROKES

I played Civil War golf. I went out in 61 and came back in 65.

—HENNY YOUNGMAN
COMEDIAN

CHAPTER SEVENTEEN

Major Tournaments:
From the Masters to the Ryder Cup

The word (psst: *tournament*) is enough to add three or four shots to our score. Farther up the food chain, one need only confirm the severity plastered across their faces to sense how different a kettle of fish the major championships present the dogged victims. The spoils are so much greater as is, of course, the challenge. Another day at the office? I don't think so. No bigger sport fans can be found outside the PGA Tour. And they know full well that the majors are one of those few times all year when golf eschews its second-class status with the other minor sports to legitimately become front page news.

At stake are not just column inches, money, exemptions, endorsements, better tee times and pairings but glory, even—gulp—a shot at immortality. Some seem to wrestle with the specters of patriotism or history. What hand will they be dealt? What swing will they leave the range with today?

A PGA Champion once assessed his odds in the major championships. He figured "someone like him" might qualify to play in ten or twelve. In half of those he could expect to be on his game, free of injury, food poisoning, depression, marital problems, etc. On half of those again would he be playing courses where he thought he had a realistic shot. That leaves the pragmatist with three good chances over the course of a career. Many never get one shot. Others seem to dangle tantalizingly in contention but are held back by . . . what? The mercurial Fates? Their own demons? One bad swing? A moment of indecision or ambivalence? No wonder the smiles are so taut, the brows creased, the expressions vacant.

* * * * *

Every kid learning to play golf dreams about winning the Masters, and about winning the Open, not about being the leading money winner.

—TOM KITE

———•—•———

I always get a kick out of the guys who say they're getting their game ready to peak at the majors. I'm not that good. Hey, I went into the Masters with low expectations. Look what happened there.

—MARK O'MEARA
1998 MASTERS WINNER

———•—•———

Ninety-seven percent of the field, myself included, are not equipped to play this course. We just don't have the shots. I heard Byron Nelson say on television that 272 would win here. I couldn't shoot 272 if I got a mulligan every hole.

—GEORGE ARCHER
ON MERION BEFORE THE 1971 U.S. OPEN

———•—•———

I held the putter in a vice-like grip and from the moment I took it back from the ball I was blind and unconscious.

—TOMMY ARMOUR
ON HOW HE HOLED THE PUTT THAT WON HIM
THE 1931 OPEN CHAMPIONSHIP

619

It was kind of a process of self-isolation, of going into a shell, of putting away outside things. Crack American women golfers . . . brought it to the point of perfection. They never talk . . . they seem to press a button and all at once, in their own minds, nobody else exists.

> —PAM BARTON
>   PREPARING FOR THE 1936 U.S. WOMEN'S AMATEUR

I kept getting tears in my eyes. It happened to me once at Baltusrol. But here, it happened to me four or five times. I had to say to myself, Hey, you've got some golf to play.

> —JACK NICKLAUS
>   ON THE 1986 MASTERS

I used to think you could win just a bunch of other tournaments, but, well, I never would have said it, but I guess you have to win Majors to be up there. The longer you play, the more you realize that they are more important.

> —ANDY BEAN

A major golf tournament is 40,000 sadists watching 144 masochists.

> —THOMAS BOSWELL

That gives me the Greater Slam.

—MARK BROOKS
ON THE GREATER HARTFORD, GREATER GREENSBORO, AND GREATER
MILWAUKEE BEING THE THREE VICTORIES OF HIS CAREER

Having never been there, I guess I can't say anything good or bad about the Masters, so don't get me wrong. I've dug myself a hole with the people at the Masters. If I do get to the Masters, maybe I should let Gary McCord caddy for me.

—BRAD BRYANT

The finishes of the Masters Tournament have almost always been dramatic and exciting. It is my conviction that this has been because of the make-or-break quality of the second nine.

—ROBERT TRENT JONES, SR.
GOLF IS MY GAME

Today was the best I've played in weeks. I didn't lose with bogeys. I lost to birdies, and that's the way you should lose.

—BRANDIE BURTON
AFTER LOSING THE US WOMEN'S AMATEUR TO VICKI GOETZE
AT PINEHURST NO. 2

I wish it could have been a 54-hole tournament—the last 54.

> —JoAnne Carner
> AFTER SHOOTING AN OPENING-ROUND 81 AND LOSING THE US
> WOMEN'S OPEN BY ONLY A FEW

We needed good performances from the whole team and we got them. All the team played majestically. It's getting almost too much to bear, this Ryder Cup.

> —Bernard Gallacher
> ON THE 1995 RYDER CUP

It's tough to see a grown man beg—unless it's a U.S. Open winner momentarily letting down his guard and entreating the mercy of the golf gods.

> —Jim Apfelbaum

At my age I've got to think positively. I'm 43 next week, and it's nice I can come back to this tournament and do well again, and I look forward to coming back here again next year and trying another U.S. Open disaster.

> —Colin Montgomerie

I don't play great golf a lot. I do it every now and then like in the British Open last year when I finished third so I know I can do it . . . It's just a matter of going out there and doing it again.

—FRED COUPLES

When I'm through, I'll really miss kicking myself to get it done. I can live without playing the Masters. But the really satisfying time is the three weeks leading up to the Masters when I'm preparing for it.

—JACK NICKLAUS

I'm a big believer in fate . . . I have a good feeling about this.

—BEN CRENSHAW
THE NIGHT BEFORE HIS AMERICAN TEAM OVERCAME A
FOUR-POINT DEFICIT TO BEAT EUROPE AT THE RYDER CUP

I think you all know pretty well how much I feel. I suppose the sun got me a little. I got a little tired, I guess I got a little emotional coming up 18.

—ARNOLD PALMER
AT A PRESS CONFERENCE AFTER HIS FINAL U.S. OPEN
AT OAKMONT IN 1994

To this day Taylor has extremely strong views about that bunker, and he has been heard to suggest that its creator should be buried in it with a niblick through his heart.

—BERNARD DARWIN
ON J.H. TAYLOR'S REACTION TO THE FOURTH HOLE AT PRESTWICK,
WHERE HE MADE A 7 IN THE 1914 BRITISH OPEN

If I knew what was going through Jack Nicklaus's head, I would have won this golf tournament.

—TOM WEISKOPF
ASKED IF HE KNEW WHAT JACK NICKLAUS WAS
THINKING ON HIS WAY TO WINNING THE 1986 MASTERS

You've got a fairly good idea as to what the questions are going to be. But how to record the best answer is another matter.

—NICK FALDO
EQUATING THE U.S. OPEN TO AN EXAM

At its worst, the Open eradicates the difference in ability between a Tom Purtzer and a Tom Watson and throws both in the same jail of high rough and high risk shots. . . .

—THOMAS BOSWELL

It was a good shot, but it was a bad mental mistake.

—RAYMOND FLOYD
DESCRIBING HOW A BAD SHOT COST HIM A CHANCE AT
VICTORY IN THE 1990 MASTERS AGAINST NICK FALDO

If I could just putt, I might just scare somebody. Maybe me.

—JACK NICKLAUS
AFTER THE SECOND ROUND OF THE 1986 MASTERS,
WHICH HE WON AT AGE 46

Of the big four, the PGA is the most fair and the least fun. Basically, it's just the U.S. Open set up by nice, rather than nasty, fellows.

—THOMAS BOSWELL

I've got no business going to the U.S. Open this week and playing a hard course like Medinah.

—LOU GRAHAM
BEFORE HIS VICTORY AT THE 1975 U.S. OPEN

If I can't play this last nine in thirty-seven strokes, I'm just a bum and don't deserve to win the Open.

—RALPH GULDAHL
AT THE TURN BEFORE WINNING THE 1937 U.S. OPEN

Bobby [Jones] was playing some good golf in spots. He's got everything he needs to win any championship, except experience and maybe philosophy. But I'll tip you off to something. Bobby will win an Open before he wins an Amateur.

—WALTER HAGEN
JONES WON THE 1923 U.S. OPEN AS HIS FIRST MAJOR TITLE

The British Open probably would have died if the American stars hadn't started going over to play in it more regularly the last fifteen years. Arnold Palmer saved it, but as far as I'm concerned he didn't do us any favours.

—DAVE HILL

Gentlemen, the defense rests. I think the hole is eminently fair.

—ROBERT TRENT JONES, SR.
AFTER SCORING A HOLE-IN-ONE ON THE PAR-3 HE DESIGNED
FOR THE U.S. OPEN AT BALTUSROL, WHICH WAS UNDERGOING
CRITICISM FOR ITS TOUGHNESS

For an amateur, standing on the first hole of the Masters is the ultimate laxative.

—TREVOR HOMER

✦

I'm coming home and I'm bringing home the trophy and it's a big one.

—JULIE INKSTER
TO HER DAUGHTERS AFTER WINNING THE 1999 US WOMEN'S OPEN

✦

You start to choke at the Masters when you drive through the front gate.

—HALE IRWIN

✦

I looked up and there was a streaker on the course, running back and forth on the green, dodging the cops. When he turned and ran toward me, I just nailed him—I did my great Jack Lambert imitation.

—PETER JACOBSEN
ON TACKLING A STREAKER AT THE 1985 BRITISH OPEN

I just feel that the Ryder Cup, if it were left to the players, would be a wonderful event. The players would compete and have fun. It would be what it was meant to be, which is good will between two golfing organizations. The Ryder Cup has become a war.

—JACK NICKLAUS
GOLF DIGEST (1991)

It's the old American thing from the Ryder Cup matches. The Americans wear Foot-joys and all the English players stand together admiring their shoes and their slacks and their clubs. How can you beat a man if you can't afford his shoes?

—NICK JOB

At Augusta National they bikini-wax the greens.

—GARY MCCORD
A COMMENT THAT SAW HIM BANNED FROM THE MASTERS
AS A TELEVISION COMMENTATOR

One of the prerequisites to win a major championship is to enter the damn thing. You are not going to win the British Open by correspondence.

      —TOM KITE
         CRITICIZING EXEMPT AMERICAN PLAYERS WHO
         DO NOT PLAY IN THE BRITISH OPEN

The logic is that every sport ends with a bonanza, and ours doesn't. The Tour Championship is going up against football and the World Series. We need to stand on our own.

      —BILLY ANDRADE

Any time you save par out of the rough in this tournament, you feel like you've escaped from jail. It's like a get-out-of-jail-free card.

      —TOM LEHMAN
         ON THE U.S. OPEN

There's no reason to compare apples to oranges. But this is one hell of an orange.

> —JUSTIN LEONARD
> WHEN ASKED TO COMPETE AT THE BRITISH OPEN
> AND THE PLAYERS CHAMPIONSHIP

By the time I got to the first tee in my first Masters, I was so scared I could hardly breathe. If you're not a little nervous there, there isn't anything in life that can make you nervous.

> —ROGER MALTBIE

You just can't miss putts and win tournaments, whether it's the Atlanta Classic or the Masters.

> —FRED COUPLES

If you're going to be a player people will remember, you have to win the Open at St. Andrews.

—JACK NICKLAUS

———◆———

Playing in the U.S. Open is like tippy-toeing through hell.

—JERRY MCGEE
MEMBER OF THE PGA AND CHAMPIONS TOUR

———◆———

At 11 o'clock I bathed and shaved and ate a big breakfast here at the club and killed time in the locker room and hit a few shots down the practice fairway, and then it was nearly 1:42. I thought it would never come.

—CARY MIDDLECOFF
ON THE FINAL WAIT BEFORE THE LAST ROUND OF THE 1955 MASTERS

———◆———

Where the hell's Jane?

—NICK FALDO
AFTER CLIMBING A TREE TO PLAY A SHOT IN THE 1992 U.S. OPEN

The Ryder Cup is a hard face-to-face match, and because [players] are not used to that kind of confrontation, they feel the heat. And it shows.

—JOHNNY MILLER
GOLF DIGEST

Form goes out the window at the Ryder Cup. On the Friday morning, on the first tee, it's not how's your form but whether you can stand up.

—COLIN MONTGOMERIE

I had a fifteenth club in my bag this week. It was Harvey Penick.

—BEN CRENSHAW
WHO WAS VICTORIOUS AT THE 1995 MASTERS AFTER
SERVING AS PALLBEARER FOR HARVEY PENICK

On the 17th and 18th greens of the regulation playoff, Els holed devilish putts on top of Roberts that could only have been made by a fearless 24-year-old or a blockhead who didn't know better.

—DAN JENKINS
ON HOW ERNIE ELS'S AND LOREN ROBERTS'S PUTTING
KEPT THEM IN THE 1994 U.S. OPEN PLAYOFF

Like unhitching a horse from a plow and winning the Derby.

—JIM MURRAY
ON ORVILLE MOODY'S UNEXPECTED WIN AT THE 1969 U.S. OPEN

The lord hates a coward.

—BYRON NELSON
TO HIMSELF DURING HIS 1937 MASTERS VICTORY

You don't come to Augusta to find your game. You come here because you've got one.

—GENE SARAZEN
ON THE MASTERS

It tasted a little chemical at first.

—PATTY SHEEHAN
ON DRINKING FROM THE LPGA TROPHY
AFTER WINNING THE 1993 CHAMPIONSHIP

I finally found the guy I used to know on the golf course. It was me.

—JACK NICKLAUS
AFTER WINNING HIS 6TH MASTERS IN 1986

At its best, the U.S. Open demands straight drives, crisp iron shots, brilliant chipping and putting, and strategic position play. Plus the patience of St. Francis and the will of Patton.

 —THOMAS BOSWELL

I think the great thing about the Ryder Cup is that the players are really playing for their countries and not playing for money. I think that is the important essence of the Ryder Cup.

 —BERNARD GALLAGHER
  PGA PRO, AND EUROPEAN RYDER CUP TEAM CAPTAIN

In fishing terms, this was a mackerel in the moonlight—shining one minute, smelly the next.

 —GREG NORMAN
  ON HIS "UGLY" ONE-OVER-PAR WIN AT THE 1993 PGA CHAMPIONSHIP

I didn't want to [shoot for the pin] but there's this thing in my brain that just shoved the ball over there.

 —FRED COUPLES
  DESCRIBING HOW HE ALMOST HIT A SHOT INTO RAE'S CREEK
  IN THE FINAL ROUND OF HIS 1992 MASTERS WIN

It's the only pure golf tournament we play in, including all of the other major championships. No skyboxes here or anything like that. You see the same faces in the gallery come tournament time. Over the years, I get to know the people and where they sit.

—GREG NORMAN
ON THE MASTERS

In America, the Ryder Cup rates somewhere between the Tennessee Frog Jumping Contest and the Alabama Melon-Pip Spitting Championship, although the players themselves have always taken it seriously—until Tom Wieskopf declined to play in favor of a week's holiday shooting sheep.

—PETER DOBEREINER
1978

Nobody wins the [U.S.] Open. It wins you.

—CARY MIDDLECOFF

Before I hit that shot I remember standing there thinking that all I needed to win was a 4 . . . That's where I made my mistake, thinking about something besides the ball. If I'd kept my mind on swinging the club. . . .

 —ARNOLD PALMER
  ON HIS DOUBLE BOGEY ON THE 72ND HOLE,
  COSTING HIM THE 1962 MASTERS BY ONE STROKE

Instead of putting pressure on myself and thinking, 'I've got to make this shot,' I just thought, 'Go ahead and make it.' It's a subtle difference but a big one.

 —COREY PAVIN
  AFTER MAKING A CRITICAL 141-YARD IRON SHOT
  IN THE 1993 RYDER CUP

When the British Open is in Scotland, there's something special about it. And when it's at St. Andrews, it's even greater.

 —JACK NICKLAUS

The things I have seen in the Ryder Cup have disappointed me. You are hearing about hatred and war.

 —GARY PLAYER

If you like root canals and hemorrhoids, you'd love it there.

—NICK PRICE
ON THE RYDER CUP

———◆———

This was one of the rare occasions when I was so keyed up my stomach was upset, even during the night. I lost my breakfast the next morning, which I thought might be a good sign because I had always played well when I became that sick beforehand.

—BYRON NELSON
BEFORE HIS 18-HOLE PLAYOFF WIN AGAINST
BEN HOGAN IN THE 1942 MASTERS

———◆———

The emotion is unbelievable. After my second shot at 18 it blows my head. Then I hole the putt. Give me another chance. The putt, nobody is supposed to hole that putt.

—COSTANTINO ROCCA
ON MAKING A 60 FOOT, 72ND HOLE BIRDIE AT ST. ANDREWS TO GET
INTO A PLAYOFF FOR THE 1995 BRITISH OPEN TITLE WITH JOHN DALY

———◆———

The first time I played the Masters, I was so nervous I drank a bottle of rum before I teed off. I shot the happiest 83 of my life.

—CHI-CHI RODRIGUEZ

We all say majors are just another 72-hole tournament. In a way, they are. But we're really just saying that to keep ourselves from getting too fired up.

—Curtis Strange

Well son, we had a good best ball, anyway.

—Denny Shute
to Dow Finsterwald after Shute made a birdie 2 and Finsterwald an 11 at the 12th hole in the 1951 Masters

When Christ arose, God placed a Masters jacket on him.

—Sign at the Woodlawn Baptist Church in Augusta, Georgia 1972

You gotta sneak up on these holes. Iffen you clamber and clank up on 'em, they're liable to turn round and bite you.

—Sam Snead
on Oakmont, during the 1953 U.S. Open

I played horrible and putted just as bad. On the back nine I had an opportunity to put everybody away, and I just didn't do it. The only consolation is that I didn't lose the tournament.

—CURTIS STRANGE
ON HIS WAY TO BEATING NICK FALDO IN A PLAYOFF
AT THE 1988 U.S. OPEN

Maybe you think I'm a stupid Argentine, but you spell my name wrong on the seating plan, the place cards and the menu—and different each time.

—ROBERTO DE VICENZO
AT AN OFFICIAL DINNER AFTER HE FAILED TO TIE FOR THE
1968 MASTERS, SIGNING AN INCORRECT SCORECARD

We're not trying to humiliate the worst players in the world . . . we're trying to identify them.

—FRANK TATUM
USGA PRESIDENT, ON THE SELECTION OF U.S. OPEN COURSES

If that's golf, I'm in the wrong damn league.

—FUZZY ZOELLER
COMPLAINING ABOUT THE CONDITIONS OF THE GREENS
AT THE MASTERS

Sometimes you're so into a putt that when you miss it, it's like a stab in the heart.

—TOM LEHMAN
ON MISSING AN IMPORTANT PUTT AT THE 15TH HOLE
DURING THE FINAL ROUND OF THE 1994 MASTERS

Hell, man, Ray Charles could play here . . . and it still wouldn't make no difference.

—LEE TREVINO
ON THE SUBTLETIES OF MUIRFIELD DURING THE 1972 BRITISH OPEN

I'm sitting there with the press, all pleased and comfortable, and when Arnie holes the thirty-footer they leave me like I got the pox.

—KEN VENTURI
AFTER ARNOLD PALMER MADE A 30-FOOT BIRDIE PUTT
ON THE FINAL HOLE TO WIN THE 1960 MASTERS

I knew it would be a big play that won. But if you'd put us in the same position, with 18 to play the next day, Johnny [Miller] might have won, or I might have. It's like tossing a coin when you're all playing that well.

—TOM WEISKOPF
ON THE 1975 MASTERS, WON BY JACK NICKLAUS

The last year's champion serves as the host. He chooses the menu and picks up the tab. When I discovered the cost of the dinner was more than the prize money, I finished second four times.

—BEN HOGAN
ON THE MASTERS DINNER

We don't want to get anybody killed. Of course, if we could pick which ones, it might be a different story.

—HORD HARDIN
CHAIRMAN OF AUGUSTA NATIONAL (1981–1991), AFTER LIGHTNING
HAD POSTPONED PLAY IN THE 1983 US MASTERS

I'll probably shoot 85 tomorrow.

—CHARLIE COE
SHOWING HIS PESSIMISM AFTER SHOOTING A
FIRST-ROUND 71 IN THE 1966 MASTERS

There is absolutely nothing humorous at the Masters. Here, small dogs do not bark and babies do not cry.

—GARY PLAYER

The greatest natural laxative in the world.

—FUZZY ZOELLER
ON THE FIRST HOLE OF THE MASTERS

My wife will find ways to spend $16,000 first-prize money in sixteen minutes.

—JULIUS BOROS
ON WINNING THE 1963 U.S. OPEN

All those who turn in 36-hole scores will make the cut.

—RAFAEL ALARCON
TOURING PRO, ON THE HORRIBLE CONDITIONS
IN THE FIRST ROUND OF THE 1986 MASTERS

In other sports they don't do anything differently than they have done all year, but golf is the only game that changes for a major event.

—RAYMOND FLOYD

I must admit the name was born of a touch of immodesty.

—BOBBY JONES
THE FOUNDER OF THE MASTERS

Leave all the social significance aside. This is like watching Babe Ruth in the 1920s.

—GEORGE WILL
ON TIGER WOODS WINNING THE 1997 MASTERS

I want the Masters bad! I'm going to Augusta in April and eating crow on the front steps.

—LEE TREVINO
AFTER YEARS OF CRITICIZING THE MASTERS

You get the feeling that Bobby Jones is standing out there with you.

—LEE JANZEN
ON THE MYSTIQUE OF THE MASTERS

They talk about the majors and how important they are. But you're playing the same guys you play every week, just on another golf course.

—SAM SNEAD

My God. I've won the Open.

—KEN VENTURI

AFTER WINNING THE 1964 U.S. OPEN

The only good job I've done this week is making a perfect fool of myself.

—SANDY LYLE

ON MISSING THE MASTERS CUT AFTER WINNING THE YEAR BEFORE

The USGA makes sure that every [US] Open is a paramount test of a player's ability to use the game's most definitive clubs, the driver and the putter.

—THOMAS BOSWELL

They keep trying to give me the championship, but I won't take it.

—LEO DIGEL

ON CHOKING IN THE LAST ROUND OF THE 1933 US OPEN

Winning the Open is the greatest thing in golf. I have come close before. This time I thought I'd won. But I didn't. Golf is played by the rules, and I broke a rule. I've learned a lesson. And I have two broad shoulders.

—JACKIE PUNG
  AFTER BEING DISQUALIFIED IN THE 1957 US WOMEN'S OPEN
  FOR RECORDING AN INCORRECT SCORE ON A HOLE

He's going to win more of these [Master's titles] than Arnold [Palmer] and I combined.

—JACK NICKLAUS
  AFTER A PRACTICE ROUND WITH TIGER WOODS
  AT THE MASTERS IN 1996

There should never, ever be a sense of inevitability about golf. Too much can go wrong, especially in a major championship. One half-bad swing, one gust of wind, one silly club selection can unravel it all, can turn apparent victory to disaster.

—MICHAEL WILBON
  "IT'S ALL BUT IN THE BAG," *WASHINGTON POST*

How's my name going to fit on that thing?

  —MARK CALCAVECCHIA
   ON WINNING THE CLARET JUG

I haven't even figured out what club I'm going to hit off the first tee.

  —FUZZY ZOELLER
   ASKED WHAT CLUB HE WOULD GIVE TO AUGUSTA TO
   PUT ON DISPLAY IF HE WON THE MASTERS

Is winning The Open worth a million pounds? Well, it's worthwhile winning it—I would recommend it to anybody.

  —SANDY LYLE

The majors are what golf's all about. The other ones you play for the prize money. These you play to get your name on a piece of silver.

— NICK FALDO

Maybe if I knock on the door enough, the door will open one day.

— COLIN MONTGOMERIE
ON COMING CLOSE TO WINNING A MAJOR TOURNAMENT

When I woke up Sunday morning at the Open and stepped outside and felt the wind and rain in my face, I knew I had an excellent chance to win if I just took my time and trusted myself.

— TOM KITE
ON FINALLY WINNING A MAJOR, THE 1992 US OPEN

Perhaps the best explanation is that Mac was harried in these events by some psychic injury . . . that, fed by his subsequent failure to produce in the Opens, grew into a complex of such obstinate proportions that the harder he fought to defeat it, the more viciously it defeated him.

— HERBERT WARREN WIND
ON WHY MACDONALD SMITH NEVER
PRODUCED IN THE MAJOR TOURNAMENTS

But here, the 100-player, the 80-player, the 75-player, has only one shot to play from the sand; and neither boldness nor skill will help him correct a position which may not have been his fault in the first place. He has one shot—the blast. That is all.

—TED RAY
ON THE UNFAIRNESS OF OAKMONT'S BUNKERS IN THE 1927 U.S. OPEN

How about that, amigo? I just come over to see my friends and I win ze bloody championship.

—ROBERTO DE VICENZO
ON WINNING THE 1967 OPEN CHAMPIONSHIP

I suggested that Ghezzi begin play and I would join him on the third hole conceding him wins on the first two . . . The kid was just mad enough to beat me on the first two holes anyway, then I began to play. I finally caught him and won.

—WALTER HAGEN
DESCRIBING HIS VICTORY IN THE 1940 PGA CHAMPIONSHIP
AFTER VIC GHEZZI SUGGESTED BEFORE THE MATCH
THAT HAGEN HURRY IT UP

Golfing excellence goes hand in hand with alcohol, as many an Open and Amateur champion has shown.

> —HENRY LONGHURST

Only Opens.

> —TOM WATSON
> WHEN ASKED IF HE COLLECTED ANYTHING SCOTTISH FOR LUCK

Throwing up on myself.

> —CURTIS STRANGE
> ON WHAT HE FELT LIKE DOING AFTER LOSING THE 1985 MASTERS

I'm not sure. I think it's 27.

> —RIVES MCBEE
> ASKED HIS AGE, AFTER SHOOTING A 64 IN
> THE SECOND ROUND OF THE 1966 US OPEN

I hit every shot the way I dreamed about today. But that's the strange thing about golf. You don't have any control about what your opponent does.

> —TOM KITE
>   LOSING THE 1986 MASTERS TO JACK NICKLAUS

I wasn't scared at the British. I didn't step down. I stayed strong. When I think back, there were a lot of testy putts . . . You know, in putting, it isn't so much the break as the speed. It's who wants to win. Pure willpower.

> —JESPER PARNEVIK
>   ON THE PUTTING CONDITIONS AT THE 1994 BRITISH OPEN

This lie is tighter than an Italian tenor's trouser buttons.

> —KEN BROWN
>   COMMENTATING ON THE 2004 OPEN CHAMPIONSHIP

He had that look today . . . I could all of a sudden see it in his eyes. It's this stary look, a blank . . . He saw me, but didn't see me. And I knew he had it under control . . . I've seen him win before without that look, but I've never seen him lose with it.

—MARIE FLOYD
ON HER HUSBAND, RAYMOND FLOYD, DURING THE FINAL ROUND OF
THE 1986 US OPEN

Were you in prison in 1984? Maybe you didn't get copies of the newspaper there?

—LEE TREVINO
1984 PGA WINNER, UPON BEING TOLD BY A REPORTER DURING THE
1986 US OPEN THAT HE HADN'T WON A MAJOR IN A LONG TIME

If the U.S. Ryder Cup team got washed up on a desert island, they would build twelve separate huts and go off and grill their own swordfish.

—MARTIN JOHNSON COLUMNIST, CRITICIZING THE
SELFISH ATTITUDE OF AMERICAN PROS

I played 36 holes today with a kid who should have won this Open by ten shots.

—BEN HOGAN
ON THE AMATEUR JACK NICKLAUS AT THE 1960 US OPEN

I have seen men who have won a dozen or more tournaments, upon teeing off for their first USGA Open Championship, come close to vomiting. And golf is no easy game when you are trying to hole a downhill three-footer and throwing up at the same time.

—CHARLES PRICE

I can't see how I'm going to get out of it.

—NICK JOB
SURPRISED SECOND ROUND LEADER OF THE 1981 BRITISH OPEN WHEN ASKED HOW HE WAS GOING TO HANDLE BEING IN THE FINAL GROUP

I was so nervous today I was almost jumping out of my skin all day. Usually when I'm playing decent, I'm nervous.

—TOM WATSON
ON WINNING THE 1981 MASTERS

———— ✦ ————

A million thoughts went through my mind. What a little mind I have.

—FUZZY ZOELLER
AFTER WINNING THE MASTERS

CHAPTER EIGHTEEN

A Passion for Golf:
Why We Love This Game

I must remind those who stand accused that despite dispensing with the formality of again swearing you in, each of you remain under oath. Counselor, you may proceed.

Thank you, your Honor.

The above exchange is purely hypothetical. Were a trial to take place to determine the extent of the commission of crimes of golf passion, the dock would be crowded, the evidence damning. Any hope of exoneration for the brazen offenders, particularly from an unsympathetic, non-golfing jury, must be considered remote at best. (One may hold out hope that judge plays but that's not much to go on.)

The list of alleged first-degree felonies is long and lengthy.

You, sir, the pathetic soul said to have thrown his clubs into the sea only to nearly drown trying to retrieve them. We find the defendant guilty. Mr. Michael Jordan, the suit alleges that you were a "no-show" for the presentation of your first NBA Most Valuable Player award, that you were playing thirty-six holes at Pinehurst at the time. Throw the book at him!

The golfer who participated in a tournament with his right arm in a full cast? Guilty! The sap who owns 150 putters? Guilty! The golfer who played seven courses in one day? The traveler who teed it up in London, New York and Los Angeles on a single day. Guilty! Guilty! Guilty!

Let the record reflect that no similar eccentric devotion exists elsewhere in sport. Not hardly. So, in conclusion, before we throw ourselves on the mercy of the court in the matter of Humanity v. Golf, we ask only that the judge recall the finding of the late Abigail Van Buren. Her precedent-setting ruling with respect to enforced ultimatums remains worthy of your consideration. Thank you, your Honor. With that, the defense rests.

* * * * *

The pleasures of golf are increased a thousand-fold when it is played correctly.

—ALEXANDER "SANDY" HERD
BRITISH GOLFER AND INSTRUCTOR

If they don't have golf in heaven then I'm not going.

—AN INSCRIPTION ON A PILLOW IN ARNOLD PALMER'S HOME

I play because I like it, very much. I play golf for money when I play an exhibition. But when I play in a tournament I'm there because I enjoy it.

—SEVE BALLESTEROS
GOLF DIGEST

The amateur has an infectious, contagious enthusiasm for golf and life.

—MAC O'GRADY

Man blames fate for other accidents but feels personally responsible for a hole in one.

—MARTHA BECKMAN

How can you get tired of playing golf?

—RAYMOND FLOYD

It's a faithless love, but you hit four good shots and you've started your day right.

—DINAH SHORE

I live for the loud smacking sound I hear when the clubface comes into the ball at high speed and contacts its center back portion, hard.

—JOHN DALY
FROM *GRIP IT AND RIP IT* BY JOHN DALY AND JOHN ANDRISANI

I love golf, but I'm not going to sacrifice everything for the game. If some people want to, I think it's wonderful.

—GLORIA ARMSTRONG
LPGA PROFESSIONAL

It's not a big risk to me . . . My sites are really so well-located, in such great areas, that if the golf were to fail, I could probably make more money putting housing on them. But I won't do that. I enjoy golf too much.

    —DONALD TRUMP
    GOLF DIGEST

Woods and Kite play golf because they love it. To them it is art. They paint pictures with their clubs. Neither one can wait for the next day of golf.

    —JIM McLEAN
    FROM *THE EIGHT-STEP SWING*

What made him the most special wasn't all the tournament and awards he's won. It was his pure unequaled love for the game.

    —NICK PRICE
    ON ARNOLD PALMER

What other people may find in poetry or art museums, I find in the flight of a good drive.

    —ARNOLD PALMER

I can only tell you one thing that I do know for sure, I am a dreamer . . . I continue to get up in the morning, enthusiastically, and go pick up a golf club with a thought that I can somewhere find that secret to making the cut.

—ARNOLD PALMER

Golf may be a hussy, but I love her.

—DON HEROLD
AMERICAN HUMORIST, WRITER, ILLUSTRATOR AND AVID GOLFER

The great thing about golf—and this is the reason why a lot of health experts like me recommend it—you can drink beer and ride in a cart while you play.

—DAVE BARRY

Golf to me is not a business; it's an art form, like a Picasso or a Steinbeck novel.

—TOM WATSON

The steps you hit your drive past your opponent are the most golden you'll walk in your life.

— PAUL BERTHODY

My love of golf is part of my religion. I introduce the game to friends and other people constantly, hoping they will get from it what I have.

— BILL BLUE
LPGA COMMISSIONER

The fun you get from golf is in direct ratio to the effort you don't put into it.

— BOB ALLEN

Golf may be . . . a sophisticated game. At least, it is usually played with the outward appearance of dignity. It is, nevertheless, a game of considerable passion, either of the explosive type, or that which burns inwardly and sears the soul.

— BOBBY JONES

When you fall in love with golf, you seldom fall easy. It's obsession at first sight.

—THOMAS BOSWELL

If there were no professional football, you wouldn't find four or five guys to put out there. People pay to play golf. Nobody plays football for anything, at least not after the age of 21.

—JOHN BRODIE
ON WHY GOLF IS A PARTICIPANT SPORT
AND FOOTBALL IS A SPECTATOR SPORT

I like it for the same reason a lot of other busy people don't: I like it because it takes so much time.

—PRESIDENT BILL CLINTON
GOLF TODAY

Just having fun. Got to do it while I've still got it.

—TIGER WOODS

This game is great, and very strange.

—SEVE BALLESTEROS

———•———

I love golf. It is a wonderful game, one that at any given moment, with any given shot, you can do as well as the best player in the world.

—BOB COSTAS

———•———

I try to play every day and when I don't play—if you'll excuse the expression—I feel like a bear with a sore tail because of it.

—ARNOLD PALMER
FROM *A GOLFER'S LIFE WITH JAMES DODSON*

———•———

This is the best. This is just too perfect, so serene, so peaceful. There's nothing like it.

—BEN CRENSHAW

Love is the ultimate outlaw. It just won't adhere to any rules. The most any of us can do is sign on as its accomplice.

—TOM WATSON

ON GOLF

Golf is my life and I love it. I'd play with rocks if I had to.

—MARGARET CURTIS

I simply wanted to do nothing . . . My nothing meant simply to play golf . . . This may seem incredible to those who have never fallen hopelessly in love with the game.

—BERNARD DARWIN

I just love to play golf. I try to play 365 days a year. I don't care if it's January or June. I wanted to play on Christmas Day, but my wife looked at me kind of funny, so I thought I'd better not.

—LEE TREVINO

I make my living out of golf, but it is still a game to me. When it becomes work and not fun, I'll go into something else.

—JIMMY DEMARET

Golf is more than a mere game. It is a religion.

—WALTER TRAVIS

Life is a journey and it must be enjoyed—and, like golf, part of the fun is that you never know where it might take you.

—DR. BOB ROTELLA
SPORTS PSYCHOLOGIST

I feel very fortunate to make a living playing a game I love and look forward to the next ten years.

—TIGER WOODS

The simple truth is I love Scottish golf and all the peculiar experience that embraces.

—JAMES DODSON
IN HIS 1997 ESSAY, "GOLF IN THE HOMELAND"

In vain will a player with a woebegone countenance endeavor to go a round. Before he has played a couple of holes, he will brighten up, his whole aspect will become changed and happiness will shine forth on his face.

—Dr. Proudfoot
1890

They will take out this volume from its secret hiding place and they will say: 'There is no question, son, that these were unholy places in an evil age. Unfortunately, I had a whale of a time.'

—Alistair Cooke
ON THE DAY THAT GOLF ENDS

Golf obviously provides one of our best forms of healthful exercise accompanied by good fellowship and companionship.

—President Dwight D. Eisenhower

I'm just playing for the love of the game. And for the little cups.

—Nick Faldo
From Peter Allis's *Golf Heroes*

I don't like going to the mall. I'm not really like the other girls. I just like to go out on the golf course and play. Golf is fun and feels really good.

  —MICHELLE WIE

I play golf so I can fly. At $2 a gallon for fuel, I have to support my habit somehow.

  —BILL GLASSON

I owe everything to golf. Where else would a guy with an IQ like mine make this much money?

  —HUBERT GREEN
  PGA TOUR PRO

Adeline was looking up at him tenderly. 'May I come, too, and walk round with you?' Cuthbert's bosom heaved. 'Oh,' she said, with a tremor in his voice, 'that you would walk round with me for life!'

  —P.G. WODEHOUSE
  THE CLICKING OF CUTHBERT

The game lends itself to fantasies about our abilities.

—PETER ALLISS

At Westward Ho! we step straight into the pure air of sanctity, an open plain and limitless sky; and if we are capable of an emotion worthy of the occasion we shall hear the sound of an invisible and celestial choir echoing in our ears.

—H.N. WETHERED AND TOM SIMPSON
ON THE GOLFING EXPERIENCE

Everything about golf has been a challenge to me, a great and wonderful riddle wanting to be solved. It's been that pursuit that has been my lifeblood.

—JIM HARDY
FROM *THE PLANE TRUTH FOR GOLFERS*

As someone who loves the game and owes his livelihood to it, I value the fact that golf, more than any other sport, is built on honor, integrity, and playing within the rules.

—SHAWN HUMPHRIES
FROM *TWO STEPS TO A PERFECT GOLF SWING*

I am a slave to golf.

—ENID WILSON
WINNER OF THE 1925 BRITISH GIRLS' TITLE

———◆———

After all, as every golfer in every land will attest after a good round, it may well be the best game ever invented.

—HERBERT WARREN WIND

———◆———

Golf is just so much fun. I don't see how anybody can't have a great time out here doing what we're doing.

—PETER JACOBSEN

———◆———

There is a basic fascination with golf unlike other games. No ordinary person could go one round with the heavyweight boxing champion . . . But a golfer may at any time hit that one spectacular shot just as well as Ben Hogan, Arnold Palmer, or Greg Norman.

—PETE DYE

671

A tolerable day, a tolerable green, a tolerable opponent supply, or ought to supply, all that any reasonably constituted human should require in the way of entertainment.

—ARTHUR JAMES
FIRST EARL OF BALFOUR, IN *GOLF*

Regardless of what the Tour pros think, golf is a rich and varied game, and what all of us awkward fools do on weekends is what golf is truly all about.

—DAN JENKINS

I'm a golfaholic, no question about it. Counseling wouldn't help me. They'd have to put me in prison. And then I'd talk the warden into building a hole or two to teach him how to play.

—LEE TREVINO

It is the whole man, mind and body. That is the meaning of the temperamental factor in golf, and that is why a great match at golf is great indeed.

—HENRY LEACH

When I look on my life and try to decide out of what I have got most actual pleasure, I have no doubt at all in saying that I have got more out of golf than anything else.

—LORD BRABAZON
THE BRABAZON STORY

———◆———

The great thing about this game is that the bad days are wonderful.

—PRESIDENT BILL CLINTON

———◆———

No athletic game affords such opportunity for cool calculation or such occasion for self-examination and self-castigation as golf.

—JOHN L. LOW

———◆———

Unlike the other Scotch game of whisky-drinking, excess is not injurious to the health.

—SIR WALTER SIMPSON

It is almost impossible to remember how tragic a place the world is when one is playing golf.

—ROBERT LYND
SOCIOLOGIST

When I get out on that green carpet called a fairway, manage to poke the ball right down the middle, my surroundings look like a touch of heaven on earth.

—JIMMY DEMARET

Golf charms by its infinite variety.

—THEODORE MOONE

One of the beauties of the sport is the inspirational heart-stopping move that reminds us of possibilities yet unguessed.

—MICHAEL MURPHY
FROM *GOLF IN THE KINGDOM*

Like other forms of compulsive behavior, for true golfaholics even nine holes are more then they should attempt, yet 18 holes are not enough to satisfy their insatiable craving for humiliation and self-abuse.

—MARK OMAN

Golf is deceptively simple and endlessly complicated; it satisfies the soul and frustrates the intellect. It is at the same time rewarding and maddening— and it is without a doubt the greatest game mankind has ever invented.

—ARNOLD PALMER

In golf you've got to try to cover all the bases, just like in life. It's the best microcosm of life I know. That's why we all love this game so much.

—DAVE PELZ
FROM *DAVE PELZ'S SHORT GAME BIBLE*

No one will ever have golf under his thumb. No round ever will be so good it could not have been better. Perhaps this is why golf is the greatest of games. You are not playing a human adversary; you are playing a game. You are playing old man par.

—BOBBY JONES

Obviously yet mysteriously, [golf] furnishes its devotees with an intense, many-sided, and abiding pleasure unlike that which any other form of recreation affords.

—HERBERT WARREN WIND

Shall the married man play golf? This admits of no argument. Certainly. Of all the plagues to a woman in the house is a man during the day.

—DR. PROUDFOOT

They don't offer me a championship sitting on my butt back in New Jersey. I like playing golf. I got nothing better to do. You play the greatest golf courses in the country and they're in great shape. It's a lot of fun.

—JIM MCGOVERN
ON PLAYING 67 TOURNAMENTS IN 1991 AND 1992

Golf is the most fun you can have without taking your clothes off.

—CHI-CHI RODRIGUEZ

The pleasure I get from hitting the ball dead center on the club is comparable only to one or two other pleasures that come to mind at the moment.

—DINAH SHORE

The beauty of golf, you're in charge out here.

—MIKE WEIR

My only fear is that I may have to go out and get a real job.

—FUZZY ZOELLER

Some of us worship in churches, some in synagogues, some on golf courses.

—ADLAI STEVENSON

I like golf because I can go out and hit a little white ball that doesn't move and doesn't hit back. It should be easy, but it isn't.

—LAWRENCE TAYLOR
PRO FOOTBALL HALL OF FAMER

Golf will grow so long as it's fun.

—TOM WATSON

It is really a great thing to know that although a man can be paid for playing a game he loves, he can at the same time play for the honor of his team and his country.

—SAMUEL RYDER

That's my business [real estate], you understand? This golf thing isn't my business. I love it, but I'll make more money from selling A-Rod a place than I'd make all year from a golf course. But I get a kick out of the golf thing.

—DONALD TRUMP
GOLF DIGEST

Golf has so many virtues: it is not too strenuous; it is healthy; it can be played, anyhow in our climate, practically the whole year round. It has so many advantages over all other games that it must endure and prosper.

—LORD BRABAZON

One reason I love golf is, it puts you in the moment. It's like rock climbing or kayaking or skiing. There's something in the immediacy.

  —MIKE UDAL
   U.S. CONGRESSMAN

Golf appeals to the idiot in us and the child. Just how childlike golf players become is proven by their frequent inability to count past five.

  —JOHN UPDIKE

I think at that time I really fell in love with the game. I'd always loved golf, but now it was a new type of love that I could have.

  —TOM WATSON
   AFTER BEATING JACK NICKLAUS BY ONE
   STROKE IN THE 1977 BRITISH OPEN

I feel like I'm good enough to play as good as I did five or six years ago. But I think the difference is now that I might really enjoy it—not that I never appreciated—I just didn't understand how good I was playing. Now if I get that form going, I think I'll really enjoy it.

  —KARRIE WEBB

I like golf cause—well, I reckon I jes' love to play the game.

—Sam Snead

The older inhabitants of St. Andrews may be indifferent to catastrophes, but all of them are golfers bound together in one common enthusiasm for the game.

—Joyce Wethered

Go out and have fun. Golf is a game for everyone, not just for the talented few.

—Harvey Penick

No inconvenient reminiscences of the ordinary workaday world, no intervals of weariness or monotony interrupt the pleasures of the game.

—Arthur James
Golf

Beyond the fact that it is a limitless arena for the full play of human nature, there is no sure accounting for golf's fascination . . . Perhaps it is nothing more than the best game man has ever devised.

—HERBERT WARREN WIND

What is love compared with holing out before your opponent.

—P.G. WODEHOUSE

Golf to me isn't just something to do. I love this game. It's like a drug I have to have.

—TIGER WOODS
FROM PETER ALLIS'S *GOLF HEROES*

I could only have met these people through golf. No football player or baseball player can get close to people through the playing of their game. Golf brings people together like no other sport.

—JIMMY DEMARET
FROM *JIMMY DEMARET: THE SWING'S THE THING*,
BY JOHN COMPANIOTTE

I'm a guy who'll play with amateurs. A $50 Nassau, $500, $5,000 or nothing. It doesn't matter. I just like to play.

—LEE TREVINO
GOLF DIGEST

Golf is just one thing to me—the pure pleasure of the golf swing.

—MICKEY WRIGHT
WINNER OF 82 LPGA TOURNAMENTS

I don't want the money if I have to make it this way. I want to live my life outdoors. I want to play golf.

—BABE ZAHARIAS
TO HER SISTER ESTHER NANCY, ON HER DECISION TO GIVE UP A
DEPRESSION-ERA VAUDEVILLE CONTRACT TO PLAY COMPETITIVE GOLF

I've never been to Heaven, and thinkin' back on my life, I probably won't get a chance to go. I guess the Masters is as close as I am going to get.

—FUZZY ZOELLER

There are no guarantees in this game—not to mention this life—and we have only a short time to enjoy it. Even when I'm not playing particularly well, I enjoy what I do.

  —Scott Simpson

There is no type of miracle that can't happen at least once in golf.

  —Grantland Rice

Few things draw two men together more surely than a mutual inability to master golf, coupled with an intense and ever-increasing love for the game.

  —P.G. Wodehouse

You can get close enough to mastering the game, to feel it, to breathe it, maybe to smell it. But you can't master it, not for a long time.

  —Tom Watson

A day of clubs, a silver town or two,
A flask of scotch, a pipe of shag—and thou
Beside me caddying in the wilderness—
Ah, wilderness were paradise enow.

  —H.W. BOYNTON
   IN *THE GOLFER'S RUBAIYAT*

Its [golf's] fascinations have always been gratefully acknowledged, and not a few of its worthier practioners have from time to time in prose and verse, rehearsed its praises.

  —ROBERT CLARK

To dwell near a good course and work hard at the game; to go away whenever the spirit moved one . . . to some paradise by the seas with a pleasant companion or two; to stay as long as one liked . . . even to think of it is still to feel faintly the old desire.

  —BERNARD DARWIN
   ON PARADISE

It matters not the sacrifice which makes the duffer's wife sore. I am the captive of my slice, the servant of my score.

—GRANTLAND RICE

You're only here for a short visit. Don't hurry, don't worry. And be sure to smell the flowers along the way.

—WALTER HAGEN

CHAPTER NINETEEN

Celebrities on the Links:
From Movie Stars to Presidents

They enter talking, readily identifiable by their sun-drenched skin, lifted laugh lines, square jaws, and their spiked highlights accented by the light just so. They laugh a little too loud, infuse their surroundings with just a bit too much bonhomie. You'd think we'd be used to it by now. But, no. The celebrity golfer is mildly distressing even after all these years. The problem is they're out of context, on the wrong set, bereft of a laugh-track, participants in an unscripted reality show. Mugging for the camera gives them points. They're putting it on the line, sans publicist, make-up, best boy. It can't be easy.

If somewhat less reluctant to publicly embarrass themselves, political golfing luminaries have similar concerns. Just as unfairly, the top dogs are held to a ridiculous standard. Carry a few extra clubs, take an extra mulligan, pick up a putt and they're branded with the scarlet letter. Bump the regular Tuesday seniors from the course, or play better than they have any right to expect, well then, what's HE doing playing golf? We've got budget deficits that need reducing. Back to work!

Both enthusiasts assuredly suffer for their golf, sharing an inability to play nearly enough as they might like. We could be more sympathetic. They can't help themselves playing the fool, and to be fair, neither can we. This is not necessarily a bad thing. When the famous, the serious, the self-important—and the genuinely important—fall on their face, there is a silver lining. The prospects are good for their coming away with a little humility along with the sand in their glistening pearly whites from the third attempt to escape from a greenside bunker. This is all to the good, receiving the occasional refreshing sting from the slap from reality, just as it is for the rest of us.

* * * * *

Finally I'm vindicated. I'm certainly one of the most talented athletes ever to come out of the Chicago area, and I've been largely unappreciated . . . but at least I'm able to claim the glory that is rightly mine . . . I am now recognized as a true athletic hero.

—BILL MURRAY
AFTER DEFEATING MICHAEL JORDAN AND
D.A. WEILBRING IN A CHARITY EVENT IN CHICAGO

A fidgety player who addressed the ball as if he could reason with it.

—AN ANONYMOUS CHARACTERIZATION OF
PRESIDENT WOODROW WILSON'S GOLF GAME

It took me seventeen years to get 3,000 hits in baseball. I did it in one afternoon on the golf course.

—HANK AARON

I can't hit a ball more than 200 yards. I have no butt. You need a butt if you're going to hit a golf ball.

—DENNIS QUAID
ACTOR

I played one of the days with Sam Jackson, George Lopez and Cheech Marin . . . Sam is over there contemplating the game of golf and what it means . . . and Cheech and George are trying to figure out who has had the best one-liner so far. That just cracks me up.

—Justin Leonard
about a Pro-Am

When golf season comes around, I get like a piano player who doesn't shake hands with anybody for fear of hurting himself . . . I haven't reached an accommodation with that phobia, so here I sit, fat and soft.

—Bryant Gumbel

Sometimes when I look down at that little white golf ball, I just wish it was moving.

—Dusty Baker
Former Major League ballplayer and Manager

I've always said basketball players are the greatest athletes in the world, but I think golfers are the greatest professional performers because they have no teammates.

—SPARKY ANDERSON
HALL OF FAME BASEBALL MANAGER

———•———

It's nice to get outside. And it's a great thing to do on tour, especially in cities I've visited so many times I know the animals at the zoo by their first name.

—AMY GRANT
SINGER, ON TAKING UP GOLF

———•———

It's amazing how many people beat you at golf now that you're no longer president.

—PRESIDENT GEORGE H. BUSH

———•———

Here's the man who won the Lunar Open, and his closest competition was 250,000 miles away.

—GENE CERNAN
ASTRONAUT, ON ALAN SHEPARD

George Plimpton always said the smaller the ball, the better the writing.
—DAVE ANDERSON
THE NEW YORK TIMES

You can't do well if you're thinking about anything else . . . This is the nearest I ever am to being a normal person.
—PRESIDENT BILL CLINTON
ON GOLF, FROM *GOLF TODAY*

The terrible beauty is that in the brotherhood of golf (feminists please excuse the term) we are all the same—certifiable.
—SEAN CONNERY

The problem with golf is I have to deal with a humiliation factor.
—PRESIDENT GEORGE H. BUSH

I think golf is good for boxing, but the reverse is far from being the case.
—MAX BAER
FORMER WORLD HEAVYWEIGHT CHAMPION

It would have been like a friend of mine coming out of the stands to pass the time of day when I was at bat.

—JOE DiMAGGIO
WHEN ASKED WHAT HE THOUGHT OF TALKING
TO GOLFERS WHILE THEY WERE PLAYING

———◆———

I really like Bill, but I don't think I'd ever go down to a set where he's shooting a movie and jump and scream like a maniac.

—FRED COUPLES
ON THE ANTICS OF BILL MURRAY AT THE PEBBLE BEACH PRO-AM

———◆———

Bob Hope's swing? I've seen better swings on a condemned playground.

—BING CROSBY

———◆———

Some players would complain if they were playing on Dolly Parton's bed-spread.

—JIMMY DEMARET

I'm a 16 at Sleepy Hollow, up in Westchester [N.Y.]. Won one tournament there, and got a trophy—Headless Horseman. Figures. Best score ever: 79.
—BILL MURRAY

On one hole I'm like Arnold Palmer, and on the next like Lilli Palmer.
—SEAN CONNERY

Lots of golfers spend their time wondering whether to lay up or go for it. I'm always going for it because that's the way I play football.
—BRETT FAVRE
QUARTERBACK, GREEN BAY PACKERS

He has a good swing, he hits it hard, a little erratic, but I understand that.
—PRESIDENT GERALD FORD
ON BILL CLINTON

Your financial cost can best be figured out when you realize if you were to devote the same time and energy to business instead of golf, you would be a millionaire in approximately six weeks.
—BUDDY HACKETT
ON PLAYING GOLF

At least he can't cheat on his score because all you have to do is look back down the fairway and count the wounded.

—BOB HOPE
ABOUT GERALD FORD

I would like to deny all allegations by Bob Hope that during my last game of golf, I hit an eagle, a birdie, an elk and a moose.

—PRESIDENT GERALD FORD

Give me my golf clubs, fresh air, and a beautiful partner, and you can keep my golf clubs and the fresh air.

—JACK BENNY

That's Jack Benny. He's always out there on bad days like that looking for golf balls.

—BING CROSBY
AFTER A SKIN DIVER CAME OUT OF THE WATER
AT THE 16TH HOLE OF THE CROSBY PRO-AM

Where I play, the greens always break toward the bar.

  —GEORGE GOBEL
   WRITER

When someone has a bad day like that on the golf course, you say, Greg, you look good, you look fantastic. I like your shoes, I like your pants, I like your . . . well, the hat's okay. I mean, you need to keep it light. Instead they say, Greg, what's next? Suicide? Alcoholism? Drugs?

  —BILL MURRAY
   ON THE MEDIA'S CRITICISM OF GREG NORMAN
   AFTER HIS MASTERS LOSS

Either he is an unbelievable athlete or I have a career as a golf instructor.

  —PRESIDENT BILL CLINTON
   TO PRIME MINISTER TONY BLAIR AFTER
   HIS FIRST ROUND OF GOLF EVER

Here Eddie, hold the flag while I putt out.

  —WALTER HAGEN
   TO THE PRINCE OF WALES

Doook! Doook! You forgot to pay your green fee!

—BESSIE FENN
MANAGER OF THE BRAKERS GOLF OPERATIONS, RUNNING AFTER THE
DUKE OF WINDSOR AFTER HE HAD FINISHED THE FIRST HOLE

You know, this is like having Billy Martin in your pocket.

—MICKEY MANTLE
ON USING A DEVICE ON THE GOLF COURSE THAT
UTTERS CURSES AT THE PUSH OF A BUTTON

I think if I were going to pick three people I could spend the day talking to, it would be Lincoln and the two Roosevelts.

—PRESIDENT BILL CLINTON
GOLF DIGEST

One lesson you better learn if you want to be in politics is that you never go out on a golf course and beat the President.

—PRESIDENT LYNDON JOHNSON

He hits the ball 130 yards and his jewelry goes 150.

> —Bob Hope
> on Sammy Davis, Jr.

That does look like very good exercise. But what is the little white ball for?

> —President Ulysses S. Grant

I was three over—one over a house, one over a patio, and one over a swimming pool.

> —George Brett
> Baseball Hall of Famer

One time I was complaining that my shot was going to wind up in the water. So my friend Kevin Carroll told me that I should think positive. I told him okay, I was positive my shot was going to wind up in the water.

> —Yogi Berra
> from *Trump: The Best Golf Advice I Ever Received*

I don't have any handicap. I am all handicap.

—President Lyndon Johnson

Welcome, grave stranger, to our green retreats,
Where health with exercise and freedom meets.

—Sir Walter Scott

I can only thank Davis Love III for turning me on to golf and showing me
it isn't a sissy game.

—Michael Jordan
NBA superstar, who took up golf in his college days

I'll be playing center for the Bulls before Michael plays on the tour.

—Peter Jacobsen
describing Michael Jordan's shot at joining the Tour

The King's guards shall attend him at the church and also when he goeth
to the fields to walk or goff.

—Lord Lothian
on Charles II

Absolutely not. I would have let him fall on his face.

—ANDREW MAGEE
WHEN ASKED IF HE WOULD HAVE CAUGHT PRESIDENT CLINTON IF
HE HAD FALLEN IN MAGEE'S HOUSE INSTEAD OF GREG NORMAN'S

———

My golf is woeful but I will never surrender.

—BING CROSBY

———

My best score is 103. But I've only been playing fifteen years.

—ALEX KARRAS
FORMER NFL GREAT

———

Before I got out of the rough in one tournament it had turned into a shopping center.

—BOB HOPE
ON HIS PLAY IN A PRO-AM TOURNAMENT

———

Every time I look down, I think I'm in the rough.

—JACK LEMMON
ON GROWING A MOUSTACHE

A typical day in the life of a heavy metal musician consists of a round of golf and an AA meeting.

—BILLY JOEL

First of all, unless you're Charles Barkley, you have to have a low handicap. I don't want to go just to go—I want to have fun. I go to Pebble Beach to have fun, but I also think I can win. Did I just say that again?

—BILL MURRAY

I'd rather make the cut in the Crosby than win another Oscar.

—JACK LEMMON

Mr. Agnew, I believe you have a slight swing in your flaw.

—JIMMY DEMARET
TO VICE PRESIDENT SPIRO AGNEW

I'd love to see John McEnroe join the PGA Tour, just so we could kick him out.

—PETER JACOBSEN

I have an insane desire to shave a stroke or two off my golf handicap.

—ALISTAIR COOKE
ON WHY HE WAS RETIRING

Not even Barbra Streisand celebrates herself as tirelessly as golf celebrates itself.

—BRUCE MCCALL
"THE CASE AGAINST GOLF," FROM *ESQUIRE*

Some golfers fantasize about playing in a foursome with Arnold Palmer, Jack Nicklaus, and Sam Snead. The way I hit I'd rather play in a foursome with Helen Keller, Ray Charles, and Stevie Wonder.

—BRUCE LANSKY
AUTHOR

Most of these guys only want to grow up and mature. When I retire, I'm going to enjoy being a black multi-millionaire.

—CHARLES BARKLEY
ON THE CELEBRITY GOLF TOUR

I play in the low 80s. If it's any hotter than that, I won't play.

> —JOE LOUIS
> FORMER HEAVYWEIGHT CHAMPION OF THE WORLD

Once when I was golfing in Georgia, I hooked the ball into the swamp. I went after it and found an alligator wearing a shirt with a picture of a little golfer on it.

> —BUDDY HACKETT
> COMEDIAN

By the time you get dressed, drive out there, play 18 holes, and come home, you've blown seven hours. There are better things you can do with your time.

> —PRESIDENT RICHARD NIXON

The actual distance a bad golfer is going to hit the ball with any club obviously depends on many factors, not the least of which is whether the ball was actually hit at all.

> —LESLIE NIELSEN

In golf, when we hit a foul ball, we got to go out and play it.

    —SAM SNEAD
        TO BASEBALL GREAT TED WILLIAMS

I would have been worried if they played well. It would have meant they were spending too much time playing golf and not enough time running the country.

    —SEVE BALLESTEROS
        AFTER PLAYING WITH PORTUGAL'S PRESIDENT
        AND MINISTER OF JUSTICE.

I would rather play Hamlet with no rehearsal than play golf on television.

    —JACK LEMMON

Find a man with both feet firmly on the ground and you've found a man about to make a difficult putt.

    —FLETCHER KNEBEL
        AUTHOR

In golf, you keep your head down and follow through. In the vice presidency, you keep your head up and follow through. It's a big difference.

  —DAN QUAYLE

There we go! Miles and miles and miles!

  —ALAN SHEPARD
   AFTER HITTING A TEE-SHOT ON THE MOON

At the end of the day he had an 82 on his score card, but it took him two hundred swings to get there.

  —DON VAN NATTA
   DESCRIBING BILL CLINTON'S GOLF GAME, CNN

The Secret Service is in front of you. And the Air Force is flying over you. But the worst part is that the Marines are digging sand traps for your balls.

  —BOB HOPE
   ON PLAYING GOLF WITH PRESIDENTS

707

I have no ambitions, no goals. I just want to maintain enough celebrity status so they'll keep inviting me to golf tournaments.

—LESLIE NIELSEN
ACTOR AND COMEDIAN

Swing hard in case you hit it.

—DAN MARINO

He plays such a great game of golf for a guy wearing skis.

—BOB HOPE
ABOUT PRESIDENT GERALD FORD

Got more dirt than ball. Here we go again.

—ALAN SHEPARD
PREPARING TO TAKE ANOTHER SWING DURING
HIS FAMOUS MOON WALK IN 1971

If everybody in Washington in government service who belongs or has belonged to a restricted [golf] club was to leave government service, this city would have the highest rate of unemployment . . . in the country.

—PRESIDENT RICHARD NIXON

How about a little noise. How do you expect a man to putt?

—BABE RUTH
WHEN THE CROWD BECAME SILENT AS HE LINED UP A PUTT

You've heard of Arnie's Army. Well, those are Dean's Drunks.

—DEAN MARTIN
ON HIS FOLLOWERS ON THE GOLF COURSE

If I swung the gavel the way I swung that golf club, the nation would be a helluva mess.

—THOMAS "TIP" P. O'NEILL
FORMER SPEAKER OF THE HOUSE OF REPRESENTATIVES

I've done as much for golf as Truman Capote has done for sumo wrestling.

—BOB HOPE

Stick your butt out, Mr. President.

—SAM SNEAD
ADVICE TO PRESIDENT EISENHOWER WHEN THE
PRESIDENT ASKED WHY HIS SWING WAS RESTRICTED

President [George H.] Bush does not take mulligans. That family plays by the rules.

—Ben Crenshaw

Don't ever walk in front of them.

—Scott Hoch
ON WHAT HE LEARNED FROM PLAYING GOLF WITH
PRESIDENTS BUSH, CLINTON, AND FORD

Grass? Give me a bucket of balls and a sand wedge. Sure I like grass.

—Ivan Lendl
ON CLAIMS HE DIDN'T LIKE PLAYING ON GRASS

What surprised me is how often these presidents reveal themselves and their style of leadership on the golf course.

—Don Van Natta
CNN

Probably I'm a hell of a lot more famous for being the guy who hit the golf ball on the moon than the first guy in space.

 —ALAN SHEPARD
  ASTRONAUT

I just can't find it when I hit it.

 —JERRY WEST
  NBA HALL OF FAMER, ON HIS GOLF GAME

The best perk of this office is who you get to play golf with. I've played with Jack Nicklaus, Arnold Palmer, Raymond Floyd, Amy Alcott.

 —PRESIDENT BILL CLINTON

I was like, 'Oh my God, it's the secretary of state. They put me in charge of driving her around [in the golf cart]. I was like, if I crash, the secretary of state goes down with me.'

    —MICHELLE WIE

Baseball reveals character; golf exposes it.

    —ERNIE BANKS
      BASEBALL HALL OF FAMER

Whenever I play with him, I usually try to make it a foursome—the president, myself, a paramedic, and a faith healer.

    —BOB HOPE
      ON PRESIDENT GERALD FORD

The best part is I've taken five strokes off my golf game.

    —ELLEN DeGENERES
      ON COMING OUT OF THE CLOSET

If Bill Clinton is an 8-handicap, I'm Bobby Jones.

—PRESIDENT GEORGE H. BUSH
ON CLINTON'S CLAIM OF BEING AN 8-HANDICAP

———•———

I may not know enough about being President, but I do know that a lot of decisions can be made on the golf course.

—PRESIDENT WARREN HARDING

———•———

Golf is fine relief from the tensions of office, but we are getting a little tired of holding the bag.

—ADLAI STEVENSON
ON PRESIDENT EISENHOWER'S LOVE OF GOLF

———•———

Every time you swing you have a chance for greatness.

—KEVIN COSTNER

———•———

I'm not feeling very well—I need a doctor immediately. Ring the nearest golf course.

—GROUCHO MARX

Hit till you're happy.

>—PRESIDENT LYNDON JOHNSON
>ON HIS GOLF STRATEGY

I play boring golf. I don't hit it far, but I hit it straight. I just plod along.

>—CHRIS CHOCOLA
>U.S. CONGRESSMAN

The greatest thrill of my life—even better than getting elected.

>—PRESIDENT RICHARD NIXON
>ON HIS FIRST HOLE-IN-ONE

I think my skills are at that level. Plus, Birmingham has some nice golf courses.

>—MICHAEL JORDAN
>ON BEING SENT TO THE BIRMINGHAM BARONS,
>THE WHITE SOX DOUBLE A AFFILIATE

I envy that man. Because he makes a hundred thousand dollars a year like I do, but nobody knows him.

—MICKEY MANTLE
ON GOLFER MILLER BARBER

Orville was on the Tour a year before he stopped saluting his caddy.

—BOB HOPE
ON ORVILLE MOODY, AN EX-MARINE TURNED GOLF PRO

Golf isn't like politics when Clinton can get to the center just by throwing Hillary over the side. Golf takes work.

—TONY KORNHEISER
WASHINGTON POST COLUMNIST

Congress.

—PRESIDENT LYNDON JOHNSON
WHEN ASKED HIS HANDICAP WHEN HE SHOWED UP AT THE MASTERS

My golf game reminds me of Woody Hayes's football game—three years and a cloud of dust.

    —BILL DOOLEY
        FORMER HEAD FOOTBALL COACH, WAKE FOREST UNIVERSITY

It should be in when the opportunity arises, as every man who has played the game knows that it rejuvenates and stretches the span of life.

    —PRESIDENT WILLIAM HOWARD TAFT

If you drink, don't drive. Don't even putt.

    —DEAN MARTIN

Drugs are very much a part of professional sports today, but when you think about it, golf is the only sport where the players aren't penalized for being on grass.

    —BOB HOPE

I sold three memberships, at $350,000 apiece . . . at Trump International, just standing on the tee hitting golf balls. People walked up and gave me checks. I know that if I'm not there, those three people don't join . . . It's called the owner's touch. You have to have that personal touch.

    —Donald Trump
    From *Golf Digest*

The tour is a juggernaut. But there's a reason why people flock to see Sergio Garcia. Yeah, these guys are good. How about, these guys are good and fun?

    —Bill Murray

The only time my prayers are never answered is on the golf course.

    —Billy Graham

I'm a vice president in charge of special marketing. That means I play golf and go to cocktail parties. I'm pretty good at my job.

    —Mickey Mantle

All I've got against golf is it takes you so far from the clubhouse.

—ERIC LINKLATER
SCOTTISH AUTHOR

On the practice range, he drives it to places that make your head spin. After he got warmed up and got a sweat going, he started hitting balls over the fence at the end of the range. Everyone oohed and aahed.

—BILLY ANDRADE
ON GOLFING PARTNER AND BASEBALL GREAT MARK MCGWIRE

Obviously a deer on the fairway has seen you tee off before and knows that the safest place to be when you play is right down the middle.

—JACKIE GLEASON

Well, I think it's the game's uncompromising difficulty that really appeals to the American presidents . . . I think they really like the fact that on a golf course they're on their own.

—DON VAN NATTA

I was hot. I was smoking 'em. Even a blind pig finds an acorn sometimes.

—PRESIDENT BILL CLINTON
ON SHOOTING HIS FIRST 79

You have to let a little air into the war room now and then.

—PRESIDENT DWIGHT D. EISENHOWER
ON ENJOYMENT OF GOLF

If that ball were wrapped in bacon, Lassie wouldn't find it.

—DAVID FEHERTY
ON A SHOT COMEDIAN GEORGE LOPEZ HIT INTO THE WOODS

Don't ask what I shot.

—PRESIDENT DWIGHT EISENHOWER

I'm actually a little nervous, like it's my first pro tournament. The first swing might be a little scary.

—JIMMY CONNORS
ON PLAYING AT THE PEBBLE BEACH PRO-AM

How has retirement affected my golf game? A lot more people beat me now.

—President Dwight D. Eisenhower

I tried everything mental and physical I could to help him out. After three or four holes, there was nothing I could do. I ran out of ideas. I just told him, 'I feel for you. I really do.'

—Tom Watson
    after being paired with NBA player
    Charles Barkley at a pro-am

It keeps guys like Jack Lemmon from making an 8 or a 9 on national television.

—Fuzzy Zoeller
    on the idea of moving tees up for amateurs
    in celebrity tournaments

My God, he looks like he's beating a chicken!

—Byron Nelson
    On actor Jack Lemmon's swing

Forget that I am president of the United States. I am Warren Harding, playing with some friends, and I'm going to beat the hell out of them.

—PRESIDENT WARREN HARDING

* * *

Charley hits some good woods—most of them are trees.

—GLEN CAMPBELL
ON HIS FRIEND CHARLEY PRIDE

* * *

You look perfect. That beautiful knitted shirt, an alpaca sweater, those expensive slacks. You've got an alligator bag, the finest matched irons, and the best woods money can buy. It's a damn shame you have to spoil it all by playing golf.

—LLOYD MANGRUM
TO GEORGE BURNS

CHAPTER TWENTY

Legendary Players, Legendary Moments

Honest, injun, we could care less about the spoils, the long road that came before, or the inevitable letdown to follow. The number on the card? Bean counting, a sterile pleasure. We're gluttons for the adrenalin, that's what we are. The celebrity, the bucks, the applause? All very nice but keep 'em. All we're about is the thrill—vicarious, surreal—a chance to share in the rush of destiny sweeping us along in the avalanche, taking us all the way there if just for a moment—that's it.

We forget how good we have it. Arnold hit the big 5-0 in Masters appearances before he'd finally had enough; not that he was in contention in most of them, sure, but the thought that even a great football player might appear in more than, say, one or two Super Bowls, or that a baseball player might make it to more than a couple of World Series just shows how much of an anomaly golf truly is, and, also, how well the game treats its royalty.

We have them longer so we remember longer. Some of the shots are etched in stone, others are etched in memory. We hold on to the special ones. The best, like holiday classics, return every year, highlights we never get tired of revisiting. We know what's coming but we never tire of the ending. The silence, the pressure, the concentration, the execution, the waiting, the exhilaration! The joy! We remember, as clear as when it happened. There can be no arguments, no disputes, no controversy. Nothing obscures the view. There is only the iconic moment, the player and the shot. Now and forever.

* * * * *

I never played a round when I didn't learn something new about the game.

—BEN HOGAN

◄—•—►

I don't know very much. I know a little bit about golf. I know how to make a stew. And I know how to be a decent man.

—BYRON NELSON

◄—•—►

I'm glad we don't have to play in the shade.

—BOBBY JONES
RESPONSE TO BEING TOLD IT WAS 105 DEGREES IN THE SHADE

◄—•—►

People always ask me about one shot that won a tournament, and I really have trouble recalling a specific shot. But I will always remember that shot right there. I'll remember that putt because I don't know how it went in.

—RAYMOND FLOYD

◄—•—►

Seve Ballesteros and Greg Norman are the modern giants, the Michelangelos, the Picassos, the da Vincis. We are lucky we have them.

—MAC O'GRADY

To me [Seve Ballesteros's] swing was perfect.

—Tom Weiskopf

To say aloud the words 'Seve Ballesteros' conjures up in one's mind images of a swashbuckling player; a modern-day Arnold Palmer, a man driven by a rich vein of inspiration.

—David Leadbetter
From his book *David Leadbetter's Lessons from Golf Greats*

To me, he's very boring. He's never in the trees or in the water. He's not the best driver, not the best putter. He's just the best at everything.

—Fred Couples
On Nick Faldo

All you had to do was look at her. She has all the ability in the world. She can drive, chip, putt. All her shots are top class. And her temperament. She's an ice-cool Swede, one of the best talents in the world.

—Laura Davies
On Annika Sörenstam's talent

Babe Zaharias was a remarkable person. She was no pantywaist, I'll tell you. She definitely was stronger than most men. When she walked, her muscles just rippled under her skin. She could hit longer than I could; so could Mickey Wright.

  —Paul Runyon

One player asked me, 'Who's Mickey Wright?' I felt like slapping her.

  —Kathy Postelwait, 1993
   At Mickey Wright's first tournament in eight years

Because that's how goddamn good Bobby Jones was.

  —Tommy Armour
   Explaining why, as 1927 US Champion, he had
   to have a stroke a side to be competitive in betting
   games with Bobby Jones

In his most useful and tempestuous days he had never been angry and not often, I think with Fate, but he had been furiously angry with himself. He set himself an almost impossibly high standard . . . but he became outwardly a man of ice, with the very best of golfing manners.

  —Bernard Darwin
   On Bobby Jones in *The Darwin Sketchbook*

Jones: Mr. Vardon, did you ever see a worse shot than that?
Vardon: No.

—HARRY VARDON
RESPONSE TO BOBBY JONES WHEN HE SKULLED
A NIBLICK IN THE 1920 US OPEN

A match against Bobby Jones is just as though you got your hand caught in a buzz saw. He coasts along serenely waiting for you to miss a shot, and the moment you do he has you on the hook and you never get off.

—FRANCIS OUIMET

Golf without Jones would be like France without Paris—leaderless, lightless and lonely.

—HERBERT WARREN WIND
ON BOBBY JONES

It is nonsense to talk about who was the greatest golfer in the world. All you can say that there have been none greater than Bobby Jones.

—TOMMY ARMOUR

Well, what more can I say for my hero? He was a gentleman and there was laughter in his heart and on his lips, and he loved his friends.

—PAUL GALLICO
FROM *FAREWELL TO SPORT*, ON BOBBY JONES

He was a magnificent putter, standing straight up, noticeably far from the ball, and hitting it straight in. It really looked as if the ball knew better than to disobey him.

—BERNARD DARWIN
ON BRITISH GOLFER MURE FERGUSON'S PUTTING STYLE

Ben Hogan would rather have a coral snake rolling inside his shirt than hit a hook.

—CLAUDE HARMON

There is a special delight in seeing the kind of divine fury with which he laces into the ball, and yet the wonderful accuracy with which the club meets the ball.

—HORACE HUTCHINSON
ON JAMES BRAID

Deeply regretted by numerous friends and all golfers, he thrice in succession won the championship belt and held it without rivalry and yet without envy, his many amiable qualities being no less acknowledged than his golfing achievements.

—INSCRIPTION ON THE GRAVE OF YOUNG TOM MORRIS
WINNER OF FOUR BRITISH OPENS,
AND THE DOMINANT PLAYER OF HIS ERA

Tiger is the dragon out there. Somebody had to slay him.

—JEFF MAGGERT
ON BEATING TIGER WOODS

He's playing a game I'm not familiar with. Of course, I'm playing a game I'm not familiar with.

—JACK NICKLAUS
ON PLAYING PARTNER TIGER WOODS

The only thing that can stop him is an injury or a bad marriage.

—DAN JENKINS
ON TIGER WOODS

I didn't want to be the bad guy. I wasn't trying to end the streak per se. I was just trying to win the golf tournament.

—PHIL MICKELSON
AFTER BEATING TIGER WOODS AT THE BUICK INVITATIONAL (2000)

I don't know . . . I never played there.

—SANDY LYLE
WHEN ASKED WHAT HE THOUGHT OF TIGER WOODS

I would rather play a man who is straight down the fairway with his drive, on the green with his second, and down in two putts for his par. I can play a man like that at his own game, which is par golf.

—BOBBY JONES
AFTER LOSING TO WALTER HAGEN IN MATCH PLAY IN 1926

I said, 'That's all right, Mr. Hagen, I am the best caddie in Brisbane.'

Hagen looked down at me. 'OK son, then you and I are a pair, because I am the best golfer in Brisbane.'

—NORMAN VON NIDA
RECALLING HIS MEETING WITH WALTER HAGEN

If it were not for you, Walter, this dinner would be downstairs in the pro shop and not in the ballroom.

—ARNOLD PALMER
AT A DINNER IN HAGEN'S HONOR

Walter broke 11 of the 10 Commandments.

—FRED CORCORAN
ON GOLFING GREAT WALTER HAGEN

When I dine with Mr. Snead he always suggests that I order as if I was expecting to pay for it myself. I have known many great destroyers of money, but Mr. Snead is not among them.

—GEORGE LOW
ON SAM SNEAD

Sam Snead once told a very funny story about gambling at golf. He laughed so loud you could have heard a pin drop.

—PORKY OLIVER

If this tour is a blood bank, he's going to be a Count Dracula having a gory feast.

—GARY MCCORD
ON TOM WATSON'S SENIOR TOUR DEBUT

His control of the ball was such that he seemed to allow it no option but to go where he wanted it to go.

—AL LANEY
ON BEN HOGAN

Gray-blue, they had a piercing quality. They were the eyes of a circling bird of prey: fearless, fierce, the pupil no more than a dot in their imperious center. They were not the eyes of a loser.

—JIM MURRAY
ON BEN HOGAN'S EYES

Actually, Ben didn't leave himself much time for laughter. I can't recall him ever finding humor in anything that happened on the golf course. Golf was his business—a tough business, full of disappointments.

—FRED CORCORAN
ON BEN HOGAN

I've seen a lot of pros drop their clubs to go over to watch Ben Hogan practice. But I never saw Hogan drop his clubs to watch them practice.

—TOMMY BOLT

When you played with Hogan, he made you feel like you were holding your clubs upside down.

—BILL COLLINS
FORMER GOLF PRO

For what [Ben] Hogan meant, it's the old story. For those who know golf, no explanation is necessary. For those who don't, no explanation is possible.

—JIM MURRAY

Put today's players against me in 1945, and I would have won more than six [tournaments]. I think I would have won nine tournaments. I was playing very well.

—BYRON NELSON
GOLF DIGEST
ON HIS RECORD-SETTING EIGHTEEN VICTORY CAMPAIGN IN 1945

So how did Nicklaus win so much? Because he could finish a hole better than anyone else. As a player he's the greatest of all time but as a golfer I can't even put him in the first fifty.

—"WILD" BILL MEHLHORN

Some things cannot possibly happen, because they are both too improbable and too perfect. The US hockey team cannot beat the Russians in the 1980 Olympics. Jack Nicklaus cannot shoot 65 to win the Masters at age 46. Nothing else comes immediately to mind.

—THOMAS BOSWELL

It's hard not to play up to Jack Nicklaus's standards when you are Jack Nicklaus.

—JACK NICKLAUS

When Jack Nicklaus plays well, he wins. When he plays badly, he finished second. When he plays terribly, he finished third.

—JOHNNY MILLER

I would say with the technology we have today, with the equipment, if you put that in Jack Nicklaus's hands, he'd be a better golfer than Tiger Woods.

—GREG NORMAN

The only equivalent plunge from genius I could think of was Ernest Hemingway's tragic loss of ability to write. Hemingway got up one morning and shot himself. Nicklaus got up the next morning and shot 66.

—IAN WOOLDRIDGE
WHEN NICKLAUS FOLLOWED A FIRST ROUND 83 IN THE
OPEN CHAMPIONSHIP WITH A 66

If I had to have someone putt a 20-footer for everything I own—my house, my cars, my family—I'd want Nicklaus to putt for me.

—DAVE HILL

My nickname? Lighthorse? Damon Runyon put that on me in 1926 at the Los Angeles Open when I won the first $10,000 Open. George Von Elm and I played the last round in two hours and a half with 5,000 people following us.

—HARRY "LIGHTHORSE" COOPER

I can't thank the game enough for what it did for me. I've been different all my life and the game let me be myself. I did it my way.

—MOE NORMAN
ON BEING INDUCTED INTO THE CANADIAN HALL OF FAME

Lloyd [Mangrum] could get down in two from off the earth.

—TOMMY BOLT

I've studied golf for almost fifty years now and know a hell of a lot about nothing.

—GARY PLAYER

Sir Walter Hagen was the greatest golfer that ever lived. I truly believe this, greater than even Vardon, and Vardon went three and one-half years without hitting a sandtrap.

—WILFRED REID

Michael Jordan strikes me as one of the greatest athletes who ever lived, but Sam Snead still goes down as the greatest. He's performed in his teens, his twenties, his thirties, his forties, his fifties, his sixties, and at seventy he finished second.

—GARY PLAYER

Hagen played in tournaments as though they were cocktail parties.

—CHARLES PRICE
ON WALTER HAGEN

When I'm through with my career, I'm going to look back and say, hey, I was part of this little chapter of my life of golf, for instance, but I'm enjoying that because I'm on top of all that. It's a great moment in my life, anyway.

—VIJAY SINGH

Julius Boros died on a golf course one quiet May afternoon and took the swing of our dreams with him . . . No one ever swung a club with such nonchalance as Boros. He had, more than any other player of his time, the game's most exclusive quality: effortless power.

—JERRY TARDE, 1994
EDITOR OF *GOLF DIGEST*

I remember playing the match and how excited Ken [Venturi] and I were to be playing [Ben] Hogan and [Byron] Nelson. I know we played some fantastic golf that day, all of us, but I don't remember much else.

—HARVEY WARD
TWO-TIME U.S. AMATEUR CHAMPION

———◆———

That's the equivalent to a duffer shooting par 72 after one lesson.

—DEL MILLER
ON ARNOLD PALMER DRIVING A PACER A MILE IN 2 MINUTES
AND 9 SECONDS AFTER ONLY AN HOUR OF TRAINING

———◆———

I saw him take one swing on the practice tee and I said that's the best golfer I'd ever seen . . . That's the first time I saw a spark fly when the club hit the ball.

—GARY PLAYER
ON THE VERY FIRST TIME HE SAW ARNOLD PALMER
SWING A GOLF CLUB

———◆———

If that guy ever wins a tournament, it will set golf back one hundred years.

—HERBERT CHICK
COMMENTING ON NEWCOMER ARNOLD PALMER
AT THE 1954 US AMATEUR

You made all this possible, Arnold. We're all here because of you.

—ROCCO MEDIATE
TO ARNOLD PALMER AFTER PALMER FINISHED HIS
LAST US OPEN IN 1994

You figured out who you thought you could beat and you challenged him. And you hoped you didn't get Leonard Dodson because he'd pay a guy to follow you around with a camera and click it on your backswing.

—JIMMY DEMARET
ON HOW PAIRINGS WERE MADE DURING THE SAN FRANCISCO
MATCH PLAY CHAMPIONSHIP IN THE 1930S

He is on the whole a very good putter, though inclined in moments of stress to be short. How familiar is the picture of Sandy urging on his ball with frantic wavings of his putter on the last few inches of its course.

—BERNARD DARWIN
ON SANDY HERD

Never saw one who was worth a damn.

—HARRY VARDON
DESCRIBING LEFT-HANDED GOLFERS

There are hitters who are reminiscent of howitzers in action, beneath whose feet the earth trembles; Braid seems to impart the velocity of a bullet. It must have been a strain on the solid ball to have to pull itself together and refrain from bursting into pieces.

—H.N. WETHERED
ON JAMES BRAID

They made people play better by having to live up to their standard, but they did not make people play like them.

—BERNARD DARWIN
COMMENTING ON THE TRIUMVIRATE:
BRAID, TAYLOR, AND VARDON, WHO AS
A GROUP WON 16 BRITISH OPENS

Harry Vardon was a big man with huge hands. My own was practically lost in his hand shake. He was reserved, quiet, with almost nothing to say. But I learned plenty from watching him swing a golf club.

—WALTER HAGEN
OBSERVING HARRY VARDON AT THE 1913 US OPEN

Harry Vardon stands alone in all the glory that his performances testify.

—J.H. TAYLOR

He smiles as he plays, but it is not a broad smile, just a faint flicker over his features. It is what you might call the Vardonic Smile. He was never a worrier, or recounter of lost strokes . . . He sank into the game but there was nothing grim about him.

—ANDREW KIRKALDY
BRITISH GOLF PRO, ON HARRY VARDON

It could be worse; I could be allergic to beer.

> —GREG NORMAN
> ON BEING ALLERGIC TO GRASS

Greg Norman looks like the guy they always hire to kill James Bond in the movies.

> —DAN JENKINS

Who does Norman think he is, God?

> —MARK MCCUMBER
> ON NORMAN'S PROPOSAL FOR A WORLD TOUR

You know what we should have done? Taken Greg skiing.

> —BRAD FAXON
> ON GREG NORMAN EASILY WINNING THE TOURNAMENT PLAYERS
> CHAMPIONSHIP AFTER MARK CALCAVECCHIA, PHIL MICKELSON,
> AND MARK WEIBE WERE ALL INJURED SKIING

One of the remarkable things about Walter Hagen was the fact that, even in their defeat, his opponents all had tremendous affect for him.

—Fred Corcoran

———◆———

He is the most immeasurable of golf champions. But this is not entirely true because of all he has won, or because of that mysterious fury with which he has managed to rally himself. It is more than anything because of the pure unmixed joy he has brought back to trying.

—Dan Jenkins
on Arnold Palmer

———◆———

In the opinion of many people, of all the great athletes, [Bobby] Jones came the closest to being what we call a great man.

—Herbert Warren Wind

———◆———

On being asked how good Young Tom Morris really was, an aged golfer replied: 'I cannot imagine anyone playing better.'

—Anonymous

Walter Hagen was the greatest loser and the greatest winner and the greatest golfer.

—CHICK EVANS
LEADING AMATEUR GOLFER OF THE 1910S AND 1920S

Hagen was the first professional to make a million dollars at the game— and the first to spend it.

—FRED CORCORAN

Before Hagen broke down the walls of prejudice, a professional golfer had no standing whatever.

—GENE SARAZEN
1950, IN HERBERT WARREN WIND'S *THE COMPLETE GOLFER*

He was a cold, detached artisan on the course, likened by some observers to an undertaker wearing a shroud of defeat for his adversaries.

—WILL GRIMSLEY
ON BEN HOGAN

A professional at sixteen and a dominant force in world golf throughout the 1980s, Seve's self-educated genius is not so much in the consistency of his ball-striking, but his ability to conjure shots out of thin air and seemingly will the ball into the hole.

—DAVID LEADBETTER
FROM *DAVID LEADBETTER'S LESSONS FROM GOLF GREATS*

Hidden under that famous straw hat of his is a slick spot as wide as some fairways I've seen.

—TOMMY BOLT
ON SAM SNEAD

The only reason I ever played golf in the first place was so I could afford to hunt and fish.

—SAM SNEAD

I know I had a couple of drinks last night, but I didn't expect to wake up in Sun Valley, Idaho.

—Jimmy Demaret
ON PARTYING THE NIGHT BEFORE A FLUKE SNOWSTORM
AT THE CROSBY PRO-AM IN MONTEREY, CA

Arnold Palmer is an early riser. He is anxious to get the day going because who knows how many good things might happen.

—Mark McCormack

CHAPTER TWENTY-ONE

The Back Nine:
On the Senior Tour and
Getting Older

Women may refer to fifty as being the new forty, but golf officially trumped Father Time long ago, transforming the over-the-hill mob into fashionable golden oldies savoring their new lease on life, turning fifty into what?—the new thirty? The Sansabelted seniors are laughing all the way to the bank. No longer must they fear green bananas, clip coupons or wrap themselves in blankets of wistful memories.

Some of their reflections, yes, invite a Vaudevillian rim shot. Truth be told, they're really just too busy to stop and reflect; too busy making birdies, friends, and money as they take advantage of their mulligan to play some of their best golf. Of course we resent them; they've still got game—in spades—but we also cherish seeing them, and can't help but marvel over and be encouraged by their golf. What other game could be so generous, so permissive, as to let the old boys go out and play on the fields of youth without making fools of themselves? And for their maturity, for playing sensibly, "within themselves," for applying the game's lessons neglected long ago when blinded by swagger, they are rewarded.

They've received what every athlete, what every one of us desires. A second chance (not to mention plum tee times). Applause, courtesy cars, respect, what have they got to be sore about? Retirement? Hardly. Nothing more than a few more aches and pains. As long as they can go, old is a state of mind, the competitive gene requires no prescription. No wonder they're in a hurry, and no wonder we follow in hot pursuit.

* * * * *

There is no special age for learning to play golf, but it is better not to postpone the attempt till after fifty.

—ARNAUD MASSEY

The great thing about starting golf in your forties is that you can start golf in your forties. You can start other things in your forties but generally your wife makes you stop them, as Bill Clinton found out.

—P.J. O'ROURKE

I just hope I don't have to explain all the times I've used His name in vain when I get up there.

—BOB HOPE
ABOUT HIS GOLFING

If you drink, quit. If you smoke, cut down. That covers the physical end of it. Then you've got to get your brain in shape, which is even harder to do and more important . . . Forget hitting balls, it's lifestyle that will get you.

—LEE TREVINO
ON JOINING THE SENIOR TOUR

We're going to have a lot more gray hair, but the thing that isn't going to change is that the same good players are going to make all the money.

—DANA QUIGLEY
ON THE SENIOR PGA TOUR

I guess I'm getting too old, but it took a long time for them to catch up with me.

—SAM SNEAD
AT AGE SIXTY-FOUR, ON YOUNG PLAYERS

You know you're on the Senior Tour when your back goes out more than you do.

—BOB BRUCE
SENIOR PGA TOUR MEMBER

Somebody is going to wake up one morning and realize the Senior Tour is not a bunch of over-the-hill guys.

—HALE IRWIN

What's so nice about our tours is that you can't remember your bad shots.
—BOBBY BRUE
COMMENTING ON THE SENIOR TOUR

I'm getting so old, I don't even buy green bananas anymore.
—CHI-CHI RODRIGUEZ

Everyone used to say to me, 'Glad you won the tournament'…and now they say, 'Glad you made the cut.'
—ARNOLD PALMER

For the retired warrior there are no anxieties, no agonies, no thwarted ambitions, no wretched little jealousies, no bitter regrets. Never again will he toss and tumble, thinking of the match that is before him on the morrow.
—BERNARD DARWIN
FROM *THE DARWIN SKETCHBOOK*

That's the easiest 69 I ever made.

—WALTER HAGEN
ON TURNING SIXTY-NINE

One of the nice things about the Senior Tour is that we can take a cart and cooler. If your game is not going well, you can always have a picnic.

—LEE TREVINO

I've known you longer than anyone in golf. I can only tell you there is no help. I can only get worse, but you are not to keep thinking of it. You know that in golf we play the ball as it lies. Now, we will not speak of this again, ever.

—BOBBY JONES
REPLY TO WRITER AL LANEY WHO WAS DISTRAUGHT OVER JONES'S
DEBILITATING AFFLICTION, WHICH CONFINED HIM TO A
WHEELCHAIR UNTIL HIS DEATH IN 1971

Some of these Legends of Golf have been around golf for a long time. When they talk about having a good grip, they're talking about their dentures.

—BOB HOPE

I probably hit the ball as far today as I did 40 years ago. That just shouldn't be.

—GENE LITTLER

***

I play by memory. If somebody tells me to hit the ball 150 yards, I hit it 150 yards.

—SAM SNEAD
ON HIS POOR VISION

***

There may be a certain amount of pleasurable excitement in running up to the top of a hillock in the hope of seeing your ball near the flag, but this kind of thing one gets tired of as one grows older.

—ALISTER MACKENZIE
ON BLIND SHOTS

***

I felt like I was walking naked, like the grass was taller than me. I tried to walk with my head high. It was really hard.

—IAN BAKER-FINCH
BAKER-FINCH CRIED IN THE LOCKER ROOM THAT AFTERNOON,
WITHDREW FROM THE TOURNAMENT AND QUIT COMPETITIVE
GOLF AT AGE 35, THE PRIME OF HIS CAREER.

I'm so tired of getting operated on. I'd rather die almost than have another operation, but I may not have another choice.

—JOHNNY MILLER

I don't want to be eulogized until I'm dead.

—BEN HOGAN
TURNING DOWN AN INVITATION TO BE THE HONOREE
AT JACK NICKLAUS'S MEMORIAL TOURNAMENT

The older I get the better I used to be!

—LEE TREVINO

We saw elderly citizens playing at the Old Scots game of golf, which is a kind of gigantic variety of billiards.

—PETER MORRIS, 1819
FROM PETER'S *LETTERS TO HIS KINSFOLK*

We stop, sometimes, because of age. More often because we can't tolerate how badly we have come to play the game. The clubs come home and never go out again.

—MICHAEL HOBBS,
ON QUITTING GOLF, FROM *GOLF FOR THE CONNOISSEUR*

I'm just tired. It has been a long grind. There were days when I thought I would scream if I had to go to the course. It was week-in, week-out for years. I tried to give my best to golf. Now I want to realize a dream . . .

—BYRON NELSON
RETIRING FROM THE PRO TOUR IN 1946, AT AGE THIRTY-FOUR

His nerve, his memory, and I can't remember the third thing.

—LEE TREVINO
ON THE THREE THINGS AN AGING GOLFER LOSES

Like a lot of fellows on the Senior Tour, I have a furniture problem: My chest has fallen into my drawers.

—BILLY CASPER

761

People have always said, 'Jack, I wish I could play like you.' Well, now they can.

> —Jack Nicklaus, 1994
> On how at age fifty-four he is struggling with his game

Bruce Lietzke is talking seriously about retiring from the PGA Tour, which begs the question—How will anyone know?

> —Steve Hershey

I don't want to get old, but I don't have much choice, so if it will help my golf like these guys, then it won't be so bad.

> —Jose Maria Olazabal
> After falling to Greg Norman and Nick Price
> in the 1994 Grand Slam of Golf

That's life. The older you get, the tougher it is to score.

> —Bob Hope

You know you're getting old when all the names in your black book have 'M.D.' after them.

—ARNOLD PALMER

I don't think I'll live long enough to shoot my age. I'm lucky to shoot my weight.

—BRUCE LANSKY
AUTHOR

If we don't change them, pretty soon there's going to be a bunch of old ladies in there, and then pretty soon those old ladies are going to die, and then it's just going to be a dead Hall of Fame.

—PATTY SHEEHAN
ON THE LPGA'S DEMANDING HALL OF FAME REQUIREMENTS

When you die, what you take with you is what you leave behind. If you don't share, no matter how much you have, you will always be poor.

—CHI-CHI RODRIGUEZ
RECIPIENT OF NUMEROUS COMMUNITY SERVICE AWARDS
FOR HIS WORK WITH JUNIOR GOLFERS AND OTHERS

I'm old enough to be most of their fathers. They don't know whether to call me Mr. Sigel or to call me Jay.

—JAY SIGEL
AT AGE FORTY-NINE, WHILE PLAYING HIS TWENTY-SEVENTH
CONSECUTIVE US AMATEUR IN 1993 AGAINST A FIELD
OF COLLEGE-AGE PLAYERS

My game is not for display right now. I do, however, get great pleasure from playing and replaying holes in my mind.

—BEN HOGAN
ON RETIREMENT

I sure was glad I ran out of holes. I looked down at my hands and arms to see if it was me when I finished with the score.

—DON JANUARY
AFTER SHOOTING A 67 AT A RECENT SENIOR TOUR EVENT

There aren't many fifty-year-olds beating twenty-year-olds. I was born at night, but it wasn't last night.

—LEE TREVINO
· ON BEING IN THE MASTERS HUNT AT THE AGE OF FIFTY

When you get this old, you wake up with a different pain each day. Besides, it's a grind trying to beat sixty-year-old kids out there.

—Sam Snead

Anyone who says he plays better at fifty-five than he did at twenty-five wasn't very good at twenty-five.

—Bob Brue

Baseball players quit playing and they take up golf. Basketball players quit, take up golf. Football players quit, take up golf. What are we supposed to take up when we quit?

—George Archer

Then I was skinnier, I hit it better. I putted better and I could see better. Other than that, everything's the same.

—Homero Blancas
on the Senior Tour versus his younger days

What do I do better now? Probably sleep.

—LARRY ZIEGLER
WHEN ASKED WHAT HE DOES BETTER NOW
THAN HE DID TWENTY YEARS AGO

This is the kind of putt an old guy can make.

—FRED COUPLES

I'm going to be around until the Atomic Energy Commission finds a safe place to bury my liver.

—PHIL HARRIS
ON HOW LONG HE WILL CONTINUE GOLF

It's a lot nicer looking down on the grass instead of looking up at it.

—ARNOLD PALMER
ON PLAYING HIS 43RD MASTERS

It's always good to see Arnie in an event. It means I'm not the oldest one in the field.

—DON JANUARY
ON ARNOLD PALMER

When you get up there in years, the fairways get longer and the holes get smaller.

  —Bobby Locke
   South African golfer

When you get older, your body is supposed to go. Mine is finally starting to come. I've been waiting twenty-one years for my body to come, and finally it's here.

  —Chi-Chi Rodriguez
   at age forty-five

I never dreamed about golf when I was an active player. The dreams started after I quit. There was a pattern to them: They started out good and ended bad.

  —Byron Nelson

Once a guy gets past fifty, if he misses one day of playing, he goes back two.

  —Sam Snead

Time goes by and people forget all the tournaments I've won. Only my wife and my dog remember.

> —GARY PLAYER

The older you get, the stronger the wind gets—and it's always in your face.

> —JACK NICKLAUS

In golf, as in other sports, youth is a great helper, but if you cannot start at three, or twelve, or even thirty-five, start at forty-five or fifty. Remember that it's better to have golfed and foozled than never golfed at all.

> —JEROME TRAVERS

It gets easier as you get older.

> —JOE JIMENEZ
> SENIOR TOUR PLAYER, ON SHOOTING HIS AGE

Why the hell would people love that? I don't know. So Lee Trevino can make some more millions. It's a farce.

> —JOHN MCENROE
> ON THE SENIOR TOUR

—◆—

I'm going to die in a tournament on the golf course. They'll just throw me in a bunker and build it up a little bit.

> —LEE TREVINO

—◆—

I'll shoot my age if I have to live to be 105.

> —BOB HOPE

—◆—

I can talk to the cows and get them to go, but that golf ball, it doesn't listen to me at all.

> —ROBERT LANDERS
> SENIOR TOUR PLAYER AND PROFESSIONAL FARMER

I hope in ten years' time I'm out of touch with golf altogether, sitting on my tropical beach. Or at least knocking it round for an absolute laugh.
—NICK FALDO
FROM *PETER ALLIS: GOLF HEROES*

———•———

It just shows this old bottle of wine hasn't turned to vinegar yet.
—TOM WATSON
ON WINNING THE DUNLOP OPEN IN JAPAN AT AGE FORTY-EIGHT

———•———

Guys, when you get to seventy, you're allowed a mulligan.
—GARY PLAYER

———•———

I went to bed September 4, 1992, and I was old and washed up. I woke up a rookie. What could be better.
—RAYMOND FLOYD
ON TURNING FIFTY AND BEING ELIGIBLE TO PLAY ON THE SENIOR TOUR

I forget when it happened but in the middle of a round, which I was regarding with the usual distaste, a small voice within me said: 'You don't *have* to do this,' and I thought, 'No, by God, I don't.'

—HENRY LONGHURST
ON QUITTING GOLF, *MY LIFE AND SOFT TIMES*

Retire to what? I already play golf and fish for a living.

—JULIUS BOROS
WHEN ASKED IF HE WOULD EVER RETIRE

The road's getting shorter and narrower, but I'll play wherever pigeons land.

—SAM SNEAD, 1994
AT AGE EIGHTY-ONE

Take two weeks off and then quit the game.

—JIMMY DEMARET
WHEN ASKED FOR ADVICE BY A STRUGGLING GOLFER

I'm not a real smart guy. But I've got enough brains to realize that when I'm sixty years old and play a sport, that it's downhill.

—LEE TREVINO

The golfer is never old until he is decrepit. So long as providence allows him the use of two legs active enough to carry him round the green, and of two arms supple enough to take a 'half swing' . . .

—ARTHUR JAMES
FIRST EARL OF BALFOUR, *GOLF*

Don't ever get old.

—BEN HOGAN, 1971
WHEN HE WITHDREW FROM THE HOUSTON OPEN
BECAUSE OF PAIN AND FATIGUE

One of the glories of golf is that people can continue to play it long after the marathon runner is hobbling at home on his worn-out ankle and knee joints.

—DEREK LAWRENSON
FROM *STEP-BY-STEP GOLF TECHNIQUES:*
MASTERING THE LONG AND SHORT GAME

Golf is like love. One day you think you are too old, and the next day you want to do it again.

  —ROBERTO DE VICENZO

The old fellas can still win.

  —LEE TREVINO
   AFTER JACK NICKLAUS WON THE MASTERS AT AGE FORTY-SIX

I've been playing the game so long that my handicap is in Roman numerals.

  —BOB HOPE

I'm afraid the old man has had it.

  —JIMMY DEMARET
   AT AGE FORTY-SEVEN, AFTER LOSING HIS LEAD AT THE
   U.S. OPEN ON THE 15TH HOLE OF THE FINAL ROUND

I continue to play because of the tradition. I'm not here to be competitive. I'm here to be part of the history. I would never go over and play a regular Tour event because I'm not competitive.

  —RAYMOND FLOYD

I've been doing the sword dance for parts because I don't make enough birdies. That's when I know my game has gone bad.

—CHI-CHI RODRIGUEZ
ON HIS SENIOR TOUR SLUMP IN 1996

When I got back from Pebble Beach, people said, 'Good playing, Jack.' When I used to finish sixth in a tournament, people would say, 'Too bad, Jack.' I want to hear that again.

—JACK NICKLAUS
AFTER FINISHING SIXTH IN 1995

Because once you sit on your ass, you die. I've got to keep active. It's what keeps me young, keeps me going to the gymnasium, setting goals for myself in business and in life. It's all part of my life—traveling, meeting people. That's the big thing. I love people.

—GARY PLAYER
ON WHY HE CONTINUES TO PLAY GOLF COMPETITIVELY

What I want is Fred Couples's face. And I want Fred Couples's body. And Fred Couples's swing. His hair . . . I want anybody's hair.

—ROCKY THOMPSON
SENIOR TOUR PRO

I'm looking forward to not competing. Pride takes over after a while. You remember how you used to play and how you used to perform shots that you can't play now. That's what's frustrating—knowing you were at a certain level at one point in your career, and you're not there.

—KATHY WHITWORTH

I'm never satisfied. Trouble is, I want to play like me—and I can't play like me anymore.

—JACK NICKLAUS
AT FIFTY

Acknowledgments

This book would not have been possible were it not for the Herculean researching efforts of Jared Lafer.

Jeremy Selengut, Lee Transue, Brando Skyhorse, and Laura Hazard Owen of Skyhorse Publishing were all instrumental in the organization of this project.

Special thanks go out to Arnold Palmer for his wonderful foreword, and to my editor, Mark Weinstein, for pulling this whole thing together.

—J.A.

Those Quoted